Video Editing

Video Editing

A Postproduction Primer
Fourth Edition

Steven E. Browne

Focal Press
An imprint of Elsevier Science

Amsterdam   Boston   London   New York   Oxford   Paris   San Diego
San Francisco   Singapore   Sydney   Tokyo

Focal Press is an imprint of Elsevier Science

 Recognizing the importance of preserving what has been written, Elsevier Science prints its books on acid-free paper whenever possible.

Library of Congress Cataloging-in-Publication Data

Browne, Steven E.
  Video editing : a postproduction primer / Steven E. Browne.—4th ed.
    p.   cm.
  Includes bibliographical references and index.
  ISBN 0-240-80402-3 (pbk. : alk. paper)
  1. Video tapes—Editing.   I. Title.

  TR899 .B725 2002
  778.59′3—dc21

                                        2001058576

British Library Cataloguing-in-Publication Data
A catalogue record for this book is available from the British Library.

The publisher offers special discounts on bulk orders of this book.
For information, please contact:
Manager of Special Sales
Elsevier Science
225 Wildwood Avenue
Woburn, MA 01801-2041
Tel: 781-904-2500
Fax: 781-904-2620

For information on all Focal Press publications available, contact our World Wide Web home page at: http://www.focalpress.com

10 9 8 7 6 5 4 3 2 1

Printed in the United States of America

To Michele, the best friend and wife imaginable.

Contents

Introduction

Since the first edition of *Video Editing*, postproduction has grown and prospered. Computers, once a small part of the fledgling video industry, are now the mainstay of on-line and off-line editors as well as special effects and graphics.

Linear editing and the old familiar NTSC 4×3 ratio image developed in the 1950s are being replaced with a high-definition 16×9 image, recorded on digital video with awesome sound quality. Along with this image will come new channels on your television and new postproduction challenges.

But with all the new technical innovations, the process of choosing and editing the most appropriate images for any visual project has not changed; only the tools that are used have changed. These tools will continue to evolve, but assemble recordings, time code, dissolves, wipes, edit decision lists, and control track still exist and continue to be used on a daily basis.

Even though the technology of video editing has moved away from the linear world and into the quick-paced monitors of nonlinear editing, much of this text, especially those areas concerning the esthetics of postproduction, has remained extremely accurate and reliable even in the nonlinear world.

Ultimately, it is the story that holds a program together and keeps the audience's interest. The choosing of images and sound that promote a show's purpose will always be the driving force behind any show. The technical tools with which visual effects and chosen images are physically (or electronically) placed into a program will continue to change. It will always remain the editor's ability to tell the story, not the equipment used, that determines the success of the program.

As in previous editions, this book is designed to build knowledge, not flood the reader with information. At first glance this process may seem repetitive, but it makes difficult ideas much easier to understand.

Acknowledgments

There is no way any significant project can be accomplished by one individual. Whether it is through technical information, support, advice, love, or friendship, a book of this nature could never be finished without help.

I would like to take this opportunity to personally thank a few people who have made a significant contribution to this book as well as to my life. For technical advice I thank Mark Cooan, Arthur Payson, Barton Durfee, and especially Michael Clow. I want to thank Dale Carroll and Scott Brown for their help in the photography shoots. Finally, special thanks go to Paul Apel for providing steady friendship, support, and the freedom to make this book possible.

PART I

Technical Aspects of Videotape

A Brief History of Videotape

Videotape has been in existence for over half a century. Though its start was tenuous and hesitant, it is now used everywhere in the world. After capturing the television industry, videotape invaded the home and, after much resistance, moved into the creative aspect of filmmaking. Computerized storage and retrieval of picture and audio changed the editing room environment. Films were shot on film, transferred to and then edited on video. Rapid advances in computers allowed the actual editing to be done on nonlinear editing systems. Now, with the new high-definition formats, the original image is being captured on videotape. Following is a brief history of the rapid growth of this technology.

AMPEX AND QUAD

In 1956, Ampex announced that it had developed a new device: the videotape machine. A team of six men (see Figure 1-1), including Ray Dolby (who later created the Dolby sound system), had invented what is now referred to as *quad*. These large tape machines used four record heads (hence the name quad) and two-inch-wide tape. On November 30, 1956, CBS broadcast the first program using videotape. The live New York show, *Douglas Edwards and the News*, was recorded, and then rebroadcast three hours later on the West Coast.

The machines were first used to record live programs for rebroadcast at a later time, but it did not take long before producers and directors wanted to edit the taped programs. In late 1958, Ampex began marketing a videotape splicer. By sprinkling a small amount of magnetically active tracing powder on the tape,

Figure 1-1 The Ampex team that created the original quad tape machine. Pictured from left to right: Fred Pfost, Shelby Henderson, Ray Dolby, Alex Maxey, Charles E. Anderson, and Charles Ginsburg. Photo courtesy of Ampex Corporation.

an editor could locate the video frame line with the aid of a microscope. The tape could then be physically cut at this line and new material spliced onto the tail of the original tape.

Five years later, Ampex introduced a device called Editec. An audio cue tone recorded on a secondary audio track of the quad tape signaled Editec to make the quad machine go into edit. Engineers (not editors) placed the cue tone at the beginning of the edit. The engineers would manually back up the playback and record machines, and put the machines into play mode simultaneously. Editec would electronically perform the edit.

TIME CODE EDITING

NASA provided the next advance in video editing. The space agency was using a time code system based on Greenwich Mean Time (hours, minutes, and seconds) to record telemetry information on audio tapes to keep track of the vast amounts

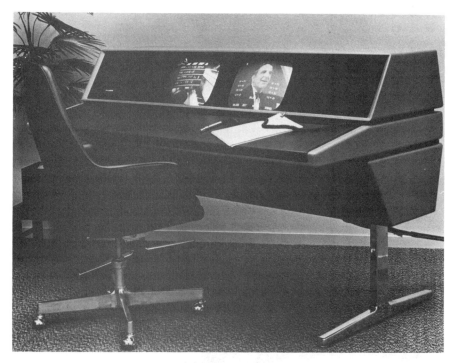

Figure 1-2   The CMX 600, the first random-access editor. Instead of using a keyboard, the operator controlled the machine by placing a light pen on the screen. Photo courtesy of CMX Corporation.

of data from their instruments. A company called EECO modified this system to accommodate the 30-frames-per-second playing speed needed for videotape. In 1967, EECO introduced the time code technique to the video industry and began marketing editing devices based on this highly accurate coding system.

The popularity of the time code editing concept lead several other manufacturers to follow suit, each with its own type of code. In 1972, the Society of Motion Picture and Television Engineers (SMPTE) standardized the format for time code.

In 1971, CBS Laboratories and the Memorex Corporation created a company named CMX as a joint venture. That year, CMX introduced the CMX 600, the first random-access video editing system (see Figure 1-2). The system worked by copying original video onto huge mechanical computer disks. The CMX 600 could then randomly access any frame from the disks. Because the CMX 600 was expensive and prone to failure, it was not a financial success.

A year later, the same company introduced the CMX 300. Although the CMX 300 was limited in its functions and speed compared to today's editors, it was frame accurate, and it became the industry standard for computerized video editing.

TAPE FORMATS

During 1962 and 1963, manufacturers introduced a variety of helical-scan video machines, none of which followed any universal standard. Whereas quad machines record video frames perpendicularly to the edge of the videotape, the helical-scan format records video on a slant. This diagonal recording pattern made physically cutting videotape on the frame line impossible. Early helical-scan machines were not accepted in the broadcast industry because engineers were unwilling to replace their expensive quad machines with these nonstandardized units.

In 1969, Sony™ introduced its EIAJ-standard three-quarter-inch U-Matic series, which proved extremely popular in the United States, both in the industrial market and for broadcast editing. In 1974, Sony announced its VO-2850 three-quarter-inch editing deck, which was capable of recording both insert and assemble edits. CMX incorporated the VO-2850 into its next product, the CMX 50 (see Figure 1-3).

The CMX 50 used 3 three-quarter-inch U-Matic cassette machines: one record machine and two playbacks (the minimum number of decks required to create a dissolve or a wipe). The CMX 50 used three-quarter-inch tape copies of the orig-

Figure 1-3 The CMX 50, the original off-line editing system. Photo courtesy of CMX Corporation.

inal two-inch quad videotape, with identical video and audio and matching time code. The off-line computer logged all edits performed on the three-quarter-inch work print and printed out a list on paper tape. When this list was fed into the CMX 300, the computer repeated the edits that had been performed on the CMX 50, using the camera-original two-inch quad tapes as playbacks. This process mimicked the film editing process (creatively edit with copies of the camera original, called *work print*, then conform the camera negative to the work print).

What made the CMX 50 such a success was that the creative editing process was done on a less expensive system. If a paper punch tape containing all the edits was brought from a CMX 50 to the CMX 300 on-line editing session, the costly CMX 300 and quad tape machines were needed only for final editing chores. Using the CMX 50 saved producers thousands of dollars per show.

In 1974, CMX introduced the CMX 340X, which enhanced computerized time code editing. The 340X simplified keyboard instructions and was easier to operate than the CMX 300. The 340X could be used for either off-line or on-line editing.

ONE-INCH TAPE

In 1975, Bosch-Fernseh introduced its BCN one-inch videotape format. The next year, Sony and Ampex brought out their broadcast-quality one-inch machines. The problem of machine incompatibility stopped broadcasters from parting with their large two-inch quad machines. During an SMPTE conference in 1977, ABC and CBS executives said that they would not adopt one-inch tape until some standard was established.

As a result of that meeting, two committees were formed. One committee focused on nonsegmented (one drum revolution per video field) recordings and the other group concentrated on segmented (more than one drum revolution per video field) recordings. The committees eventually defined three categories of one-inch recording: Type A was the original Ampex recording; Type B was the Bosch-Fernseh segmented standard; and Type C was the compromise standard to which Ampex and Sony agreed. Type C became the de facto standard of one-inch production and editing.

VIDEO EXPANDS

In the 1970s, sitcoms became extremely popular. Many of these shows were recorded and edited on videotape. This increased use of video for production created a substantial market for videotape editing machines, inspiring other manufacturers to compete with CMX. During the same period, the control track editor came into its own. Control track editors used the electronic frame pulses on the tape to keep track of tape location and edit points, rather than time code. By the late 1970s, many producers had purchased their own editing systems.

At the end of the decade, television news departments began to switch from 16 mm film to videotape production to bypass the time-consuming process of developing film footage. Several popular prime-time network and syndicated programs increased the reputation of three-quarter-inch editing by using the format for show segments. The mass movement toward video as a medium had begun.

HALF-INCH VIDEOTAPE AND RANDOM-ACCESS EDITING

By 1984, broadcast-quality half-inch videotape had been accepted by the broadcasting industry. The picture quality of the half-inch tape was far superior to that of three-quarter-inch and incredibly close to that of one-inch, thanks to the technique of composite recording. An added advantage was that the recorder could be built into the camera, eliminating a crew member as well as the cumbersome wires that ran from the camera to the record deck (called the camcorder).

Newer editing systems began mixing two-inch quad with one-inch videotape, and three-quarter-inch tape cassettes. Video, which had once been a very expensive process used almost exclusively by the networks, was becoming a flexible, fast, and relatively inexpensive production medium. Yet despite its improved signal, video still lacked the resolution to compete with film as a feature film medium. Blown up on the big screen, the picture was full of horizontal lines and was extremely blurry.

In the mid-1980s, several companies began to take advantage of microcomputers in the editing process. One company modified an IBM PC to control videocassette recorders and switchers (see the Glossary). To meet the growing pressure to provide low-cost editing systems, some manufacturers created less-expensive edit controllers that could be upgraded. As a result of this technological innovation, editing videotape became more affordable. Now postproduction companies could build more editing bays. Corporations could afford to establish their own video departments to produce newsletters and public service programs.

As the cost of video editing dropped, the rate of technological change increased. By the middle of the 1980s, much of the film industry's resistance to videotape had evaporated. VCRs were becoming a common household appliance, and the marriage of the video and film industries appeared to be a lasting one. Television shows were shot on film, then edited and delivered on videotape.

The 1980s also brought the rebirth and growth of random-access video editing. *Random access* means that specific segments of tape, dispersed through one or more reels, can be defined and accessed independently and almost immediately, usually through the use of a computer. Random-access video editing became popular because of its speed and re-editing ease. In addition, the high-end random-access systems could provide film key numbers in order to conform the film negative. Random-access systems began to capture television film business and in the 1990s major feature films were being edited on this type of system.

Figure 1-4 A display taken from Apple's nonlinear editor, Final Cut Pro. This editor is used for all types of projects from motion picture promotion to home video projects. Photo courtesy of Apple Incorporated.

By the mid-1990s, tape-based linear off-line editors had become obsolete. Computer prices had dropped and systems had been upgraded to hold hours of picture and audio information. Shortly after the turn of the century, powerful, cost-effective editors like Speed Razor, Final Cut Pro, and Adobe Premiere became popular (see Figure 1-4).

THE MTV/AMERICAN HOME VIDEO IMPACT

The cost of video editing equipment continually dropped which, in turn, increased the number of consumers who bought their own cameras and home editing systems. Music videos were shot on VHS, Hi-8, or eight-millimeter film. In the latter part of the 1980s, complete shows built around home videos premiered. ABC's *America's Funniest Home Videos* revealed that the entire country was taping and editing everything that moved. Videotape had strengthened its hold on both sides of the economic equation.

DIGITAL VIDEO ARRIVES

A growth pattern similar to the one-inch standards problem emerged as digital video entered the marketplace in the late 1900s. Digital video, which defines images by a series of electronic pulses rather than by voltage levels (analog), offered superior image quality over traditional analog formats, especially when it came to duplication and multigeneration editing. However, because of its high cost, digital video did not offer an economic advantage over existing formats; thus, its acceptance by the production and editing community was selective.

One-inch tape machines had replaced two-inch machines because one-inch was cheaper and provided higher quality. Digital videotape was technically far superior to one-inch tape, but much more expensive to purchase and maintain. The competition between several digital formats further divided the potential users.

The split between two digital formats segmented the high-end video market. One-inch, already firmly entrenched, continued to be the workhorse of tape production and postproduction. D1, an expensive, extremely high-end product, was used for effects and graphics. D2, a less-expensive digital medium, made inroads into the higher-budgeted production and postproduction environment and as a film-to-tape mastering format.

Productions with large budgets used D1 as their recording medium. D1 was also used for mastering home video products, while D2 was used for some graphic and animation product creation. Although one-inch tape remained the most widely accepted economical standard for almost all programming needs, the advantage of multiple generations with little loss of quality, combined with D2's ability to play back and record at the same time, caused a growing acceptance of D2.

In the 1990s, additional digital formats came onto the editing scene. D3, a Panasonic product, is a digital video format on a half-inch-wide tape, designed to compete in the digital domain as an economically feasible alternative to D1 or D2. The Ampex DCT also gained a foothold in the postproduction environment. DCT is a component system with the advantages of being cheaper than D1 but more expensive and of higher quality than D2. It has an incredibly quick lockup time and excellent picture quality.

At the same time that digital video was changing video postproduction, further fragmentation of formats was created by component-versus-composite recording techniques. Composite video combines the luminance (black and white) and chrominance (color) portions of the video signal. Component video recording keeps the luminance and chrominance portions of the signal separate, which results in superior image quality.

Composite recording and editing had been the standard method of video production. However, the introduction of the component formats D1, DCT, and Betacam SP brought component recording and editing into the commercial mainstream. In the late 1980s and early 1990s, many component editing bays found uses ranging from graphics to feature film effects to show postproduction, often combining digital and analog signals in a component environment.

With no clear standard, no one tape or recording format was dominant. Finally, Sony became the de facto standard with their 2:1 compressed Digital Betacam. The format was component digital with enough resolution to satisfy purists and accountants. An added advantage was that the "Digi Beta" was compatible with Betacam and Betacam SP. The format caught on.

At the turn of the century, random access on-line had taken hold. With Discrete Logic's Fire, Smoke, and Inferno and Quantel's Edit Box and Domino, more and more effects and editing companies began to eliminate linear video postproduction and moved into nonlinear editing, compositing, and graphics creation. As computer costs dropped, the power of nonlinear increased.

A disadvantage in using nonlinear editing emerged. For quick changes on long programs, nonlinear editing was less efficient than linear editing. For example, to transfer a half-hour scene, add a five-second card, and continue for another half-hour took half as long as it did to digitize an hour program, add a card, edit for five minutes, then rerecord the project onto tape for the necessary hour and ten seconds. The linear transfer process of editing still had its creative and financial place in the video editing world. Many facilities, heavily invested in digital linear editing equipment, continued to operate their linear editing equipment, because each process had its advantages and disadvantages.

In the early 2000s, Sony introduced their Betacam SX. This format records its signal in digital format, but it is more severely compressed (10:1 versus digital Betacam's 2:1). It does not have the capability to do variable speed playback, but most SX editors have built-in hard drives, and the SX format can be transmitted and up- or downloaded into a computer at four times play speed. Sony is hoping that this format, able to shoot in 16×9 or 4×3 format, will help broadcasters in their transition into the digital broadcasting era. Some of these decks can also play Betacam and Betacam SP tapes.

In the early part of 2001, the computer editor/graphics systems had taken a firm hold of the off-line as well as the on-line process. Then came the multiple standard of digital broadcasting with the lure of 16×9 widescreen format. With the federally mandated switch to an entirely digital broadcast system by 2007, with 18 digital format options, the entire editing world had been fragmented again and was on the lookout for a format leader.

Thus, from a few farsighted people at Ampex, to linear computerized editing pioneered by CMX, to the smaller formats of one-inch, three-quarter-inch, and now digital videotape, video has come a long way in five decades. And since videotape is an electronic medium, even more exciting developments are on tap as progress in electronic and computer technologies continues unabated. It will only be a matter of time before film disappears from the production and post-production scene altogether.

2

Videotape, Control Track, and Time Code

Videotape consists of a Mylar® backing covered with a thin layer of ferrous oxide (see Figure 2-1). Mylar is a strong, flexible plastic material that provides a base for the oxide. This oxide is easily magnetized and is the substance that stores video and audio information. Metal tape is highly refined videotape that uses metal particles instead of ferrous oxide to enhance recording sensitivity. Metal tape is used in digital videotape Betacam SP, S-VHS, Hi-8, and almost all digital formats. Videotape is very similar in composition to audiotape.

When videotape is purchased it is usually blank. (A prerecorded tape has a signal on it.) When a blank tape is played on a video machine, the viewer sees either snow or a blank screen. The same condition exists after the viewer erases a recorded tape by putting it next to a very strong magnetic field, which destroys the video signal on the tape. The machine that does this is called a *bulk eraser*.

Tape can be bought both new and used. One should be very careful when buying used or off-brand tape. Videotape, like any manufactured material, can be created under various conditions and still perform the task of recording signals. Cheaper tape tends to have more *dropouts*, minute spots that have a lack of oxide attached to the base. These dropouts, which look like white horizontal scratches, are easy to spot on lower grades of VHS tape.

Professional-quality tapes are manufactured under more stringent procedures than consumer tapes. High-quality tape is not that expensive. Since it is the medium on which original pictures and audio are stored, buying quality tape

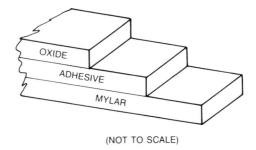

(NOT TO SCALE)

Figure 2-1 Cross section of videotape.

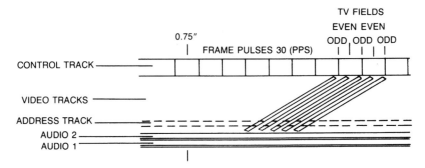

Figure 2-2 Diagram of three-quarter-inch recording tracks.

is worth the extra expense. For off-line editing one might consider using recycled tape or a cheaper brand because if the tape is faulty, the dub (from original material) can be remade.

CONTROL TRACK

Control track is a pulse recorded onto a track of the videotape. Because the pulse, which is only created during an assemble recording, marks each revolution of the record drum and the beginning of each frame, it is called the *frame pulse*. The control track could be called the electronic sprocket holes of video, since its purpose is to act as a guide for the playback of the video signal (see Figure 2-2).

Since the pulses on the control track are recorded in evenly spaced intervals at each revolution of the recording drum, the playback machine must maintain the same relationship to display the signal properly. If the spacing of the control track pulses is altered, the picture will roll until the spacing becomes even again. During this roll, the playback machine will change the tape speed and drum rotation in an attempt to keep the control track pulses constant.

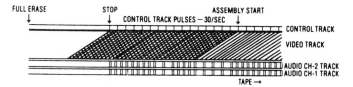

Figure 2-3 Diagram of an assemble edit.

All video formats use different but similar control track signals. Some video machines are capable of playing video that has a damaged control track. This is accomplished by locking to the video signal rather than the control track pulses.

TAPE RECORDING AND EDITING

Two important types of video recording are used: assemble and insert.

Assemble Recording

Assemble recording erases *everything* on the tape, from the beginning of the assemble edit, replacing it with the new picture, audio, and (most importantly) control track (see Figure 2-3). This method is not very useful if you want to record audio from sources other than the original picture. It is, however, a very effective way to make a direct copy of another videotape or to create a control track in preparation for an insert editing session.

Another disadvantage of assemble recordings is that if a tape already has a recorded signal on it and an assemble recording is made within the original recording, the control track pulses at the end of the edit will occur either earlier or later than the previous control track pulses. This difference in spacing will cause the picture to break up or roll, as mentioned earlier. Most machines have the ability to lock to the previous control track, producing a stable continuation of an assemble edit. However, the end of the edit will not have the same spacing as the video that follows.

These two major technical disadvantages of assemble editing and recording explain why almost all professional editing is done using insert recording.

Insert Recording

Insert recording offers the advantage of clean edits and the option of performing audio- or video-only edits. Video, audio, or both can be replaced on an existing tape without disturbing the control track (see Figure 2-4).

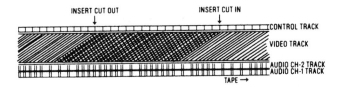

Figure 2-4 Diagram of an insert recording.

Since videotape is blank when purchased, the tape must have a control track recorded on it before an insert recording can be made. To do this, an assemble recording is made for the length of the videotape. This recording lays down a continuous, unbroken control track. An insert recording made on blank tape will not play back properly because the tape has no reference as to how to play the video.

Professional editing houses buy new videotape and have night-shift employees assemble record these blank tapes to prepare them for use. The assemble recording is usually a black picture with no audio, but it does have time code. This *black and coded* tape is used as a record master for insert recordings. Therefore, when buying a record tape from a professional editing house, you will usually find that it already has the control track and time code on it. It is more expensive than blank tape because time has been spent recording control track and time code on an expensive machine.

To repeat, *an assemble recording erases everything*—all video, audio, and control track—and replaces it with new signals. An insert recording replaces only those tracks (video, audio, or both video and audio) selected. Insert recording is the method used by most professional editing companies (on a tape that has already had an assemble recording performed on it).

Recording versus Editing

The words *insert* and *assemble* are used in several different ways in the video vocabulary. An insert recording is done according to the method described above. To insert an edit, however, means to place an edit between two other edits or to erase part of a previously recorded edit by inserting a new edit. The insert edit is made using an insert recording.

An assemble recording erases all signals on a tape and records new signals on it, as previously discussed. However, an *assembly* refers to an on-line editing session using a computer-generated edit decision list (EDL). This *auto assembly* is accomplished through the use of insert recordings. An A, B, C, D, or E mode assembly refers to different approaches to assembling an EDL (see Glossary). Almost all assemblies also are accomplished using insert recordings. To auto assemble means to have the computer editor automatically perform a series of edits in an EDL list.

VIDEO FRAMES AND FIELDS

Recorded video signals on videotape are complex and tightly structured. The standard unit of video is a frame. Similar to film, motion video is created by displaying progressive frames at a rate fast enough for the human eye and brain to perceive continuous motion. Standard broadcast video in the United States, as of 2002, records and displays approximately 30 frames per second in a 4 × 3 rectangular ratio (29.97 frames to be exact, more on this seemingly insignificant error rate later; see *drop frame time code* in the Glossary).

A frame of NTSC video is composed of two fields. These fields are recorded adjacent to each other on videotape and are interlaced during the playback process to display a full frame of video. (An alternative method is to record an entire frame of information. However, this process is more expensive than recording separate fields. See *progressive scanning* in the Glossary.)

Video images are recorded and displayed through a scanning process. When a camera records a video image, a beam of electrons sweeps across the recording surface in a progressive series of lines (think of the fine lines running horizontally across the face of an image on a TV set). The National Television Standards Committee (NTSC) defines a frame as containing 525 scan lines. Each field contains 262.5 lines. One of the two fields in each frame contains the odd-numbered scan lines, and the other contains the even-numbered scan lines. When they are interlaced, they create a full frame. Blank videotape has no frames, fields, or control track.

DIGITAL BROADCASTING AND HIGH-DEFINITION FORMATS

The introduction of the high-definition formats and their associated broadcasting formats has raised the technical standards (and confusion level) of video production. Though these various digital recording and broadcasting formats are still in their early stages of commercial use, the federal government has mandated the elimination of analog television broadcasting, with new channels assigned for digital transmission by he year 2007 when the analog spectrum is scheduled to be returned to the federal government.

Over sixteen hundred existing television broadcast stations have been assigned new digital frequencies. When the digital conversion is complete, the old analog frequencies will be reassigned to other purposes (cellular phones, etc.). Digital transmission currently (remember, digital signals and equipment can

HIGH DEFINITION DIGITAL BROADCAST FORMATS

	Total/Active Scan Lines	Pixelization	Frame Rate Per Second	Aspect Ratio
	First 3, best quality	More pixels	Three scanning choices	All high definition
1	1125/1080	1080 x 1920	24 progressive	16 x 9 (HDTV)
2	1125/1080	1080 x 1920	30 progressive	16 x 9 (HDTV)
3	1125/1080	1080 x 1920	60 interlaced	16 x 9 (HDTV)
	Next 3 still high quality	Fewer pixels, still HDTV	Three scanning choices	
4	750/720	720 x 1080	24 progressive	16 x 9 (HDTV)
5	750/720	720 x 1080	30 progressive	16 x 9 (HDTV)
6	750/720	720 x 1080	60 progressive	16 x 9 (HDTV)

Figure 2-5   High-definition broadcasting formats. Currently CBS, PBS, and NBC have chosen 1080i, ABC has picked 720p, and FOX will broadcast 480p and 720p.

improve or change with technical, but not necessarily economical, ease) has 18 separate formats in the United States.

The United States has adopted a transmissions standard called ATSC/8-VSB, but most other countries have adopted a different standard, a version of the DVD-T/COFDM. In other words, the broadcast of digital signals in the United States is different from most other countries.

High-definition television (HDTV) is a 16 × 9 format with several methods of recording (and broadcasting) its image. Note that these are recording and broadcasting formats, not videotape formats.

The six HDTV formats shown in Figure 2-5 will be the ones most utilized by feature film and HDTV broadcasting. Electronic cinematography or electronic cinema appears to be leaning toward 24p (24-frame progressive scanning) or 60i (60-field interlaced), numbers 1 and 3 on Figure 2-5. 24p is the closest format to standard film speed. This format records an entire frame of picture 24 times a second. However, the 60i, or 30 frames a second with the image interlaced, is more effective at recording motion (zooms, pans, tilts, etc.). The problem is that the film community likes the jittery motion that occurs at 24 frames of progressive scanning. Film purists think that this scanning format most resembles the film exposure process, and they are right.

Eventually, older forms of video recording and editing will be phased out. Many shows shot on film will eventually be retransferred to high-definition video.

STANDARD DEFINITION DIGITAL BROADCAST FORMATS

	Total/Active Scan Lines	Pixelization	Frame Rate Per Second	Aspect Ratio
	Less quality, 16 x 9 format	Smaller amount of data	Four scanning choices	Wide screen but not high definition
7	525/480	480/704	24 progressive	16 x 9 (SDTV)
8	525/480	480/704	30 progressive	16 x 9 (SDTV)
9	525/480	480/704	60 interlaced	16 x 9 (SDTV)
10	525/480	480/704	60 progressive	16 x 9 (SDTV)
	Same quality as above,		Four scanning choices	Not wide screen format
11	525/480	480/704	24 progressive	4 x 3 (SDTV)
12	525/480	480/704	30 progressive	4 x 3 (SDTV)
13	525/480	480/704	60 interlaced	4 x 3 (SDTV)
14	525/480	480/704	60 progressive	4 x 3 (SDTV)
	The bottom of digital	Less pixels	Four scanning choices	Not wide screen format
15	525/480	480/640	24 progressive	4 x 3 (SDTV)
16	525/480	480/640	30 progressive	4 x 3 (SDTV)
17	525/480	480/640	60 interlaced	4 x 3 (SDTV)
18	525/480	480/640	60 progressive	4 x 3 (SDTV)

Figure 2-6 Standard definition broadcasting is also a digital broadcast, but does not have the resolution that high definition contains, even though the aspect ratio can be 16×9.

Figure 2-6 shows the standard definition digital broadcasting options. Note that SDTV can be in a 16 × 9 format, not be high definition, but be a digital broadcast format. The SDTV standards are digitally broadcast, but have less resolution than HDTV (high definition).

It is interesting to note that when television first was developed, the display was in a 4 × 3 ratio, the same as film was at the time. Then, to separate itself from the upstart electronic medium, film began using various widescreen formats. Now, high-definition television, with its 16 × 9 format, is in reality a 1:77 format, very similar to the current 1:66 standard widescreen format. Most likely the HDTV formats will eventually replace the current 4 × 3 ratio recording as consumers become accustomed to the 16 × 9 widescreen formats.

INTERNATIONAL TELEVISION STANDARDS

As described in the previous section, NTSC is the video broadcast standard chosen by the United States and a number of other countries back in the 1950s. This standard is in a 4 × 3 ratio. High definition, however, is recorded and broadcast in a 16 × 9 ratio with 720 to 1080 lines of resolution.

PAL (phase alternate line) and SECAM (sequential color with memory) are the two other major worldwide television standards. Both PAL and SECAM scan 625 lines per frame versus NTSC's 525 and have a rate of 25 frames per second. They also both operate at a 50-Hz frequency versus NTSC's 60 Hz. Finally, PAL defines the black level (see the Glossary) as 0, the same as the reference level for sync. Yet, the newly defined high-definition standard can be "downconverted" to any of the above-mentioned standards: NTSC, PAL, or SECAM.

In NTSC, 7.5 is the stated black level, and 0 is the sync reference level. NTSC, PAL, and SECAM are incompatible with each other. Standards converters can convert video from one standard to another. Productions intended to be broadcast or released in different video standards are often shot on film (although now high-definition 24p may replace that international film standard), which can be converted to any video standard with little or no loss of resolution.

INTERNATIONAL HIGH DEFINITION

Countries other than the United States are also moving toward digital television broadcasting (DTV) but are not going to follow the United States' choices in HDTV standards. Though the United States has adopted what is called ATSC/8-VSB, most other companies apparently are going to apply the DVD-T/COFDM standard to their HDTV broadcasting. The DVD-T format apparently works better in mountainous terrain.

TIME CODE

The development of time code made frame-accurate, repeatable video editing possible. *Time code* is a labeling system that identifies video frames and audio signals by referencing a 24-hour clock (see Figure 2-7). Each video frame is identified by an eight-digit number in the format hours:minutes:seconds:frames; for example, 05:15:18:23. Time code enables each frame to be identified and accessed for editing or reference. The time code can be recorded on videotape in several places: on one of the audio tracks (called *longitudinal* time code), in the vertical interval portion of the video signal (*vertical interval* time code, abbreviated VITC and pronounced vit-see), or on the address track of the tape (a special area located in certain tape formats).

Figure 2-7 The time code format.

In concept, time code is very similar to the edge numbers on film. It is an ascending series of numbers assigned to each frame of video. Time code is always read (by humans) in the same format. When recorded properly, time code is synchronized to the beginning of each frame. If time code is recorded by a code generator without being locked to a video source, the code may drift across the video frame, rendering it useless.

Time code also has other data embedded in it: user information and sync information. Time code is divided into 80 digital bits recorded across the video frame. Groups of four bits create a decimal number from zero to nine. There are 32 bits reserved in the code for user information. With 32 bits, only the numbers zero through nine can be used in simple systems, or the letters A through F in more complicated systems. Four binary numbers are used to represent 16 characters (0–9 and A–F). This encoding method is called *hexadecimal notation*. User bits might indicate reels in a show; for example, reel 15 shot on September 20 at location 11 could be encoded 15 09 20 11. The coding equipment can be set to record the user information on each frame of video. The sync information defines the end of the frame of time code, which allows time code readers to determine the direction in which the tape is traveling.

In a composite video signal, the phase relationship of the color burst inverts every frame. (Component video does not require this phase reversal.) If an editor connects two frames with the same phase relationship in a composite edit bay, a horizontal picture shift occurs. When cutting to a completely new picture, this shift is unnoticeable. When cutting to the same image (to extend a freeze frame or graphic), this shift is very obvious. Color phase information is included in the time code signal, aiding computerized video editing systems in keeping the phase relationship of edited tapes consistent.

There are two kinds of time code: drop frame time code and non–drop frame time code. *Drop frame time code* is time accurate, meaning that one hour of time code equals one hour of videotape running in play mode. *Non–drop frame time code* is *not* time accurate. An hour of non–drop frame time code is equal to one hour *and 3.6 seconds* of videotape running in play mode (see Figure 2-8).

The difference between the two types of time code occurred because the National Television Standards Committee decided that the color television signal would run at 29.97 frames per second rather than 30 frames per second. When time code was first introduced, however, the code was designated with 30 frames per second. Over one hour, the 0.03-frame-per-second error adds up to 3.6 seconds. To compensate for this error, a system was devised to drop certain *numbers* from

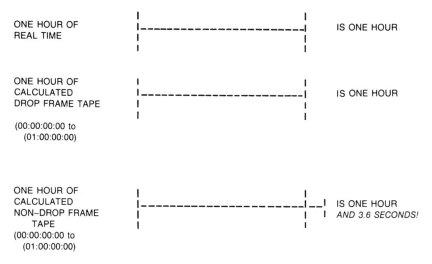

Figure 2-8 A comparison of timings between drop frame and non–drop frame time code.

the counting. This error became very apparent when producers had to deliver time-accurate program material to broadcasting companies, so drop frame time code was created to compensate for the problem.

The :00 and :01 frames are dropped at every new minute except at the 10-minute marks: 10 minutes, 20 minutes, 30 minutes, and so on (see Figure 2-9). This amounts to 108 dropped numbers (3.6 seconds), which allows drop frame time code to keep accurate time and also gives it its name. Dropping these numbers does not change any video content. Drop frame time code is used for programs that must be edited to meet certain time requirements. These shows must be edited to the second. Since drop frame time code is time accurate, it is used in these cases.

Non–drop frame time code (non–time accurate) is most often used to edit commercials and promotional tapes. Since commercials are usually no longer than one minute, there is no need to worry about the two frames dropped at the top of the minute. In addition, commercial editors like to start commercials at the start of a minute (02:01:00:00). However, there is only a true minute start in drop frame time code every ten minutes. Minutes 1 through 9 have :00 and :01 dropped. Similarly, promotional tapes are usually cut according to their content and pacing, without much concern for to-the-second timing.

Types of Time Code Recording

There are three types of time code recording, all of which originate with a time code generator. The three types are audio (longitudinal) time code, address track time code, and vertical interval time code.

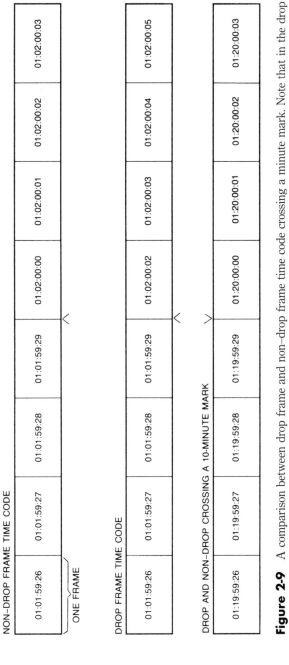

Figure 2-9 A comparison between drop frame and non–drop frame time code crossing a minute mark. Note that in the drop frame time code, the :00 and :01 numbers are dropped. The exception occurs when crossing a 10-minute mark.

Audio or longitudinal time code is digitally encoded by a time code generator and recorded onto an audio track of a tape. It can be erased or regenerated (duplicated) and then recorded onto another tape. Audio time code can be recorded during the production phase of a show or after shooting has been completed. The time code can be recorded on any available audio channel.

Address track time code is used on three-quarter-inch professional broadcast videotape formats. Address track time code can be recorded only on decks specifically designed to record and read address track and is recorded during an assemble recording. The advantage of address track time code is that it does not occupy a production audio channel.

Vertical interval time code (VITC) is a picture signal recorded in the vertical interval. The advantage of this type of time code is that, unlike audio and address track time code, it is readable even when the tape is not moving. Since VITC is recorded in the vertical interval using a video channel, it does not occupy an audio channel. VITC can also indicate the particular field on which the videotape is parked.

VITC must be recorded at the same time as the picture. Recording and decoding the code requires special equipment. More expensive decks, such as D2 and digital Betacam, often come with VITC decoders built into them. You should check the availability of this equipment before planning to use this type of time code. Also, you should take care when recording VITC to make sure that the VITC is the same as the time code on the audio time code channel. Care must be taken when editing or recording tapes with VITC time code, as there are ways to record one set of numbers on the longitudinal track and another in the vertical interval. This ability to record different time codes on the same tape is used in music video production where the sync code of the playback machine that has the music of the song is put in the vertical interval (to facilitate syncing of various takes) while the linear time code is used for creating an edit decision list. A window dub of both time codes in the picture is created to show editors both codes.

Time code should not be copied directly from tape to tape because time code is a digital signal that degrades with a straight transfer, and tape noise can render the code useless. Time code can be regenerated by feeding the original time code signal into a regenerator, which creates a clean, new signal that can be recorded onto the same tape or used to create a window dub (a copy of a tape with time code *burned* into the picture) or submaster (a copy of an original show for protection). Many decks that have time code capability also have the ability to regenerate time code internally.

Working with Time Code

As stated earlier, time code comes from a time code generator, either from an internal generator on the machine or from an external time code generator. The operator selects drop frame or non–drop frame time code on the generator, along with the specific starting point (hour, minute, second, and frame). The time code must be in exact sync with the video; thus, an external generator must be locked to the record deck or a common reference signal. Recording unlocked time code will result in *nonsynchronous* code, meaning that the code for one field will fall across two video fields, making the code impossible to use in editing situations. Some producers prefer to label videotape reels with code. For instance, reel 1 would have a one-hour time code, reel 2 a two-hour time code, and so on. If a shot is logged with a four-hour time code but the log indicates reel 3, there must be an error.

Another way to use time code is to record the time-of-day code on the tape. This is done by setting the time code generator to a clock and having it run in drop frame. For instance, time code 04:00:00:00 would indicate that the shot was made at 4 o'clock. If the editor wants to find something that happened at a particular time of day, he or she can just search the tape for that time code. A potential problem with the time-of-day method is that the code generator switches from 23 hours to zero hours at midnight. If the operator does not put up a new reel at midnight, the time code at the end of the reel will have a lower number than the time code at the beginning. The computer editor will always look for the lowest number toward the beginning of the reel. One solution is to always change the reels at midnight. Using time-of-day code also means that different reels could have the same numbers. A shot at time code 10:00:00:00 could be on any reel that was recording at 10 o'clock.

For edit master stock, most professionals start their time code at 00:58:00:00 or 09:58:00:00, both of which allow for two minutes of code for bars and tone, slates, and any other visual or audio information. The program would start at either 01:00:00:00 or 10:00:00:00 (see Figure 2-10). Most producers record time code on their production footage as they shoot as most recorders have code generators built into their circuitry. In addition, if code is displayed during the production phase, notes can be taken using the code as a reference.

Adding and subtracting time code takes a little practice, but is not terribly difficult (see Figure 2-11). There are 30 frames of video to the second, 60 seconds

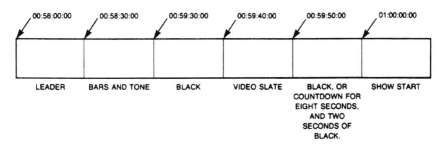

Figure 2-10 One method of placing the bars and tone, video slate, and countdown on a record tape.

$$
\begin{array}{r}
10{:}13 \\
+\,55{:}16 \\
\hline
65{:}29 \;=\; 1{:}05{:}29
\end{array}
$$

$$
\begin{array}{r}
00{:}01{.}15 \\
+\,01{:}59{:}16 \\
\hline
1{:}60{:}31 \;=\; 2{:}00{:}31
\end{array}
$$

$$
\begin{array}{r}
1{:}00{:}00{:}01 \\
+\,4{:}59{:}59{:}29 \\
\hline
5{:}59{:}59{:}30 \;=\; 5{:}59{:}60{:}00 \;=\; 5{:}60{:}00{:}00 \;=\; 6{:}00{:}00{:}00
\end{array}
$$

$$
\begin{array}{rl}
1{:}02{:}17 \;=\; & 61{:}77 \\
-\,{:}58{:}19 \;=\; & -\,58{:}19 \\
\hline
& 3{:}58
\end{array}
$$

$$
\begin{array}{rllll}
5{:}01{:}10{:}08 \;=\; & 5{:}01{:}09{:}38 \;=\; & 5{:}00{:}69{:}38 \;=\; & 4{:}60{:}69{:}38 \\
-\,4{:}59{:}20{:}09 \;=\; & -\,4{:}59{:}20{:}09 \;=\; & -\,4{:}59{:}20{:}09 \;=\; & -\,4{:}59{:}20{:}09 \\
\hline
& {:}29 & 49{:}29 & 1{:}49{:}29
\end{array}
$$

Figure 2-11 Several examples of adding and subtracting time code.

to the minute, and 60 minutes to the hour. When calculating time code, an editor usually ignores the difference between drop frame and non–drop frame time code. There are calculators available that will add or subtract time code in either drop or non-drop mode. Whichever numbering system the producer chooses, the most important consideration is finding the picture that each time code number represents.

THE COLOR VIDEO SIGNAL: COMPOSITE, COMPONENT, AND Y/C

The color video signal comprises four basic elements: the luminance or brightness (white) values within the picture, and the three chrominance or color values (red, green, and blue). These four elements combine to create the color signal.

As noted in Chapter 1, there are several methods of recording color, two of which are the component and composite formats. Composite video integrates both the luminance and the chrominance portions of the signal, and thus can be transmitted from point to point along one wire.

Standard component video divides the signal into three parts, and thus requires three wires to travel through switchers or other electronic gear. The three signals that travel in the standard component environment are the luminance signal (denoted by the symbol Y), the red signal minus the luminance (R−Y), and the blue signal minus the luminance (B−Y). With these three signals, the color green also can be represented (see Figure 2-12).

COMPOSITE, COMPONENT AND COLOR UNDER

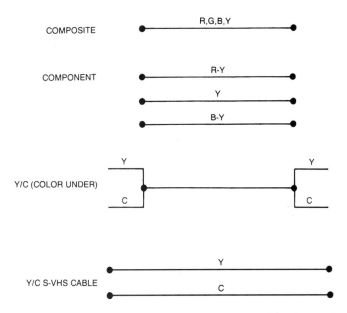

Figure 2-12 Composite video encodes the chrominance and luminance signals and sends them down one wire. Component video uses three wires to transmit the video signal. The green component of color is mathematically extracted from the information on three wires. Color under is a composite signal that is encoded and decoded at the recording and playback deck. Digital composite video is a digital signal using one wire; digital component video is a digital signal that uses three wires.

Since color information is not embedded in the component luminance signal, as it is in the composite signal, the component path and recording signal are superior to those of the composite signal. Although composite video was used first, now most productions use component videotape formats. Some of the component video formats are D1, MII, Digital Betacam, Betacam SP, Betacam SX, DV, DVC-Pro, Digi 8, and DCT.

There is a third type of color recording, called *Y/C*, which is used to record the video signal. Also called *color under*, Y/C is used in VHS, S-VHS, 8 mm, and Hi-8 recordings. Some edit systems have specific inputs to accept the separate luminance and chrominance signals. By separating the luminance from the chroma (the red, green, and blue signals), the two signals maintain a distinctness that helps to recreate the picture information during playback.

RGB (red, green, blue) is another type of video signal that provides a separate channel for output from paint systems (computers used for picture creation and/or animation) and computers. This type of signal is of extremely

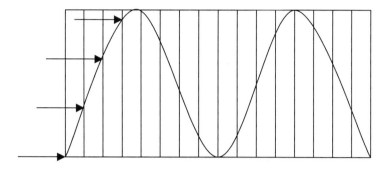

In digital sampling, the signal is examined at regular intervals and converted into numbers which are then stored on videotape. This sampling can occur millions of times a second.

Figure 2-13   A simplified example of how digital sampling works.

high quality, and in many cases carries much more information than a component signal. However, to record the output of a paint system or computer, the RGB signal moves with its accompanying luminance signal into a converter, where its information is transformed into a composite or component signal.

DIGITAL VIDEO

Digital technology has significantly altered the way video is shot, processed, and edited. Analog video signals consist of smoothly varying voltage levels. Digital technology, on the other hand, divides a signal into tiny segments of time and measures the quality of the signal within each segment (see Figure 2-13). The segments and their measurements are expressed in binary digits, a complex series of positive (one) and null (zero) values. Binary digits are more easily processed than analog signals and can be copied without the generational loss of quality that occurs with analog signals.

There are several digital formats in use. Like analog video recording, digital video can be either component or composite. In other words, the picture that is sampled digitally can be as an overall picture (composite) or as a separate recording of the three primary colors and the white level in the signal (component).

SUMMARY

Videotape is composed of a strong Mylar backing covered with a thin layer of ferrous oxide. The oxide, which is easily magnetized, is the substance that stores the video and audio information. Metal tape is highly refined videotape using metal particles to enhance recording sensitivity.

Blank tape has nothing recorded on it. You can either buy blank tape or erase previously used stock.

Control track is a pulse, recorded on the videotape in an assemble recording, that marks each revolution of the record drum and the beginning of each frame (called the frame pulse). The control track acts as a guide for the playback of the video signal.

If there is an alteration in the spacing of the control track, the picture will roll until the spacing becomes even again. All video formats use different, yet similar, control track signals. Two types of video recording are available: assemble and insert.

An assemble recording erases everything that was originally on that tape and totally replaces the video, audio, and control track. An insert recording can replace video, audio, or both video and audio, but does not disturb the tape's control track. Before an insert recording can be made, the tape must have a control track recorded on it. To lay down a continuous, unbroken control track, an assemble recording is made for the length of the videotape. Almost all professional editing situations require the use of insert recordings.

Scanning every other video field is called interlaced scanning. To record an entire frame of video is called progressive.

Most time code is a digitally encoded audio signal that numbers each frame of video. The only exception is the vertical interval time code (VITC), which is a video signal.

Drop frame time code is time accurate, meaning that one hour of time code equals one hour of videotape running in play mode. Non–drop frame time code is *not* time accurate; an hour of non–drop frame time code equals one hour *and 3.6 seconds* of videotape running in play mode. The numbers that are dropped in drop frame time code are the :00 and :01 frames at every new minute, except at the 10-minute marks (10 minutes, 20 minutes, 30 minutes, etc.).

There are three types of time code recordings: audio (longitudinal) time code, address track time code, and vertical interval time code. All three originate from a time code generator. Audio (longitudinal) time code is recorded on one of the tape's available audio tracks. Address track time code is used only on three-quarter-inch professional broadcast videotape formats. Address track time code is physically recorded in the same location as the video but at a different frequency. Vertical interval time code is a picture signal recorded in the vertical interval (the video frame line) and must be recorded at the same time as the picture.

Time code is a method of labeling frames of video.

Composite video is an encoded signal that travels along one wire. Component video requires three wires, one each for the luminance signal (Y), the red signal minus the luminance (R–Y), and the blue signal minus the luminance (B–Y). The component path and recording signal are superior to those of the composite signal.

Two other color recording formats are Y/C and RGB. Y/C recording separates the luminance from the chroma (the red, green, and blue signals). RGB often originates from paint systems and computers.

Digital video can use either component (D1, Digital Betacam, DCT, etc.) or composite (D2, D3) signals.

Videotape Formats and Their Uses

As technology has advanced, new videotape formats have come into use and older ones have disappeared. In the early stages of videotape, successive formats became less expensive and often smaller in size. In the late 1980s, this trend was reversed. The first digital video formats proved more expensive than their precursors and thus did not rapidly replace older formats. At the turn of the century, the U.S. government mandated that television stations begin broadcasting in digital format and eventually have 100 percent digital broadcasting by the year 2006. With the new digital high-definition formats creating more video format choices, producers, networks, and television stations were faced with the task of trying to guess which format would become the most commonly used. The three major networks have chosen their broadcasting formats, but the videotape format that will eventually become the de facto standard has not been determined.

With the exception of the obsolete two-inch quad, all video formats discussed here are helical-scan recordings. Two-inch quad machines rotate their record heads perpendicularly to the tape travel, whereas helical-scan machines spin the record heads at an angle to the tape. Helical scanning allows the video and audio heads to reach more of the videotape, allowing the use of narrower tape.

TWO-INCH QUAD TAPE

Two-inch quad is the granddaddy of videotape (see Figure 3-1). The name comes from *quadruplex*, which indicates that the signal is created using four record

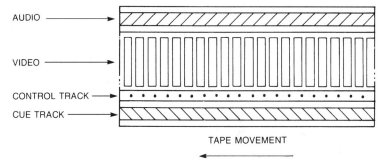

Figure 3-1 A quad (two-inch) recording.

heads. Since quad requires segmented recording, the picture could only be seen in play mode. Slow motion and freeze frames were not possible without using another device. Almost all quad machines have been put out of service.

ONE-INCH TAPE

One-inch tape came in two formats: Type B and Type C. Type B was developed by Bosch-Fernseh, and Type C was originally produced in a joint effort between Ampex and Sony. Neither the recordings nor the tape stocks of the two formats are compatible.

Both Type B and Type C used one-inch-wide tape and had three channels of audio. The first two channels, or tracks, are designed for production audio, and the third for time code. One-inch machines are being phased out, but there are many still in use.

THREE-QUARTER-INCH TAPE

In the late 1970s, the U-Matic three-quarter-inch video format became very popular in the broadcasting and industrial markets. In the mid-1980s, Sony added address track code capability to the three-quarter-inch format, which allowed time code to be recorded on the tape and left both audio tracks available for production sound.

The three-quarter-inch format replaced 16 mm film at most television news departments, as it made recording news images much faster and easier. The introduction of the Sony SP line improved this popular format still further by using metal tape and more sophisticated recording methods.

Many industrial productions and locally produced television commercials were made using three-quarter-inch machines. However, with the high resolution of the DV and DVPro formats, along with affordable random-access home computer editing, the three-quarter-inch decks are now being phased out. With so many nonlinear editing systems in use, there is a plan to use DVDs for window dubs and viewing copies.

HALF-INCH PROFESSIONAL TAPE

The Sony Betacam

This format became a very popular choice of broadcasters and high-end industrial producers because of its ability to record a quality picture that recorded the luminance (white and black) separately from the chroma (color). This process is called *component recording*. This method results in a high-quality picture and produces cleaner keys, chroma keys, and other effects.

News crews were among the first to use the half-inch format. Because the camera and recorder were contained in one unit, the camera operator could move around freely.

MII Format

Panasonic unveiled its own professional half-inch format in 1986. The MII format records a cleaner picture than the original Betacam system, and has a built-in time code generator/reader and four audio channels with more than adequate recording capabilities. The studio version also has built-in slow motion and still frame modes and can record up to one hour of video per tape.

In early 1986, Sony announced that it would upgrade its Betacam with the Betacam SP line. This improvement was a direct result of the MII introduction which addressed many of the shortcomings of the original Betacam line.

DIGITAL FORMATS

Professional digital videotape has provided producers with several new formats. All have the advantage of little or no picture degradation over multiple generations. D1 was the first digital tape format. Expensive, yet capable of excellent quality recording, D1 did not take the broadcast world by storm. D2, a composite format, made more inroads, but the "digi" Betacam was the digital format that became the standard as a result of its lower cost and backward compatibility with Betacam and Betacam SP. Several manufacturers are already marketing high-definition equipment, with the knowledge that being first could mean being an industry leader. Snell & Wilcox has brought out several HD switchers, one of which is shown in Figure 3-2.

Figure 3-2 A high-definition switcher manufactured by Snell & Wilcox. As more productions are shot on high def, more equipment to handle the postproduction chores will be manufactured. Photo courtesy of Snell & Wilcox.

More digital formats became available. Then came the confusion concerning high-definition television. The confusion comes from the issue of cost versus performance; producers, facilities, and networks are trying to figure out which format will supply economical advantages but will not be obsolete quickly, considering the possibility of advances in electronics. Several industry leaders are considering a return to 35 mm film as an acquisition format, because film can always be transferred to a new video format.

Because of the huge amount of data contained in film, to record all the information possible would take a great deal of videotape moving extremely quickly. This would result in increased cost (for making the tape drive and buying a great deal of videotape). The practical decision for broadcasters (and engineers) was to eliminate repeated information and only record information that the

Figure 3-3 A Sony HD video camera with Canon lens. Photo courtesy of Sony Broadcast.

human eye could perceive. Thus many tape formats eliminate a lot of information through a complex formula (for most digital formats it is a process called *MPEG2*) and then only record a ratio of color versus black and white information (called the *sampling rate*).

There are a number of digital videotape formats. For the sake of this discussion, let's divide the tape formats into four categories:

*   HDTV professional—professional formats designed to be used in high-definition (16 × 9 aspect ratio) television and film production (see Figure 3-3)
*   SDTV professional—established tape formats that are currently in use in standard definition (4 × 3 aspect or 16 × 9 ratio)
*   Prosumer—medium-quality formats that, if used carefully, can be considered broadcast quality
*   Consumer—lower end, low-quality home use

HDTV PROFESSIONAL FORMATS

D16

This tape format is in a class of its own. D1 tape, running at sixteen times original speed, was designed to store images from the Quantel Domino (a film

Tape Format	Sampling Ratio	Compression	Common uses - notes
HDD1000	4:2:2	Uncompressed	Top of the line HD recorder – reel to reel – very expensive
HDCAM	3:1:1	7:1	compression backward compatible
D VHS	N/A	MPEG-2	Digital wide screen viewing format firewire compatible
W VHS	N/A	Compressed analogue	Analogue wide screen VHS viewing format
D-5 HD	4:2:2	uncompressed	HD compatible for all 18 digital formats. Format used to shoot new Star Wars movie.
D-6	4:2:2	uncompressed	Digital HD recorder using D1 Tape
D-9 HD (DVCPRO HD)	4:2:2	7:1	Can shoot in 16x9 or 3x4. Some models can also play SVHS

Figure 3-4 High-definition professional digital video formats. There are relatively few choices, but this may change as HDTV becomes more accepted by producers and the general viewing audience.

resolution electronic system). This format is used mainly for transporting high-quality images in and out of the Domino into film recorders or out of film scanners.

D5 HD (Panasonic)

A modified D5, but not compatible with the standard definition model, this is the video format that is being used for shooting the second installment of the *Star Wars* movie. It has eight channels of audio and records a 4:1 compressed HD signal that, along with an optional universal format converter, can play back any of the digital broadcast formats. Newer models are backward compatible with the older D5 (SDTV).

D-6 (Phillips)

This is a cassette-based VTR that has the capability to record multiple versions of HD recording, 1125/60 and 1250/50 (Europe), and the ability to handle 1080 active lines. Also to be included is an uncompressed version of the 1080p/24 format. It is a very high-end HD format. However, with an expensive (over $350,000) price tag, its use is limited.

D9-HD (JVC)

This format is modeled after the manufacturer's D9 (Digital S) format. This high-definition format is designed to be a cost-effective answer to recording in the

Figure 3-5 A DVCPRO HD recorder. Note the backward compatibility of the deck. Photo courtesy of Panasonic Broadcasting.

widescreen format. It has no analog input or output and is compressed at 3.3:1. The D9 format can record up to eight 16-bit audio channels. It has backward compatibility to D9 (SDTV).

HDD1000 (Sony)

This machine was the first digital VTR capable of recording full-bandwidth, uncompressed high definition. These open-reel machines record a frame of video over many adjacent tracks. The format includes eight digital audio channels and an analog cue track. It is the more expensive of the two HD formats Sony manufactures.

HDCAM (Sony)

The HDCAM was developed to support a new HD camcorder based on the established Digital Betacam chassis. With an approximate compression rate of 6:1, it was the first HD format to offer a camcorder (a single unit comprising a recorder and a camera).

DVCPRO HD (Panasonic)

This format is backward compatible to D7 (DVCPRO; see Figure 3-5). One model, the HD150, is playback compatible with mini DV, DVCAM, DVCPRO, DVCPRO25, and DVCPRO50. When using a format converter, it is possible to play back any of those DV or DVCPRO formats and output either 1080i or 720p. The deck also has eight channels of audio.

D-VHS (JVC)

This format is a digital VHS capable of recording data like the kind transmitted via satellite and DTV broadcasters. D-VHS machines would provide backward compatibility with VHS machines already in use. JVC is now introducing models with built-in encoder/decoders with IEEE 1394 (Firewire) inputs/outputs. D-VHS machines are not production recorders, as the data has been far too compressed to be editable, but the format can be used for projection or regular viewing.

W-VHS (JVC)

The W-VHS is analog, and like the D-VHS though incompatible with it, is designed to play and record high-definition 1035i, 1080i, or 1125i component analog signals. W-VHS machines can record or play regular VHS tapes. The W-VHS models have assemble edit and audio dub capabilities and a VGA output. They will plug into any HD camcorder or D5-HD machine. Another benefit of the W-VHS recorder is the VGA output on the back, allowing a computer monitor to be used as an inexpensive HDTV monitor.

SDTV PROFESSIONAL FORMATS

Digital Betacam (Sony)

Digital Betacam is the de facto postproduction standard in most professional facilities. It uses a 2:1 compression and 10-bit component digital signals. Four audio channels are included. Properly optioned Digital Betacam decks can play back analog Betacam-format tapes.

One Inch (Sony, Ampex)

This format was the workhorse of video for years, but is now being replaced by Digi Betacam and D9. Open reels and two audio channels are the trademarks of this format.

MII (Panasonic)

This half-inch analog component format was a rival to Betacam SP. It too is rapidly being replaced by the new digital component formats.

STANDARD DEFININTION (4 X 3) DIGITAL TAPE FORMATS

Tape Format	Compression	Sampling ratio	Recording Format	Common uses - notes
D-1	Not Compressed	4:2:2:4	Component	Excellent top of the line SDTV format-high end graphics, mastering
D-2	Not Compressed	4:0:0	Composite	Editing, mastering, being replaced by other component formats
D-3	Not Compressed	4:0:0	Component	Editing, mastering
D-5	Not Compressed	4:2:2	Component	Excellent top of the line SDTV format-high end graphics, mastering, can play D3
D-7 (DVC PRO)	5:1	4:1:1	Component	Compatible with DVC and DVCAM
D-9 (Digital S)	3.3:1	4:2:2	Component	Can shoot in 16x9 or 3x4. Some models can also play SVHS. Becoming more popular
DCT	2:1	4:2:2	Component	Editing and mastering
Betacam SX	10:1	4:2:2	Component	Used for new broadcasting. Can play Betacam and Betacam SP
DVCAM	5:1	4:1:1	Component	Compatible with DV (the consumer digital video format) but will not play DVC PRO or PRO 50
Digital Betacam	2:1	4:2:2	Component	De facto digital editing and mastering format. Some models also play Betacam & Betacam SP
DVC Pro 50	3.3:1	4:2:2	Component	Upscale DVC format by doubling tape speed, can play DVCAM and DVC PRO
DV	5:1	4:1:1	Component	Consumer format often called Prosumer.
Digital 8	5:1	4:1:1	Component	Consumer format often called Prosumer. Can play 8mm and Hi8

4:2:2 For every 4 samples of luminance (white values) there are 2 samples each of the color difference signals, R-Y (Red minus Luminance) and B-Y (Blue minus luminance).

4:1:1 For ever y 4 samples of luminance there is 1 sample each of the color difference signals, R-Y (Red minus Luminance) and B-Y (Blue minus luminance).

4:2:0 For every 4 samples of luminance there is a sample of one of the color difference signals, followed by a sample of the other color difference signal on the next luminance sample.

4:4:4 A sampling ratio that has equal amounts of the luminance and both chrominance channels. Can also be used for RGB sampling, the color space used in most computer programs.

Figure 3-6 Standard-definition digital tape formats provide many choices, but eventually they will be phased out.

Betacam SX (Sony)

A digital, highly compressed (10:1) tape format that was designed for ENG and field work. The format can upload and download at four times sound speed, but has no slow-motion or speed-up capability, although editing stations, such as the DNWA 225 (see Figure 3-7), have built-in hard drives for dissolve and variable motion effects.

Figure 3-7 A Sony Betacam SX field editing station, Sony's DNWA 225. It features frame-accurate insert editing and Betacam and Betacam SP tape playback. It can be docked with a second or third DNWA 225. Photo courtesy of Sony Broadcast.

DCT (Ampex)

A high-quality digital tape format used in high-end postproduction houses. The Ampex CCIR 601 digital VTR uses DCT to compress the video signal before recording it to tape.

D1 (Sony)

This digital tape format records uncompressed "601" component digital format. Four digital audio channels are included. The first digital videotape format was D1. Its cost limited its use to high-end graphics and effects.

D2 (Sony, Ampex)

A quality digital composite recording which was rapidly replaced by Digital Betacam (a component recording). Four digital audio channels are included.

D3 (Panasonic)

A composite digital format that is less expensive than but similar to D2. Four digital audio channels are included. It too has limited use these days.

D4

The number four is considered unlucky in Japan. No tape formats use this designation.

D5 (Panasonic)

A component digital format similar to D1, but D5 does uncompressed component digital recording. With the proper options, D5 VTRs can play back D3 format tapes, and provide either a composite or component digital signal. However, D3 VTRs cannot play back D5 format tapes.

D7 (Panasonic, Ikegami, Phillips)

DVCPRO (see Figure 3-5) was introduced in 1995 primarily by Panasonic. It is similar to the consumer DV format except that the tape speed is twice that of DV. It is also backward compatible with the DV format. It is compressed approximately 5:1. The video data rate of this format is 25 MB/s (25 megabytes per second).

DVCPRO 50

This advancement in the DVCPRO format uses a video data rate of 50 MB/s—double that of other DV systems—and is aimed at the higher quality end of the market, designed to compete with the D9 digital format. Sampling is 4:2:2 to give enhanced chroma resolution, useful in postproduction processes (e.g., chroma keying). Four audio tracks are provided. The recording is 5:1 compression from a 4:1:1 8-bit sampled source. It includes two 16-bit digital audio channels sampled at 48 kHz and an analog cue track.

D8

There is no D8 nor will there be.

D9 (JVC)

Digital-S format uses the DV compression algorithm. It is a 601 composite digital recording compressed about 3:1. Newer machines record four audio channels.

DVCAM (Sony)

Introduced in 1996, this is Sony's improvement of the original DV format and competes with Panasonic's DVCPRO. Audio is recorded in one of two forms— four 12-bit channels sampled at 32 kHz, or two 16-bit channels sampled at 48 kHz.

PROSUMER FORMATS

The increased resolution and editing abilities afforded the consumer market blurred the boundary between professional and consumer equipment. Generally speaking, a professional camcorder has one or more of the following advantages:

- Three CCDs—Consumer camcorders only have one CCD. (The CCD is a chip that converts images into a digital signal.)
- Professional quality microphone inputs.
- Headphone jacks.
- Detachable lenses so a director of photography can pick and choose lenses that suit the production requirement.
- A video output to monitor the camera's image externally.

Lighting, camera work, set design, quality of writing, cast performance, camera composition, and audio quality of a video project indicate to the audience the level of production long before image quality does.

DV (Several manufacturers)

This consumer format uses approximately 5:1 compression to produce near Betacam quality on a very small cassette. The format was improved with increased tape speed (DVCPro and DVCam).

Digital 8 (Sony)

Sony has taken the DV format and applied it to their 8 mm standards. With backward compatibility to Hi-8 and 8 mm, consumers can play back their old tapes or can record new digital images and load them into their computers (Sony calls their IEEE 1394 transfer Ilink, as opposed to Firewire.)

CONSUMER FORMATS

With the low cost of digital prosumer formats, there is no reason to use these analog formats for any productions other than consumer home use. Generally speaking, VHS has remained a common viewing format. However, 8mm and Hi-8 are being replaced with digital 8 recorder/players because all three can be played with a digital 8 camcorder.

VHS (Various)

VHS is a fuzzy, analog format, but there are millions of players throughout the world. This tape standard is still used as a viewing format.

8 mm/Hi-8 (Sony)

These two formats are being replaced by the new Sony format Digital 8. But they are still used by consumers as production and editing formats.

S-VHS

S-VHS was an improvement over VHS, but now the DV and Digital 8 are so much better, it will probably be replaced as a high-end consumer format.

REAL AND FALSE HIGH-DEFINITION BROADCASTING

The concept of high definition is similar to that of "broadcast quality." Take for example a multigenerational dub of a VHS tape. The signal is not broadcast quality. However, if you take that tape and expand it in a digital device and record that signal on a D1 recorder, it will technically be a high-definition signal, although it will look like fuzz. Broadcast quality is a subjective term that applies to the resolution of an image. So, an image can have the technical specifications of a high-quality recording, yet be less than broadcast quality because of its appearance.

The high-definition dilemma will probably force broadcasters to fill the 16 × 9 rectangle like that shown in Figure 3-8 with an originally shot 4 × 3 picture. By expanding the original 4 × 3 picture and cropping the top and bottom, the image

Figure 3-8 Consumer model of a 16 × 9 high-definition television. More and more of these HD sets are being sold as consumers realize the outstanding visual quality of HD.

will fit the frame, but will not be high definition because the original image does not have a high resolution due to the expansion of the signal. Feature films will most likely be retransferred in the new format, but video originally shot in a 4 × 3 ratio will have to be blown up or remain in its 4 × 3 aspect ratio. These issues will be addressed as we come closer to the end of analog television broadcasting.

EDITING FACILITIES AND TAPE FORMAT CHOICES

Every editing room (see Figure 3-9a) is built in a modular fashion. Each piece of equipment is chosen and installed in accordance with the facility's demands (see Figure 3-9b). The design can allow for technological improvements and limited flexibility. Certain types of playback decks may or may not be available.

With newer nonlinear edit bays, this is becoming less of an issue. Most effects can be accomplished, and many facilities have access to a Digital Betacam, a common format that most images can be transferred to without signal degradation.

Still, it is best to use original footage to lessen the possibility of errors. It is always a good idea to edit at a facility that not only has the necessary machines

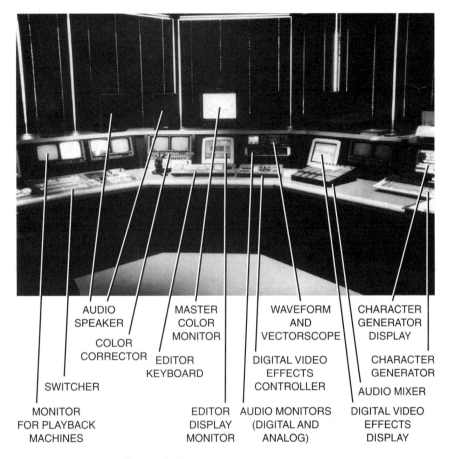

AUDIO SPEAKER	MASTER COLOR MONITOR	WAVEFORM AND VECTORSCOPE	CHARACTER GENERATOR DISPLAY
COLOR CORRECTOR	EDITOR KEYBOARD	DIGITAL VIDEO EFFECTS CONTROLLER	CHARACTER GENERATOR
SWITCHER			AUDIO MIXER
MONITOR FOR PLAYBACK MACHINES	EDITOR DISPLAY MONITOR	AUDIO MONITORS (DIGITAL AND ANALOG)	DIGITAL VIDEO EFFECTS DISPLAY

Figure 3-9a   A linear on-line editing bay.

but is familiar with the production's original format. In larger metropolitan areas, there are multiformat edit rooms that can integrate a number of source formats. Composite and component signals, like those from three-quarter-inch such as a Sony BVU-950, can be edited in the same bay through the use of converters.

The editing facilities, the available equipment, and the show's production requirements all influence the choice of video mastering format.

FORMAT USES

Here are some general guidelines concerning existing formats.

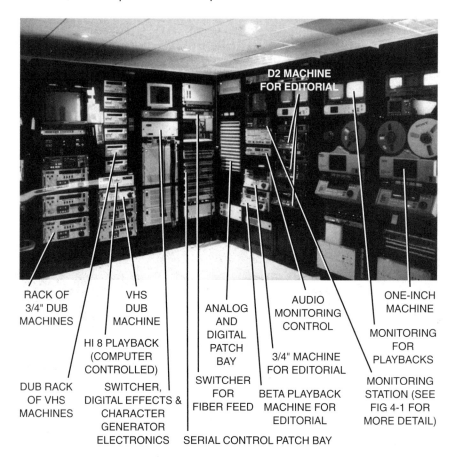

RACK OF 3/4" DUB MACHINES

VHS DUB MACHINE

HI 8 PLAYBACK (COMPUTER CONTROLLED)

DUB RACK OF VHS MACHINES

SWITCHER, DIGITAL EFFECTS & CHARACTER GENERATOR ELECTRONICS

ANALOG AND DIGITAL PATCH BAY

SWITCHER FOR FIBER FEED

SERIAL CONTROL PATCH BAY

AUDIO MONITORING CONTROL

3/4" MACHINE FOR EDITORIAL

BETA PLAYBACK MACHINE FOR EDITORIAL

ONE-INCH MACHINE

MONITORING FOR PLAYBACKS

MONITORING STATION (SEE FIG 4-1 FOR MORE DETAIL)

D2 MACHINE FOR EDITORIAL

Figure 3-9b A typical machine room in an on-line facility. Photos courtesy of New Wave Entertainment, Burbank, California.

High-Definition Formats

- D16—Only for film effects
- HDD1000, D5, D6—Top-of-the-line HD production or film production
- D9-HD, HDCAM, DVCPRO HD—Compressed HD formats positioned for broadcast use
- D-VHS, W-VHS—Taping and viewing of widescreen projects

SDTV Professional Formats

- Digital Betacam—De facto standard for 4 × 3 digital production and postproduction

Figure 3-10 The Sony D2 player/recorder. This was the standard production format for some time, but component editing replaced many of these composite machines in the mid to late 1990s. Photo courtesy of Sony Electronics, Inc.

- One-inch, MII—Becoming obsolete; buy new digital machines
- Betacam SX D9 D7, (DVPRO & DVPRO 50)—Good, economical digital production formats for news, field production
- DCT—An excellent production format, but editing facilities must be located before committing to this tape
- D1, D5—High-end graphics and effects
- D2, D3—Good quality digital composite recordings, but there are better and cheaper digital component formats available

Prosumer

- Digital 8, DV—Great for student and high-end consumer projects

Consumer

- VHS—Home viewing; being replaced in the rental market by DVD disks
- 8 mm, Hi-8—Becoming obsolete; replaced by Digital 8

SUMMARY

Analog broadcasting is coming to an end and will be replaced by DTV (digital broadcasting) by the year 2007.

With the exception of the obsolete two-inch quad, all video formats are helical-scan recordings.

The three-quarter-inch format is still used by broadcasters for viewing copies, but is being phased out.

The Betacam and MII formats became popular because of their component recording technique in which the luminance (white and black) is recorded separately from the chroma (color).

Digital formats are constantly changing and evolving. Potential editing facilities should be contacted before shooting to ensure availability of postproduction facilities that will handle any specific format.

D1 was the first digital tape format. Expensive, but capable of excellent quality recording, it has been used for high-end graphics and postproduction work. Check postproduction facilities before shooting on any format to make sure there is a reasonably priced solution to postproduction of the project.

Film remains a viable high-definition production format. However, it is somewhat expensive due to cost of developing and telecine (film to tape transfer) costs.

Compression formulas are used to keep digital format videotape and machine costs at an economical level.

HDTV tape and formats will continue to evolve. With the rapid advances in chip and electronics, these formats can quickly change and improve.

SDTV formats, will be phased out slowly as HDTV takes hold of the broadcasting world.

Prosumer formats are medium-quality digital recording schemes that, if used carefully, can be considered broadcast quality. When using prosumer formats, one should not forget to keep all the production values as high as possible.

Consumer formats are lower-end, low-quality formats intended for home use.

The transition from SDTV to HDTV will include "bumping up" of original 4×3 productions and the retransferring of film-originated productions.

4

Controlling Video and Audio

When editing with a single playback and a record machine, there is often no way to adjust the color and white values of the playback tape because the record machine makes a direct copy of the playback image. Many edit systems, however, have the ability to alter the look of a video picture. Understanding the basic ways to change the video picture is an important skill to acquire.

THE VIDEO SIGNAL

Video originates at a charge-coupled device (CCD) (see the Glossary). This device converts light into electrical pulses. The pulses include the luminance values of the image (white values); the red, green, and blue values (chroma); and synchronization pulses that keep the information together and allow the white and chroma information to be combined at a later date.

A composite signal mathematically combines the white and color values into a single pulse. This is the least desirable method of transmitting and recording a video signal. A component signal is created by transmitting the video pulses using three wires, one for the luminance signal (Y), one for the red signal minus the luminance (R–Y), and one for the blue signal minus the luminance (B–Y). This is a much more desirable method of recording color and luminance. There is a third method called Y/C recording in which color is separated from luminance. S-VHS and Hi-8 use this type of recording.

Video information can be displayed on a monitor, sent along a cable, broadcast, stored on videotape, or computer hard drive. In recording or broadcasting an analog signal (quickly becoming obsolete due to the many digital formats), electronic pulses constituting the video information are modulated, or impressed onto a radio frequency signal. *Modulating* means altering a signal at a set amplitude or frequency so that its features conform to those of the original video information. This resulting modulated signal can then be recorded to tape or videodisk or transmitted over the air.

Signals to be recorded in analog format are sent to an electromagnet within a recording head. The signals charge the electromagnet, which, in turn, charges the oxide on videotape as it passes across the top of the recording head during the recording process. Playing back a recorded tape reverses the process. The minute magnetization recorded on the tape charges an electromagnet inside a playback head. The resulting signal is amplified, and then the video information is decoded (demodulated) from the signal and sent from the playback deck.

In a digital signal, the image is converted into a series of 1's and 0's. This information is stored on the videotape, along with digital audio, and is decoded on playback. Most digital recorders and players have several options of outputting the video signal, including digital and analog.

In over-the-air broadcasting, the video signal is modulated onto a radio frequency signal. The video signal modifies an electromagnetic wave called a *carrier signal*. The carrier wave, normally a constant wave, is altered in a direct relationship to the video and audio signals. This modulated signal is amplified, and then transmitted by a radio antenna. A television set tuned to the carrier frequency picks up this wave, demodulates it, and displays the picture on its screen. Instead of televisions decoding radio frequencies, in edit bays, monitors display video from an input source.

THE VIDEO PICTURE

As noted in Chapter 2, an electron beam sweeping across the back of the picture tube creates the image we see on a television screen. The beam causes the phosphor on the tube to glow, creating a picture. When the beam returns to the top of the tube to prepare for scanning the next field, information is sent concerning which field this scan represents (equalizing pulses), and signals are sent to make sure the beam is in its proper place (vertical synchronizing pulses).

In 2007, NTSC broadcasting is scheduled to be replaced with digital broadcasting. Because the HDTV portions of this new broadcasting standard have more resolution and a wider screen format than today's NTSC standard, new frequencies have been allotted to television stations. There are currently 18 digital formats (see Figures 2-5 and 2-6). The plan is to have these formats backwardly compatible with the original NTSC formats. The digital signals will be decoded and converted into a picture. The type of television set, type of decoder, and type of broadcast signal will determine what you see at home.

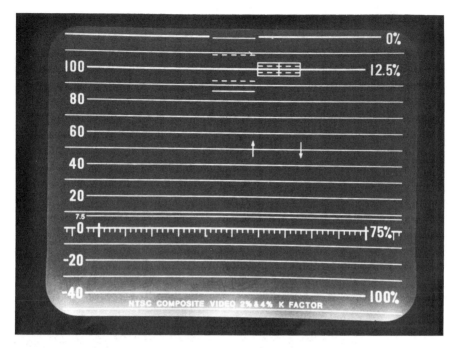

Figure 4-1 A waveform monitor. Photo by Sean Sterling.

Digital formats include options such as resolution, frame rate, and picture aspect. The frame can be interlaced (scanning the odd-numbered lines, then the even-numbered lines as described above) or in a progressive pattern (with line 1 followed by line 2). The 4 × 3 and 16 × 9 rectangle presentations are available as well as several resolution options.

VIDEO SCOPES

Video scopes are used to monitor various aspects of the video signal. To a video editor, the most important of these are the vectorscope and the waveform monitor. These two oscilloscopes display and measure the horizontal and verti-cal blanking as well as the luminance and chroma values of the video signal. The waveform monitor (see Figure 4-1) is often used to monitor the luminance portion of the video signal and the vectorscope (see Figure 4-2) is usually set up to display the color component of the video signal.

On the face of the waveform monitor screen in Figure 4-1 are various mark-ings. The left side has a series of numbers ranging from −40 to 100. These numbers represent IRE units. (IRE was a standard set by the Institute of Radio Engineers, now known as the Institute of Electrical and Electronics Engineers,

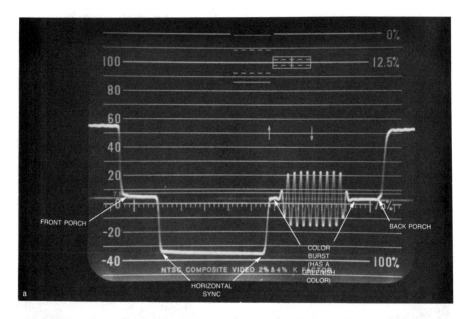

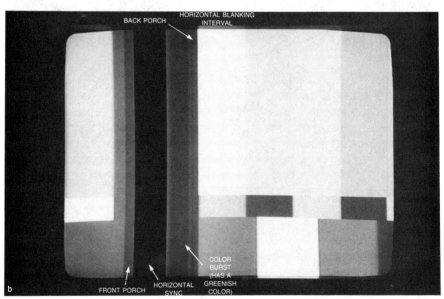

Figure 4-2 (a) A waveform monitor displaying the horizontal blanking interval. Note that the waveform portion of the display is expanded to show the horizontal blanking portion of the signal. (b) A picture of the horizontal blanking interval on a cross-pulse monitor. Photos by Sean Sterling.

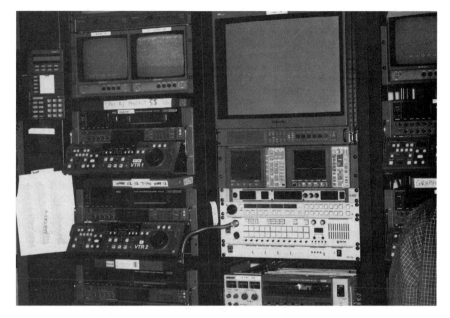

Figure 4-3 A video monitoring station. Photo by Sean Sterling.

abbreviated IEEE.) Horizontal markings are shown at zero, the baseline. The longer lines represent one microsecond, and the shorter lines are divisions of 0.2 microsecond. When looking at one full line of video on the waveform and cross-pulse monitors (see Figures 4-2a and 4-2b), you can see that the video signal is 140 units (−40 to 100).

COLOR STANDARDS

The U.S. television standard is built from three primary colors (red, green, and blue) and three secondary colors (magenta, cyan, and yellow). A mathematical formula is used to encode the color information for broadcasting. To use the formula, however, you must have a standard reference point. This point is called the *color burst*, and it appears on the vectorscope, as can the other colors in the video picture.

Color bars are produced by a reference signal created by a camera or test signal generator. This signal is usually recorded at the beginning of a tape. When the tape is played back, the time base corrector (TBC) is adjusted so that the reference signals correspond to the reference points on the vectorscope and waveform monitor. Most newer digital tape formats adjust the playback tape automatically.

UNSTABLE VIDEOTAPE SIGNALS

Since the wrap (the amount of tape) on the two sides of the videocassette or take-up reels is always changing, the video machine is continually altering the speed of the tape in an attempt to maintain a constant speed across the video heads. The result of this push-pull motion is a highly unstable signal. The TBC accepts this unstable information, delays and corrects the signal, then sends the signal out in sync with the rest of the video system. In addition to correcting time base errors, most TBCs have controls for video and chroma levels.

ADJUSTING THE VIDEO AND CHROMA WITH A TBC

A TBC can alter the color of a television signal in four areas: hue, saturation, video, and setup. The operator checks hue and saturation by examining a vectorscope, and video and setup by using a waveform monitor.

Hue is the relative phase of color and is monitored using a vectorscope. As the operator moves the hue control, all colors are rotated.

Saturation is the amount of color and is also monitored using a vectorscope. Nonsaturated pictures are dull almost to the point of being black and white. An overly saturated picture blooms with color to the point of smearing.

Video refers to the amount of white in the picture and is monitored with a waveform monitor. By dropping the video, the operator can make the shot progressively darker; by raising the video, the operator can bring out more of the white.

Setup, or *pedestal*, refers to the amount of black in the picture and is monitored using a waveform monitor. A high level of setup raises the intensity of the dark and light areas, making the black areas appear gray. The NTSC definition of video black is 7.5 IRE units. Anything below that is considered part of the horizontal blanking, not part of the picture.

Some clients prefer to adjust the chroma and luminance values of particular shots during the editing process. This is often necessary with material that has been shot under adverse or changing lighting conditions. The TBC is often used to adjust these values. If more intense correction is required, a color corrector is employed to make additional changes in the picture. To ensure that the resulting signal remains technically acceptable, many editing facilities have clipping circuitry to ensure that the luminance values do not exceed the capacity of the video machines, or that the black levels do not fall below 7.5 IRE units.

In high-end productions, the picture is *on-lined*, or finished. Then the master tape is sent through a sophisticated color correction device—often the same device is used to color correct film to tape. In a completely digital signal path there is no degradation, so the color correction pass does not harm the signal. Each shot is color corrected, and recorded onto a new tape. This method simplifies the on-line process and leaves the color correction to a specialist.

You can adjust a video signal by using these TBC controls, which are very similar to those on a television set. This is how the two sets of controls match up:

TBC Control = Television Control
hue   = tint
saturation   = color
video   = brightness
setup   = contrast

USING THE TBC AND SCOPES TO SET LEVELS

Color bars provide a playback reference to what the camera or record machine originally recorded. Once a tape has been set to bars, additional adjustments to the TBC controls may be required to enhance a particular shot. (The following procedure assumes that the scopes have been properly calibrated.)

To set the TBC to bars, load the tape into the playback machine and put it in play at the beginning of the color bar recording. Watching the waveform monitor (with the filter set on FLAT, so the scope only looks at the black-and-white portion of the signal, and on 2 H, which shows two horizontal fields of video), adjust the setup until the black level is at 7.5 IRE units. Then move the video level to 100 units. Referring to the vectorscope (see Figure 4-4a) and waveform monitor (see Figure 4-4b), you increase or decrease the chroma so that the six dots are as far from the center as the small boxes. You should use the hue control to place the dots as close to the center of the boxes as possible.

You can play the bars back and move each knob to see how each adjustment works. Moving the hue knob rotates the dots on the vectorscope, first one way, then the other. You can see how the color shifts in the bars. Moving the chroma control moves the color level in and out on the vectorscope (see Figure 4-6). Twisting the video control and watching the waveform shows the white level increasing and decreasing (see Figure 4-5). Finally, adjusting the setup knob increases and decreases the white and black levels together.

In composite video, the luminance signal carries the mathematical equation for chroma. As a result, increasing the luminance (white) value of a shot will also increase the chroma values of that shot. In component video, luminance is recorded and played back separately from the chroma information. However, since the luminance and chroma will most likely be combined for broadcast, it is important to check these monitored values in a composite environment to ensure that the chroma values do not exceed the videotape's tolerance.

After you set TBC levels, the playback tape should be ready to replay the picture that was originally recorded. But this might not always be the case. You should always check the four color aspects of the video if a vectorscope monitor is available so that you can make adjustments for technical or creative reasons.

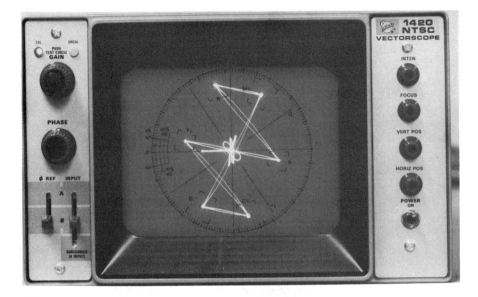

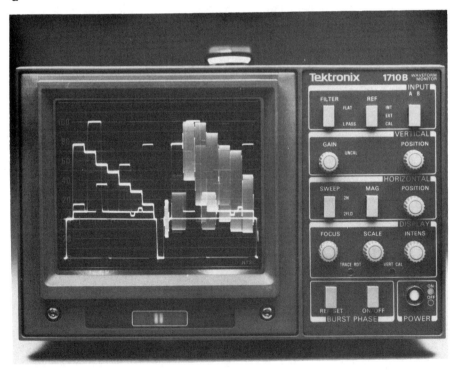

Figure 4-4 (a) Color bars displayed on a vectorscope. (b) Color bars viewed on a wave-form monitor. The left side is the signal without color information (luminance and setup only); the right side includes the chroma portion of the signal. Photos courtesy of Tektronix Corporation.

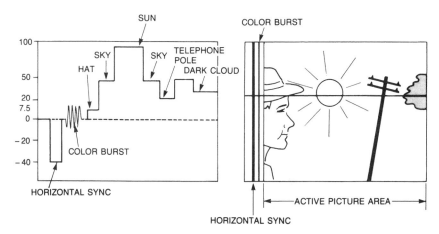

Figure 4-5 An example of reading a line of composite video on a waveform monitor. The waveform reading (left) corresponds to the video picture (right).

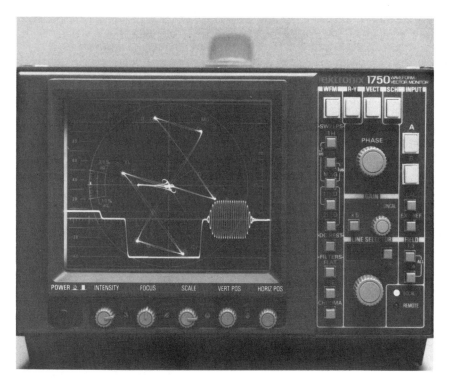

Figure 4-6 Color bars viewed on a combination waveform monitor/vectorscope. Note that the waveform portion of the display is expanded to show the horizontal blanking portion of the signal. Photo courtesy of Tektronix Corporation.

Often footage recorded in the field or on location has no relationship to the bars at the head of the tape. Many editors use skin tone to make subtle adjustments in the chroma and hue once the tape has been set up. This often occurs with tapes that are not shot under controlled situations, like news or documentary tapes. The editor often has to make adjustment to correct the look of the image. A slight hue adjustment can make a world of difference in how a person looks; be careful to ensure that a dark-skinned person does not appear green or red.

EDITING WITHOUT TBCS

Systems using only one record and one playback often edit machine-to-machine without the use of TBCs or a switcher, which eliminates the need for system timing. This type of editing occurs in news production and many industrial applications. Many three-quarter-inch and professional half-inch video decks have an output and input for dub-mode recordings. By taking the dub-mode output of the playback deck and feeding it into the dub-in of the record machine, you can transfer the video signal from the playback deck directly to the record deck without converting the signal to video and back to radio frequency. As a result, the quality of the recorded signal is greatly improved over that of a video-to-video recording.

The same situation occurs in digital and S-VHS systems. If you use dedicated cables, digital to digital editing can be transparent. In S-VHS situations, you can avoid combining the luminance and chroma by using S-VHS dub cables.

VOLUME UNIT METERS

Another important indicator in the editing bay is the volume unit (VU) meter. The VU meter measures the output of the audio signal in volume units. The goal is to keep the audio level strong enough to produce a good signal but not so strong that the sound becomes distorted.

Using Tone to Set the Record Levels

Tone is a reference signal for audio, just as color bars are a reference signal for video. Usually there is a source of audio tone in the editing bay (see Figure 4-7). At least a minute of video bars and audio tone should be recorded onto the record tape.

Riding Audio Levels

Proper levels must be maintained when recording production audio. Sometimes tone is recorded on playback tapes for reference, but this is no guarantee that the recorded levels will be the same as the tone at the head of the tape. Adjusting

Figure 4-7 A VU meter measuring audio tone at 0 dB. Photo by Sean Sterling.

audio levels during an edit keeps the meter moving and peaking at or just above 0 dB. It is acceptable for the audio to bounce into the red area of the VU meter, but the indicator should not stay there. Audio levels that remain in the red area for any length of time may become distorted.

Not only must the audio level remain consistent during an edit, but it also must be consistent from one edit to another. Nothing is more disconcerting than a sudden drop or rise in audio level.

Conclusion

Although video scopes are not used very often during the off-line editing process, VU meters are. A poor audio edit can ruin a picture-perfect master. In the on-line editing process, both video scopes and audio meters are of vital importance.

SUMMARY

Video originates at a CCD. These devices convert light into electrical pulses.

A composite signal is a picture's entire video information combined into a single signal. A component signal is picture information that uses three separate video pulses: one for the luminance signal (Y), one for the red signal minus the luminance (R–Y), and one for the blue signal minus the luminance (B–Y).

In over-the-air broadcasting, a carrier wave is altered in direct relationship to the video and audio signals. This modulated signal is amplified and transmitted by a radio antenna in all directions.

An electron beam scanning across a picture tube, causing the phosphor on the tube to glow, creates the image we see on a television screen. In NTSC video, the beam sweeps across the tube 525 times for each video frame in a process called interlace scanning. There are two fields to every frame of video. The time that the electron beam is turned off is called *blanking*.

The vectorscope and waveform monitor are oscilloscopes used to monitor various aspects of the video signal.

In composite video, luminance carries the mathematical equation for chroma. As a result, increasing the luminance (white) value of a shot will also increase the chroma values of that shot. In component video, there is no color burst. The U.S. television standard uses three primary colors (red, green, and blue) and three secondary colors (magenta, cyan, and yellow). Color bars are a reference signal created by a camera or test signal generator for the purpose of setting up the playback of a video recording.

A time base corrector (TBC) accepts an unstable videotape signal, corrects it, then sends it out in sync with the rest of the video signals. In addition to correcting time base errors, TBCs have controls that can alter video and chroma levels.

A TBC has the ability to change the video signal in four areas: hue, saturation, video, and setup. Machine-to-machine dubbing can preserve video quality if you use specialized cables (S-VHS, dub cables, digital cables).

A volume unit (VU) meter measures the output of the audio signal in volume units. The purpose of a VU meter is to keep the audio level strong enough to give a good signal but not so strong that the audio is distorted. Tone is a reference signal for audio.

The Video Edit

The remainder of this book deals with insert recordings—edits made after the record tape already has the control track and video recorded on it. Assemble recordings, as mentioned in Chapter 2, erase the control track, audio, and video.

On all linear editing systems, the record machine can only make a cut. Effects, such as picture spins, dissolves from one image to another, fades to and from black, keys, and graphics, are created by another machine. Nothing is physically cut during a video edit (see Figure 5-1). Instead, a section of video, audio, or both is copied from a source tape onto a record tape.

With the introduction of the D2 machine, followed by digital Betacam, video machines became capable of playing back and recording on the same machine. In other formats, to add visual information, you had to put the edited program into a playback machine and record an edit that combined the original footage while adding the new visual information. A deck that is capable of *prereading* can play back picture and/or sound, and then record this information at the same time. These machines have the ability to preread picture and audio information before the record head erases the original material.

For example, a complicated graphic could be preread and you could add a disclaimer to the picture without rebuilding the effect or going to an additional video generation. Since the video or audio being preread is subsequently erased, you must make sure that the system and esthetics of the edit are correctly prepared before performing the edit.

DEFINING THE CUT

Three points or locators define a simple cut:

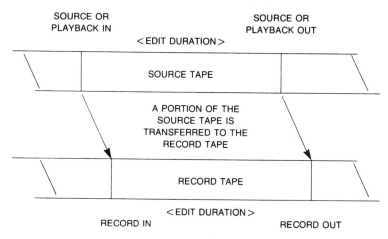

Figure 5-1   A diagram of a video edit.

1. The IN point on the record machine
2. The IN point on the source machine
3. The OUT point

The IN Point on the Record Machine

The point or location on the record tape where the image will change is the IN point on the record machine.

The IN Point on the Source Machine

The IN point on the playback or source machine is the beginning of the picture (and/or audio) that will be copied onto the record machine. This image will be recorded starting at the IN point of the record machine.

The OUT Point

The OUT point is where the edit ends. It defines the length or duration of the edit.

When an edit is performed, video and/or audio are transferred to the record tape. Without slow motion, freeze frames, or other special effects, it takes one frame of video on the record tape to copy one frame of video from the source tape. This means that the distance from the IN to the OUT point on the source

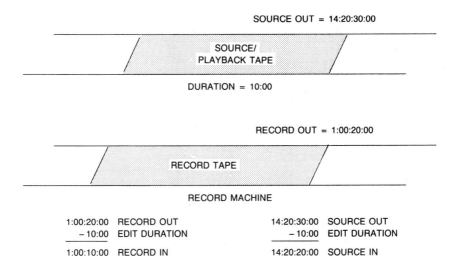

Figure 5-2 Calculation of a back-timed edit. Subtracting the edit duration from the OUT point produces the IN point.

tape is the same as the distance from the IN to the OUT point on the record tape. Thus, there need be only one OUT point, since its purpose is to define the length of the edit. You can choose the OUT point of the edit on the record tape or the playback tape, depending on the editing requirements.

If you know the duration of an edit, the location of the OUT point on the record tape, and the location of the OUT point on the playback tape, you can *back time* the edit by subtracting the duration from the OUT points (see Figure 5-2). This will give the two IN points on the source and record tapes. Similarly, if you know the IN and OUT points on the record tape and the OUT point on the source tape, you can find the IN point by subtracting the duration of the edit (the record IN point from the record OUT point) from the playback OUT point.

OPEN-ENDED EDIT

An edit that does not have an OUT point before the recording begins is called an *open-ended edit*. In an open-ended edit, the OUT point is chosen during the recording process. When the open-ended edit has been completed, the edit will have the required OUT point.

If an IN point on both playback and record has been chosen, as well as an OUT point, then an edit has been defined. This edit is a cut because only one picture source is being transferred to the record tape. If an effect requires recording from multiple sources, more source IN points must be defined. A source IN point is required for every videotape source used in an edit.

In most editing systems if two IN points have been chosen *and* two OUT points are chosen, the record OUT point will take precedence over the playback OUT point.

MULTIPLE-SOURCE EDIT

If you had a tape of a clear blue sky and wanted to add a flying saucer over the sky, you would need three IN points to perform the edit:

1. The IN point of the background (the sky)
2. The IN point of the flying saucer footage
3. The IN point on the record machine (see Figure 5-3)

If you wanted to make four digital effects boxes containing close-ups of players in a sporting event appear over the arena, you would need six IN points: one source IN point for each of the four players, a fifth source IN point for the arena background, and the final IN point on the record machine. (As an aside, nonlinear editors simply have layers. Often it is much easier to perform complicated effects on nonlinear editors because each layer can be adjusted without committing them to videotape until the effect has been completed.)

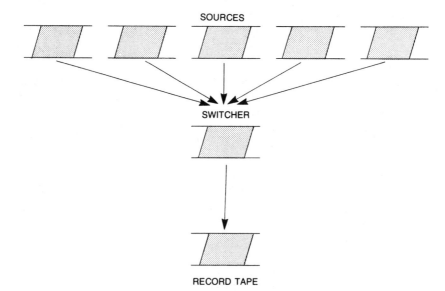

Figure 5-3 Diagram of several video signals being combined in the switcher. Multiple sources are transferred to the record tape after being combined into one video signal by the switcher.

THE EDITING PROCESS

The linear video editing process is a straightforward use of materials and tools that vary from sheets of paper describing the original footage (the master log) to computer disks with edit decision lists (EDLs) and paper printouts of the edits to be performed. The off-line process is most often accomplished using either dedicated editors (like an Avid editor) to PC- and Mac-based editors using editing software (see Figure 5-4).

Preproduction

The most important aspect of any visual program is preproduction. The crew must know where to be and at what time; the production manager must know what equipment has to be rented; the director should know where the editing will take place and who will be the editor. Problems will always occur during production, but careful preproduction preparation is one of the best ways to avoid scheduling or editing difficulties. Shooting schedules, storyboards, and an editing plan should be determined before production begins. Ninety percent of all production and postproduction is actually accomplished during preproduction.

In large productions, commercial computer programs specifically designed to help in preproduction chores are often used. In those large productions, weeks and often months are taken to resolve as many potential problems as possible. Although production seems to be the most exciting and interesting aspect of any visual project, it is the preproduction that determines how smoothly the overall strategy will be accomplished.

The Master Log

The *master log* is an organized, legible list of all available footage on each reel, the location of each shot on that reel, and the reel number. This information is noted during the shoot, along with any special instructions from the director. Special comments pertaining to each shot (such as bad audio, an audio boom in the shot, a particularly good performance, excessive dropouts, great action, or bad camera movement) are also logged. Additional information is entered in the master log while viewing the footage, before the editing session begins.

Rough Edit Notes

In order to prepare for the edit session, rough edit notes are prepared. While viewing the footage, list all the shots, in the order in which they will be edited into the show, without actually cutting the shots together. The notes include

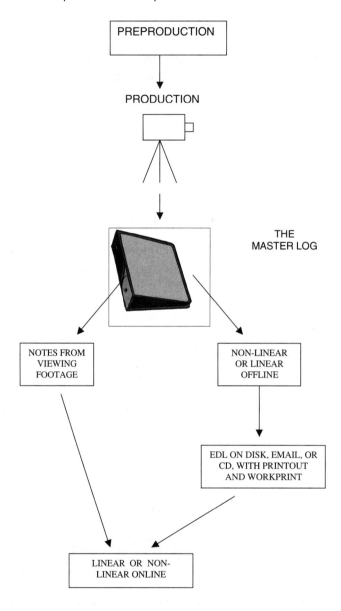

Figure 5-4 Flowchart of the video editing process and the three possible methods of preparing for the final on-line editing session.

where each shot and/or audio source is located, along with any other important information such as a general description of the shot, the time code and reel, or sound notes for the audio sweetening process. Many professionals use this method to prepare for off-line editing sessions. Some create their lists at home, viewing window dubs of their footage on VHS or three-quarter-inch decks.

Off-Line Editing

An off-line edit is a session in which a show is cut together to determine the exact order of the edits, using copies of the original footage. The off-line editor can be a linear or nonlinear system. The end result of an off-line edit is an EDL and an edited workprint that can be reviewed during or after the session. The off-line session often uses window dubs for playback material. The EDL and edit workprint are used in the on-line session to create the final version of the program.

The Workprint

The workprint, or rough cut, is videotape created as a result of an off-line editing session using a control track, computer, or random-access editor. The workprint often includes effects.

If you find that additional changes are necessary after viewing the workprint, these changes might be made in another off-line editing session. If the modifications are not too complicated, they might be performed during the on-line edit.

The On-Line Edit

During the on-line editing session, the original footage is assembled for the final time. The EDL from the off-line session is used to re-create the edits made during the off-line session. There are computer programs that can modify the EDL for optimum performance during the on-line edit session.

Some programs, such as news shows and some game shows, do not bother with the off-line editing process. The footage is viewed, logged, and edited on-line.

Organization

The key to any show's success is organization. A confusing, disorganized show will be unpleasant, difficult to shoot, and a challenge to edit.

SUMMARY

Video editing consists of copying a section of a source tape onto a record tape. The record machine can only make a cut. A composite digital machine can play back video or add video to the original picture. Once a video edit is performed on any record machine, the video that was originally there is completely erased. The following three points determine a cut on either analog or digital systems:

1. The IN point on the record machine
2. The IN point on the source machine
3. The OUT point

If an effect requires more than one playback, more source IN points must be defined. A source IN point is required for each videotape source used in an edit.

The most important aspect of any show is preproduction. Try to avoid being distracted by the excitement to be experienced later during production.

The master log is an organized, legible list of all available footage on each reel, the location of each shot on the reel, and the reel number.

The edit decision list (EDL) is used to prepare for the final, on-line edit. The list may be composed by making rough notes while viewing the footage or during an off-line edit session.

The workprint is videotape created as a result of an off-line editing session. Changes in the workprint are made in another off-line edit or in the on-line, or final, edit.

6

More on High Definition and the 16 by 9 Ratio

The world of broadcasting in the United States is in a very big transition. The U.S. government has established several digital broadcasting formats, and a timetable for the transfer from analog to digital delivery of television signals. Stations are already broadcasting digital television and by 2006 everything seen on regular television will be available digitally. In 2007, the stations you are watching regularly will, barring any major change in plan, cease to exist.

The transition to digital broadcasting has brought confusion to the production and postproduction world. However, as we work our way through this transition, new formats will begin to dominate the broadcasting spectrum. In the meantime, producers will have to deliver both a 4×3 and 16×9 master, as well as high-definition and standard definition programming. An edit on a 4×3 frame does not look the same as one on a 16×9 frame. Titles framed for 4×3 look strange in 16×9. As seen in Figure 6-1, the 4×3 image is not easily converted to the 16×9 rectangle.

So, there will be sacrifices made on either one format or the other. Eventually the 16×9 format will dominate the broadcast environment, because televisions will only be sold in a 16×9 format. The average viewers in the United States will not like black edges on their 16×9 televisions. For now, compromises will have to be made. Shooting on film is still a viable option because film can always be retransferred and the show conformed in any new format that might emerge.

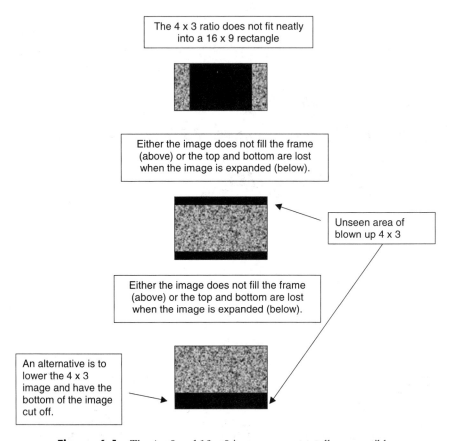

The 4 x 3 ratio does not fit neatly
into a 16 x 9 rectangle

Either the image does not fill the frame
(above) or the top and bottom are lost
when the image is expanded (below).

Unseen area of
blown up 4 x 3

Either the image does not fill the frame
(above) or the top and bottom are lost
when the image is expanded (below).

An alternative is to
lower the 4 x 3
image and have the
bottom of the image
cut off.

Figure 6-1   The 4×3 and 16×9 images are not totally compatible.

Some editors are having the 16×9 image blown up but not from the center. Often there is little interesting or valuable information at the bottom of the screen. So, rather than expanding the image from the center, the frame is lowered and the bottom of the frame is cut off.

These types of tricks and alterations will become commonplace for the transition period. And the concern for the 4×3 image will slowly give way as the majority of the viewing audience shifts from watching analog broadcasting to digital broadcasting. Eventually the analog signals will cease to be available.

LINEAR EDITING RETURNS, FOR A MOMENT

Another interesting situation will most likely occur as high-definition production and editing come in to the mainstream. Because of the wider and higher resolution of the high-definition signal, more storage will be needed for nonlinear

Figure 6-2   A high-definition color correction facility is used to color correct high-definition images to maximize the impact of each shot. Photo courtesy of Sony High Definition Center, Culver City, CA.

editors. Up until recently, the nonlinear revolution had steadily eliminated the linear edit bay. First the off-line process went nonlinear, then on-line quickly became filled with nonlinear systems like Quantel's Editbox, Descrete's Fire, Flame, and Inferno, Sony's E7s, and other brand-name nonlinear editors.

Now, for a brief time, until the large disk arrays needed to edit and composite the high-definition signal come down in price, tape may be more cost-effective for basic editorial processes. Edit bays like the one in Figure 6-3 are performing much of the high-definition postproduction editorial chores. Certainly for heavily layered shows, bumpers, commercials, and other special effects, the nonlinear edit systems will make more economic sense. But for straight ahead on-line with relatively simple graphics, the tape-to-tape environment will certainly be an option that is taken by many shows. After a program is edited, often a professional colorist will perform a tape-to-tape color-correction of the entire show (Figure 6-2).

Eventually, the cost of memory will drop and the linear bay will again be sent to the junkyard, along with two-inch, one-inch, and three-quarter-inch edit systems. Until then, as producers, directors, and editors make their way through the maze of this technical transition, every "normal" process will be examined for its technical ability and cost-effectiveness.

DIGITAL BROADCASTING FORMATS

The digital broadcasting standard consists of a series of delivery formats. Broadcasters can choose the format that suits them. A home converter will determine what signal is being received, and then decode it for viewing. Some professionals believe that one or two standards will eventually dominate the production and postproduction scene. It will take some time and experimentation until this expected shakeout occurs. Until then it is a good idea to be familiar with the various forms of the digital broadcasting formats, some of which are high-definition television.

FRAME RATE

The original color NTSC television signal is not 30 frames per second. Because of technical reasons, the frame rate was dropped from 30 to 29.97 frames per second. This slight lowering of the frame rate resulted in the creation of two different time codes: drop frame time code, which is time accurate, and non–drop frame time code, which simply counts frames and has a built-in error rate when it comes to comparing the time code to real or clock time.

High-definition frame rates are composed of even numbers (24, 30, 60). During the transition period when both analog standard definition and high-definition signals will be broadcast, machines are being manufactured so that both digital and analog signals can be generated. Many professionals believe that the high-definition rate of 24 frames, progressively scanned at 1080 by 1125 lines of resolution is going to be the universal production format. Figure 6-3 shows a high-definition, linear, 24p, 1080 edit bay. By using this scan rate, film can be easily transferred to high definition. Also, all other formats, both analog and digital, can be created from the high-definition edited master.

Figure 6-3 The Sony high-definition on-line bay. This edit bay, located in the Los Angeles area, has on-lined hundreds of high-definition programs. Photo courtesy of Sony Broadcast.

With so many cable, over-the-air, and DVD sales opportunities, one should assume that any program will be delivered to several broadcasters. Because different networks and cable broadcasters have chosen different broadcasting formats, the delivery to these companies can be complicated. This is why 24p at 1080 is considered a desired format. However, for internal use, a network or station may choose to shoot and edit in a different format.

Take, for instance, a local station that is an affiliate of the American Broadcasting Company. As of this writing, ABC has chosen the 720p format for broadcasting. The news department of that station may choose to shoot and edit 720p, ignoring the 1080 format. But a producer who is hoping to sell a program overseas or to a secondary syndication market may choose to shoot and edit in 1080p to ensure compatibility with other broadcasters, or even to transfer the product to film.

SCAN RATE

Digital television, whether high definition or standard definition, also has differing scan rates. Scan rates are defined by the horizontal line rate. There are two high-definition scan rates: 1080 and 720.

INTERLACE VERSUS PROGRESSIVE

Finally, there are two ways to display a frame of picture. The *interlace* format scans half of the picture's lines, then retraces and scans the remaining lines of information. In *progressive scanning* the entire frame is displayed at once. Interlacing is a less expensive way of recording a frame, but progressive scanning has a slightly higher resolution.

PUTTING IT TOGETHER

There is a matrix of high-definition choices for broadcasters, as shown in Figure 6-4.

16 × 9 FORMAT

High definition is recorded and broadcast in a 16 × 9 format. There are ways to create a 16 × 9 image using a 4 × 3 image. By squeezing the image anamorphically, a wider frame of view can be recorded on tape. Then, on playback, the process is reversed and the image takes on a 16 × 9 aspect. This method was first

	Total/Active Scan Lines	Pixelization	Frame Rate Per Second	Aspect Ratio
	First 3, best quality	More pixels	Three scanning choices	All high definition
1	1125/1080	1080 x 1920	24 progressive	16 x 9 (HDTV)
2	1125/1080	1080 x 1920	30 progressive	16 x 9 (HDTV)
3	1125/1080	1080 x 1920	60 interlaced	16 x 9 (HDTV)
	Next 3 still high quality	Few pixels, still HDTV	Three scanning choices	
4	750/720	720 x 1080	24 progressive	16 x 9 (HDTV)
5	750/720	720 x 1080	30 progressive	16 x 9 (HDTV)
6	750/720	720 x 1080	60 progressive	16 x 9 (HDTV)

Figure 6-4 High-definition digital broadcast formats.

used in feature film production to obtain a widescreen image in a 4 × 3 area of film. The amount of information stored in this manner is dependent on the camera and recorder.

Now comes the producer's dilemma. For several years broadcasters will be transmitting both a 4 × 3 signal and a simultaneous 16 × 9 digital signal. If you shoot a show in 16 × 9, do you frame the action for 4 × 3 putting only background and sets on the side of the image, or, do you shoot for 16 × 9 and not worry about the 4 × 3 viewer who will miss the sides of the image?

On the other side of the issue is the show that has already been shot in 4 × 3. Do you:

1. Expand the image to fill the 16 × 9 frame, thereby losing the top and bottom of the image and sacrificing image quality?
2. Stretch the image to fill the frame, making everyone look fat and losing image quality?
3. Or do you deliver the show in the original 4 × 3 and let the viewers see no image on the sides of their widescreen televisions?

IMAGE RESOLUTION

And finally there is the acquisition question. How does one actually shoot a 16 × 9 image? There are currently on the market consumer DV cameras that can shoot in 16 × 9 format. But this format certainly does not provide the same image resolution as a true 24p 1080 high-definition camera and recorder. In the middle of these two examples are a growing number of cameras and recorders that can shoot and edit 16×9 format images.

Which camera and which resolution to use will be determined by the purpose of the program. Certainly programs that are intended to be electronically projected in theaters or scanned for use in feature film effects computers will use the highest possible resolution cameras and recorders. Corporate users will use less expensive (and lower resolution) cameras and recorders. Remember, high definition is determined by certain technical requirements. One could, in theory, take a bad dub of an old VHS tape, blow it up in a digital device, make it a 16×9 image, record it on a high-definition recorder and technically it would be a high-definition signal. But as in the past, the image resolution of a picture cannot become a higher resolution than it was when it was originally acquired.

CONCLUSION

During the transition from standard definition television to digital broadcasting, there will be many challenges and questions about production format, camera selection, and program delivery. Cost is a large factor in any video program decision. So as we enter this cross-over phase, there will be choices to be made about which format to use, and how to edit it. The linear or nonlinear editing system that is used to create a video program can also affect an image's quality.

Ultimately, the cost of high-definition cameras, graphics, recorders, and editing systems will drop, as all electronics do. But in the meantime, producers, directors, and camera personnel will have to deal with the conflicting image sizes and broadcast formats.

PART II
Concepts of Videotape Editing

7

Creating and Using the Master Log

A master log will help any production during its postproduction phase. Though it takes some time to create and organize, knowing where shots are is a vital aspect of editing. When using nonlinear systems, these logging systems are often automated in bins and clip logs.

In news editing, the master log usually consists of the notes taken while viewing the footage. A news program is edited so quickly that there is no time to build an extensive shot list. In other dramatic, documentary, and informative programs, including feature news stories, the master log is a larger, more complete reference guide to the show's components.

REEL NUMBERING

It is good practice to create a reel numbering system in advance of any actual shooting. This system may be ordered in terms of location, shooting day, time code, or any method that is logical and informative.

Every reel to be used in the editing of a show should be numbered and have identifying labels that explain exactly what is inside the box. A label such as "9–15, Prebuild, hold for on-line" is useless to anyone but the original author. If the tape is a pre-edit reel, it should have a log describing the contents. The reel also should be added to the reel summary and the footage log of the master log.

THREE DIVISIONS

There are three major divisions of the master log:

1. The show script
2. The reel summary
3. The footage notes

Some postproduction professionals use a three-ring binder to hold their editing materials master log.

Copies of the script should be given to the editor along with the director's and production notes. Time code and shot composition notes are written on many dramatic and comedy scripts during production to help speed the editing process.

Reel Summary

The reel summary (see Figure 7-1) is a page or two that encapsulates the material on each reel. Note that time code indications do not include frames, because the note refers to a general location on the tape.

Footage Notes

Footage notes (see Figure 7-2) are details of each shot on each reel. These notes include technical problems, the timing of each scene, the location on the reel, and/or the time code at the beginning of the shot. Specific shots that might work well in a certain area of the show are also noted in the show script.

Footage notes are made during the shoot and in a viewing session after the production. While viewing the footage, you can add additional notes to the footage log that were not apparent or available during production.

TIMINGS

It is important to keep track of where shots are located so they can be found during editing. One method of making these timings is by viewing the tape with a watch.

Time code is the most accurate method of logging shot locations in the master log, but you need a machine that can read time code or have a window dub made. A *window dub* is an exact copy of the original footage with a visual representation of the time code burned into the picture. Some producers and

1″ SOURCE

REEL #

#50........00:58:00–01:25:00........(STOCK FOOTAGE)
#51........01:00:00–01:22:00........(CH. 4 CHROMA-KEYS)
#52........01:48:30–01:54:30........(GENERIC CHS. 1 & 4)
#53........00:58:00–01:50:00........(1810/1820 PRE-BUILD W/O TITLES)
#54........00:58:00–01:50:00........(1810/1820 PRE-BUILD W/TITLES)
#75........00:00:00–00:23:00........(GRAPHICS REEL)
#99........09:00:00–09:10:00........(MUSIC REEL)

BETA SOURCE

ON CAMERA & INSERT SHOTS

REEL #

#1..........01:00:00–01:17:00....... (CH. 2, CH. 6)
#2..........02:00:00–02:17:00........(CH. 3)
#3..........03:00:00–03:19:00........(CH. 3, CH. 7, CH. 2 & 3 VO)
#4..........04:00:00–04:19:30........(CH. 3 & 6 VO, CH. 7)
#5..........05:00:00–05:19:30........(CH. 7, CH. 8, CH. 3 VO)
#6..........06:00:00–06:19:00........(CH. 3 VO, CH. 8 VO, CH. 5)
#7..........07:00:00–07:19:30........(CH. 5, CH. 9)
#8..........08:00:00–08:18:30........(CH. 9)
#9..........09:00:00–09:19:00........(CH. 9, CH. 9 VO)
#10........10:00:00–10:18:30........(CH. 9 VO)
#11........11:00:00–11:19:00........(CH. 9 VO)
#12........12:00:00–12:20:00........(FDP/MEM PANEL CHS. 3, 5–9)
#13........13:00:00–13:21:00........(MEM. PANEL/FDP CHS. 9, 2, 3)
#14........14:00:00–14:19:30........(ECU MEM/FDP CHS. 3, 6, 7)
#15........15:00:00–15:19:00........(MEM. CHS. 7, 8/FDP ALL CHS.)
#16........16:00:00–16:18:30........(FDP CHS. 3, 5, 7, 8)
#17........17:00:00–17:21:00........(FDP CHS. 8, 2, 9/POWER CH. 2)
#18........18:00:00–18:20:00........(2ND CTRL CHS. 8, 9, 2, 3, 6)
#19........19:00:00–19:20:00........(ECU 2ND CTRL CHS. 3, 6, 9)
#20........20:00:00–20:20:00........(LOCK-OFFS CHS. 9, 5)
#21........21:00:00–21:19:00........(LOCK-OFF CH. 5/SWIVEL CHS. 2, 3)
#22........22:00:00–22:20:00........(REMOTE SHOTS ALL CHS.)
#23........23:00:00–23:10:00........((MON/VCR HK-UP CH. 9/ON-SCRN CH. 8)

VOICE OVER REELS

REEL #

#102......00:00:00–00:27:30........(CHS. 1–7)
#103......00:28:00–00:37:00........(CHS. 8, 9)

ADDITIONAL REELS

REEL #

#160......16:00:00–16:20:00........(1870 CAMERA MASTER-PLAYBACK)
#230......23:00:00–23:18:00........(1810/1820 CAMERA MASTER)
#240......01:30:00–01:49:30........(1810/1820 CAMERA MASTER)
#250......02:30:00–02:50:00........(1810/1820 CAMERA MASTER)

Figure 7-1 An example of a professional reel summary. This particular show demonstrates how to operate a Zenith VCR. Note that most of the reels have time code that corresponds to the reel number. Also note that this show uses other edited shows as playbacks, such as show 1810/1820. A lock-off is a series of shots with a camera firmly held in the same position, allowing for pop-on effects or dissolves (CH = chapter, VO = voice-over reel, ECU = extreme close-up, FDP = front display panel of the VCR, Mon-VCR Hk-Up = a recorded video playback through the VCR).

Project Title _"V.CG 1820/1820"_ Project # _2820L_ Date _2/18/86_
Client _ZENiTH_ Producer _ADAMS_ Director _NACZ_
Camera Op. _VACZ_ Camera _FR79E_ Reel # _16_ VTR
Location _entire filming_ INT EXT D N Notes

SCENE	PAGE	TAKE	AUDIO SLATE	TIME CODE	REMARKS	STATUS
				: :	Chapter 2 inserts	
12	6	1	Slate	16:01:02	right hand opening door, left hand pressing clock switch	Switch
..	'	—	—	16:01:37		
"	''	—	—	16:01:55	ECU clock adjust switch	
"	"	—	—	16:02:17	" " " "	
"	"	—	—	16:02:23	finger pushing switch to clock (left hand)	
"	"	—	—	16:02:39	" " " " "	
"	"	—	—	16:02:47	" " switch to clock adj	
"	"	— —	—	16:02:57	" " " to program	
"	"	—	— —	16:03:02	" " " to clock	
"	"	1	SLATE	16:03:46	redo w/ right hand	CU
"	"	—	—	16:04:00	switching to clock position	

REEL 16

Page No. _45_

Figure 7-2 An example of a professional footage log.

editors have window dubs made on VHS or three-quarter-inch tape and screen the material on a VCR at home.

Screening a tape and noting shots with their associated time code with a word processor allows for quick retrieval of scenes if key words are used. Using the word processor's search process will locate all those scenes using the particular key words. For those familiar with databases, these programs can be used to pull up all the reels and key words at once. There are also software programs that read time code and allow a viewer to make notes. These programs use a time code input into a computer, allowing the operator to press a single key to pick off the tape's time code and note the scene description.

DIRECTOR'S NOTES

During the production, the director often gives verbal instructions concerning shots and angles, possible editing choices, and other information. The person responsible for keeping the master log should incorporate these notes into the show script. If no script is available during the shoot, as in the case of a documentary, these notes should be kept in a separate section of the master log.

SINGLE- VERSUS MULTIPLE-CAMERA PRODUCTION

There are two very different methods of video production: single-camera production and multiple-camera production. Single-camera production is used most often for scripted and documentary location productions, while multiple-camera production is often employed in the studio. Filmed location shows, including motion pictures, use single-camera production. The exception to this rule is when a complex effect is being performed. In this case multiple cameras are set up to film all angles of the action. Concerts and sporting events are often shot with multiple cameras. Music videos and commercials are usually shot single-camera style. Sitcoms, whether shot on film or video, are most often shot using multiple cameras.

Single-Camera Production

The master log for a single-camera production is usually more detailed than the log for a multiple-camera production. This is because each scene requires more takes and more individual shots.

Trying to fit all this information into the margins of the script, as is the practice in multiple camera productions, is usually not practical. Brief notes concerning particular shots or scenes can be made in the script, with reference to the appropriate reel. The details are then recorded in the footage log.

Each reel should be viewed and logged in a viewing session. The location and running time of each take should be logged. Additional technical information also should be included in the footage notes.

Finally, as mentioned above, the script for a single-camera production contains short notes referring to the more detailed footage log. The director's or other crew members' notes also can be written briefly in the script's margins.

Multiple-Camera Production

The script is the basis of the multiple-camera log (see Figure 7-3). Different-colored lines drawn down the side of the script indicate the camera or VTR source. Timings are written in the margins, along with technical notes. When viewing the footage, you can add more notes to the script. The reel summary is also updated at this time if necessary.

Productions that do not have a script are occasionally shot with multiple cameras. These are usually interviews for documentaries or special effects shots requiring the action to be covered by several cameras. In the case of interviews, it is good practice to transcribe the dialogue, and then mark the transcription as if it were a script, using different-colored lines to indicate the camera or VTR source. Special effects shots should be logged in a viewing session after the

3.

	CAM 1	CAM 2	CAM 3

CONTINUED:

12:15:01:00 — CU NU

NU
We have heard otherwise.

WING
Mr. Maxwell, when you cashed our
check, you entered an agreement
with us. We are grateful for your
work, but there must be a change.
(beat.)
We want access to all your notes — WS
and programming.

Jake smiles and shakes his head in disbelief.

JAKE — CU JAKE
He's kidding . . . You're all
kidding.

Thunder is HEARD in the background, but no one at
the table stops to notice.

NU
No one is kidding, Mr. Maxwell
12:15:25:00

JAKE
Then you gentlemen have a
problem.

Korin gets up from the table.

KORIN
I still don't think you understand . . .

JAKE — WS
I understand perfectly, Jack. You're
not getting your paws on my
program. As far as I am concerned, — 2S KORIN JAKE
our agreement is terminated.

Jake rises and leaves the table. Korin grabs his jacket and
holds him in place.

12:15:48:00
(CONTINUED)

Figure 7-3 Multiple-camera productions often use the script to indicate the shots made by each camera at any particular time during taping. In this case, three cameras were being used, each having its own corresponding line on the script. The shots taken by each camera are labeled at the appropriate line. The time code is also indicated on the script (WS = wide shot, 2S = two shot, CU = close-up).

THE LAST FRONTIER

The Exploration of Central Brazil

VIDEO   AUDIO

REEL 7 5:06:15:00

The show opens with a wide
aerial shot of the rain
forest. Miles of untouched
land stretches for miles.

NARRATOR VO: IT IS A LAND OF
MYSTERY, A LAND TIME HAS
FORGOTTEN, A LAND THAT IS NOW
DISCOVERING IT HOLDS THE
FUTURE OF WESTERN
CIVILIZATION.

Helicopter sound

(15fr)

Dissolve to massive waterfall
as we circle the swirling
mists.   *Reel 11 - 11:15:01:00*

THERE IS ABUNDANT NATURAL
ENERGY, WATER AND RICH SOIL
TO SUPPORT A VARIETY OF
COMMERCIAL ENTERPRISES.

Water Sounds

(25fr)

Dissolve to natives eating
around their ramshackle huts.
Poverty and filth are
everywhere.   *REEL 7 5:22:00:00*

DOES CIVILIZATION OFFER HOPE
AND SALVATION TO THESE
IMPOVERISHED PEOPLES, OR
TOTAL ENSLAVEMENT TO THE
WESTERN WORLD?

Kids crying

Dissolve to World Issues
Graphic, key paint box title
over graphic.
Graphics Reel 1
1:02:00:00

TONIGHT WORLD ISSUE EXAMINES
BRAZIL, ITS PEOPLE, ITS
NATURAL RESOURCES. ARE
INTERNATIONAL CORPORATIONS
EXPLOTING THIS AREA? ARE
THERE REAL BENEFITS TO GIVE?

Music

(Flip)
DVE effect to the studio, a
wide shot of Sterling in a
bookcase filled office. He
moves to a large globe as we
dolly in. Sterling swivels
the globe to reveal South
America as he motions to
Brazil.
TAKE 5
Prod Reel 6 6:22:01:00

HELLO, I'M SEAN STERLING,
YOUR HOST FOR OUR PROGRAM,
BRAZIL THE BRIGHT LIGHT OF
SOUTH AMERICA. OUR
EXAMINATION OF BRAZIL'S
NEWFOUND POWER STARTS IN THE
MIDDLE OF THE RAIN FOREST,
AND ENDS IN A COSMOPOLITAN
CITY. THE PEOPLE OF BRAZIL
HAVE A COMMON FUTURE TIED TO
COMMERCIAL EXPLOITATION. BUT
CAN THEY CONTROL THEIR
DESTINY? OR WILL THEY BE USED
AND ABSORBED?

Figure 7-4   An example of notations on an audio-video formatted script.

footage has been shot. Careful attention must be paid to the angle of these shots,
because the action will be very similar from each angle.

KEEPING TRACK OF MATERIALS

Tracking all the source materials in a large production can be a major chore. Not
only are there videotapes, but there are also quarter-inch audio reels, title cards,

scripts, off-line diskettes, digital audio tapes (DATs), computer disks, credit lists, director's notes, and much, much more. Keeping track of every show's production elements requires an extra effort, but attempting to find a missing reel or shot during the on-line edit is even more time-consuming, frustrating, and extremely expensive.

SUMMARY

A master log should be used for every video production. Before the master log is even started, it is good practice to set up a reel numbering system in advance of the actual shoot.

The master log consists of three parts: the script, reel summary, and footage notes. The reel summary is a page or two encapsulating what material is on each reel. Footage notes are details of each specific shot on each reel.

You must keep track of where each shot is located on every reel so that it can be found during editing. Director's notes are often written in the show script (see Figure 7-4) or kept in a special location in the master log. Single-camera productions rely heavily on footage notes. Multiple-camera shoots rely more on the script.

8

Time Code, Computer, and Random-Access Editors

In this chapter we will refer to three groupings of editors:

1. Time code editors—machines that access time code but cannot remember more than two edits.
2. Linear computer editors—machines that can store more than two edits and make their edits transferring images and sound from one videotape to another videotape.
3. Random-access editors—computers that store video images, audio, and time code on hard disks and access their images instantaneously.

THE TECHNICAL VERSUS CREATIVE ARGUMENT

When videotape editing first evolved, only engineers were capable of operating the awkward editors and actually performing cuts, but the advent of computerized editors made the creation of a program incredibly easy. However, the ability to make an edit does not make it a *good* edit. To take a series of images and sounds and combine them to make a program takes more than just moving a computer mouse.

This author, who has edited longer than he wants to admit, knows that nonlinear editors are fun, easy to operate, and incredibly versatile at placing impressive effects. But often, when viewing tapes from novice editors who have used these machines, the results are less than impressive. Unmotivated effects, unnecessary flutter cuts, and a lack of a cohesive narrative immediately tell a professional that a novice with an expensive machine has not done his or her editorial homework. What is the show's message? Who is the intended audience? And, though few beginning editors realize it, effect time cannot be considered content time. An individual who is thinking of becoming an editor should take the time not only to learn the equipment that makes the program, but to learn what it takes, from pacing, to conservation of effects, when to cut, the show's intended audience, and finally, the accepted "look" any particular show has.

The editorial process is not new, nor does it employ new transitions or editorial styles easily. The successful editor knows her equipment, knows what the show needs to look like, and knows how to accomplish these tasks in an economical, timely manner.

TIME CODE EDITORS

Simple time code editing systems, as defined in this book, can read time code and, in some cases, allow the editor to create simple video sequences with minimal effects. Such systems are relatively inexpensive and are easier to operate and maintain than the more complex computer editing systems. Time code editors are often built in to many professional video decks. Time code editors are an excellent option for newsrooms and similar environments where speed and expense are primary concerns.

Basic time code editors are electronic, but do not match the processing power, speed, and memory of a full-fledged computer-based editing system. Unlike computers that possess extensive memories, these editors retain only a few edits at a time. In the case of machine-to-machine editors, no edits are stored in memory. Time code editors that use edit screens are capable of modifying the previous edit or two. If linked to a nearby printer, such systems can print out a record of the edits that have been performed. Figure 8-1 shows an example of a linear computer editor. This printout is useful for reference, as edits often are repeated exactly or approximately during an editing session. In the past, such repeatability was only available with an expensive controller.

With little memory, the time code system cannot auto assemble an edit list, but can be used as an accurate off-line system or on-line editor. In most cases, control of a sophisticated switcher or other peripheral equipment is limited or nonexistent, although some effects can be made on-the-fly. Using time code allows you to repeat an edit even if the effects device is being operated live.

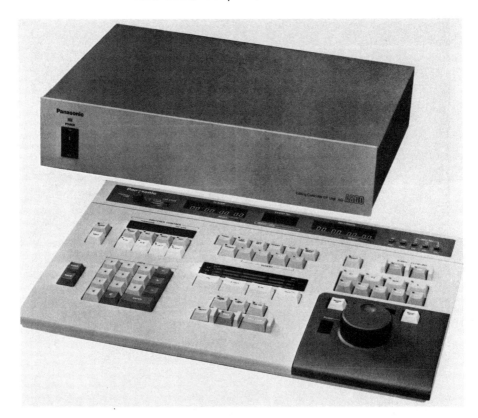

Figure 8-1 The Panasonic AG-A800 controller. This controller works with either control track or time code. This multi-event edit controller is time-code compatible. It can hold 128 edits in memory. On the left side of the controller are the keypad and external device controls. The center of the keyboard has the cue, edit enable, and mode selects. On the right side are the shuttle and machine-select controls. Photo courtesy of Panasonic Communications & Systems Company.

LINEAR COMPUTER EDITORS

Time code made it possible to perform edits repeatedly and accurately. The linear computer editor added speed and flexibility, enabling editors to focus more on aesthetics and less on technology. Linear computer editors also introduced the need for the abstract generalization of the video edit itself and the different electronic devices that make up the editing system. Eight-digit numbers represent video frames, and lines of computer information represent edits.

The linear computer editor usually requires extensive experience in controlling multiple machines while reading, analyzing, and utilizing a complex

Figure 8-2 The keyboard of the Sony BVE-9100, a large, powerful on-line editor. Photo courtesy of Sony Electronics, Inc.

cathode-ray tube (CRT) screen. The most complicated of these systems can control over ten video machines, five digital effects machines, several character generators, and sometimes more.

Accuracy and Repeatability

With a linear computer editor, edits can be performed again and again with frame accuracy. This repeatability is due to the linear computer editor's ability to store the time codes of the source and record tapes of each edit. More sophisticated linear computer editors can store switcher effects, digital video effects, and TBC settings for each edit.

By instructing the computer to save the EDL to a recording medium, usually a 3-inch diskette, you can store the list for future use or load it into another computer. For example, an off-line workprint can be created using inexpensive three-quarter-inch machines, or a random-access editor. The EDL can then be transferred to a computer on-line editing system, and the original edits can be performed during the on-line edit. The Sony 9100 (see Figure 8-2), when linked to Sony switchers and digital effects devices, is capable of storing switchers, TBC, and effects in the edit decision list. Edit decision lists can also be emailed

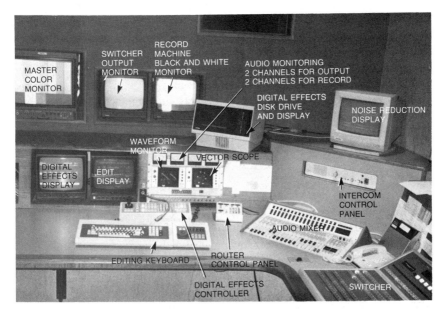

Figure 8-3 An on-line editing console. Photo by Sean Sterling.

or burned onto a CD. Because most EDL formats are in a simple ASCII format, they can be opened and edited using word processors. One should be careful to save the altered file under a different name so the original file can be accessed. Most EDLs have a file extension of ".edl."

Computer diskettes have become a common method of transferring EDLs. There are several standard EDL formats. However, many linear computer editors will accept or translate other computers' diskettes. There are also computer programs that convert diskettes.

Computer Editing Room

The linear computer editing room can be designed in many different ways (see Figure 8-3). It can be built to edit three-quarter-inch cassette video off-line or to create cassette masters. Editing rooms can handle conversions from three-quarter-inch to one-inch tape, one-inch to Betacam, D2 to digital Betacam, high definition, and so on. A room that allows editing from or to more than one tape format is called an interformat editing suite. An interformat editing suite handles several types of video formats; however, the tapes must be of the same standard. For instance, a suite may not accept both PAL and NTSC signals. There are edit bays that can edit in either PAL or NTSC, but not both formats at the same time. There are also composite analog, composite digital, and component digital bays.

The concern with so many types of configurations is that if the bay is digital, the digital signal should stay digital through the entire edit path, through patch bays and switcher, preserving the digital signal. Converting back and forth from digital defeats the format's strengths.

Most linear computer editing rooms are equipped with at least one video playback machine, a record machine, a switcher, an audio mixer, monitors, and optional equipment that the client can rent by the hour. The more elaborate the editing suite, the more varied and expensive the optional equipment will be. Chapter 9 deals with this optional equipment and explains how it relates to the computer editing room.

Random-Access Editors

Random-access editors have drastically changed the postproduction world. Random-access editors not only edit, they can also perform complicated effects. With the current power of computers, there are several very effective nonlinear editors that are even affordable for home editing. Apple Computer's "Final Cut Pro" and Adobe's "Premiere" are two such programs.

Nonlinear editing systems first gained popularity in off-line situations. Once clients and producers became comfortable with the quality and dependability of random-access editors, on-line nonlinear editing became acceptable to the broadcast community. Avid nonlinear editors (see Figure 8-4) became very popular as off-line editing systems. Because the random-access editor is an electronic device, improvements came rapidly.

There are other advantages to using random-access editors. Rather than being time code driven, the system is more visually oriented. Programs can be edited and re-edited with little concern of what the time code numbers represent; the machine takes care of remembering the actual numbers. In addition, some of the machines can correlate film key numbers, edit in 30 or 24 frames per second, and create an accurate, clean edit decision list for video on-line or negative cut list for film finishing.

Random-access editors are extremely flexible and user friendly, and foster creativity. They allow editors to make changes without having to shuttle or change tapes. Some random-access editors are capable of producing any quality output and are only limited to the amount of hard disk space available. (High-definition images take a great deal of hard disk space.)

The nonlinear editor keeps track of original time code and can output an edit decision list at the end of the session. Random-access editors can read time code and recall many complicated edits. Random-access editors are usually platformed on Silicone Graphics, Apple, or IBM computers, however, there are some systems that have their own proprietary operating systems.

The power of the random-access editor lies in its ability to retrieve audio and/or video almost instantaneously. This eliminates the "linear" aspect of

Figure 8-4 The Avid® Media Composer®, one of several random-access editors marketed by the Avid Corporation. Visuals are stored on large digital hard disks and are retrievable instantaneously.

editing. Shots can be moved here or there without reediting or dubbing entire programs.

There are drawbacks to random access editors. The process of inputting footage, editing, then outputting the finished program can be inefficient in some cases. Take for example a situation where an hour program needs only a few edits to cut it to broadcast time. With a linear editor, this process would take a little over an hour to accomplish. Using a nonlinear editor would require that the entire program be digitized, then edited, and then the resulting show put back onto tape. This would be over a two-hour process. The second item of concern is storage cost for the video and audio. Even though the cost of disk drives is dropping, to input huge amounts of video can be expensive, especially at full resolution. This is why, at least in the beginning of high-definition editing, linear bays may come back in style (although only briefly) until the cost of storage drops enough to warrant the cost for HDTV editing chores.

The random-access edit bay differs from the traditional linear computer edit bay. Since there is no need for various pieces of hardware, there is usually only a console with a computer monitor, another monitor that displays the program, a keyboard, and mouse. In larger facilities the actual computer and disk drives are in another room along with various types of playback decks.

TAKING THE TOUR

The only way to find out about a particular editing room and the equipment it offers is to take a tour, talk to the staff, watch a demo reel, and contact some of the facility's clients; then you can make an informed choice based on the program's requirements and the editing equipment available. With so many corporate and in-house editing systems, it's worth asking around.

THE HUMAN FACTOR

No matter what type of editing system is used to create a program, the individual who operates the equipment is as important as the technology used. Editors are the creative translators for the producer or director. They combine information from the production company with their own talent to create a show. Some directors will work only with certain editors or companies. Video is a highly technical and creative medium. Whoever edits the tape should have a well-balanced blend of technical and creative expertise.

SUMMARY

There are three basic ways to use a simple time code editor:

1. As a final step in the editing process
2. As an off-line or workprint editor
3. As a step before an on-line edit

The linear computer editor remembers the time codes of each edit it performs. This allows the computer editing system to perform edits over and over with frame accuracy. An EDL generated on a computer diskette can be loaded into another computer.

With a computer editor you can:

1. Edit a workprint creatively at a cheaper rate than with on-line editing
2. Edit directly in an on-line session
3. Conform original material from a cuts-only listing (a handwritten EDL), or a diskette

Diskettes for different computer editing systems might not be compatible, but there are conversion programs and established methods of transferring EDLs.

Most linear computer editing rooms come equipped with at least one video playback machine, a record machine, a switcher, an audio mixer, monitors, and certain optional equipment that the client can rent by the hour. An interformat editing suite handles several video formats; however, they must be of the same video standard (NTSC, PAL, SECAM). It is a good idea to examine and test an unfamiliar editing system before using it for an important project. As a general rule, conversion from digital to analog degrades the picture quality.

Random-access editing has changed the editing world. More effects and quick changes during the off-line process have become standard in every major video market. Home versions of these editors are becoming very powerful and relatively inexpensive.

9

Off-Line versus On-Line Editing

The purpose of an off-line edit is to create a program on a cost-effective system which allows the financial freedom to experiment. The result of an off-line editing system is an edit decision list (EDL) and a workprint of the completed program.

Effects and graphics, in a rough form, are often included in the off-line program because the tape from the off-line session will be used as a reference when the program is finished. The sources used in the off-line process are often copies of the original videotapes, with a window of the original time code burned into the image. These copies of the originals are called *window dubs* (see Figure 9-1).

Most off-line editing is accomplished on nonlinear editing systems. Usually window dubs of original footage are transferred into the nonlinear system from three-quarter-inch tapes. Additional audio and video sources can come from CDs, DA88s, or DATs. The footage and additional sources are digitized into the nonlinear editors. On-line refers to the final editing process of a production— picture and sound. An on-line session could be a simple ten-minute session that eliminates on-camera mistakes, or it could be a week-long editing session costing tens of thousands of dollars. In most cases, an off-line session precedes the on-line session, but in some cases an off-line session is not necessary or possible. In the reverse order, a prebuild on-line session could precede an off-line session so that graphics and complicated effects can be created and added to the off-line process.

Even when a program goes directly to on-line, some planning usually pre-cedes the session. Using the master log, the editor organizes a rough list of the edits before the on-line session begins. It might take a few minutes during the

Figure 9-1 A frame of a window dub with the time code burned into the picture. Photo by Sean Sterling.

session to decide in which order the shots will be edited, but pre-edit planning can help the editing session flow smoothly.

OFF-LINE EDITING

Quality Control

Because the off-line master (also called a workprint) is a reference to what will be created in the on-line session, the focus is on the editorial aspect of the show, not the technical quality of the off-line master. However, because the off-line master is often used for client approval, some consideration is given as to how the tape looks and sounds. Taking a moment or two to adjust a video or chroma level does not hurt the project unless there are terrible time constraints. Finessing a music edit can make the difference between a good program and a great one. When apparent tape damage or technical problems appear on the off-line source tapes, the location and type of each problem must be noted, and that same area must be checked on the master tape as soon as possible.

Figure 9-2 The Sony BVE-910, a small computer editor capable of performing on-line and off-line chores. Courtesy of Sony Electronics, Inc.

CREATING THE OFF-LINE MASTER

Creating an off-line master using a linear editing process is becoming less and less frequent. This transition has moved linear editors capable of performing both off-line and on-line chores (see Figure 9-2) into almost exclusively on-line editors. Because frequent changes are an integral part of the off-line process, the linear edit bay is very inefficient. Even when a program is finished in a linear on-line bay, the off-line process is often performed on a nonlinear, random-access editor.

A nonlinear editor can deal with program length changes much more easily than a linear edit bay can. But the end result is still the same: a viewing copy of the program, a paper edit decision list for reference, and an EDL floppy disk that can be loaded into another editor in order to finish the program.

When to Use an Off-Line Edit

An off-line editing session should be considered if the program is even slightly complicated. Most news stories are not off-lined because there is little time for experimentation. A two-edit commercial is not off-lined because there are few choices to be made. Most network dramas, sitcoms, commercials, and television specials use the off-line process extensively. These programs go through so many changes during the editing process that an off-line session is a necessity.

With the cost of Apple- and IBM-based nonlinear editing systems, it can be very inexpensive to create an off-line master and avoid costly decision-making time in an on-line bay. These systems are becoming powerful and cheap enough to perform a program's on-line as well, especially when digital cameras are used. The FireWire protocol used in digital video has enabled digital transfer from a playback deck into the editing system with virtually no signal degradation.

Because hard drive storage is at a premium, a program can be edited using a low resolution in the off-line stage and then the same tapes are used to re-input only the needed footage for the program at full resolution for the creation of the final tape (thus using the same system to off-line, then on-line a program).

THE EDL

The purpose of an off-line edit is to determine what visual and audio portions of the production will be included in the program. The EDL reflects all those elements, and where and how they are to be placed in the program.

With a linear on-line, there are several ways to prepare the EDL. There are also computer programs that can manipulate the EDL for quick assemblies. The Software Grille is one company that uses the prereading capability of some digital machines to optimize the assembly of the show. One of the most effective methods of assembling the footage and production audio is called D Mode. Each reel is used only once, but the computer figures out the most effective shuttle time depending on how long the program is and how far the playback and record tapes have to travel. Software Grille also markets programs for converting EDLs from one high-definition frame rate to another.

It is important to have a perfect EDL when the on-line starts. Fortunately, almost all random-access editors produce such lists. The challenge is to get the EDL in a format that the on-line editing system can accept. There are three standard linear on-line formats: CMX, Grass Valley, and Sony.

Specific edit systems can store proprietary information such as switcher settings and speed controls. Some nonlinear off-line edit systems can provide extremely detailed information that can translate directly to that same company's on-line system.

ON-LINE EDITING

Whether a show has been off-line edited or not, the most important aspect of a successful on-line edit is preparation. Planning for the on-line edit might include reviewing the footage and making a rough EDL, or it might be as involved as spending several days or weeks in an off-line session.

ORIGINAL SOURCE MATERIAL	EQUIPMENT NEEDED TO TRANSFER VIDEO	WHEN TRANSFER SHOULD TAKE PLACE
35mm film	Telecine	Before edit session
16mm film	Telecine	Before edit session
8mm film	Telecine	Before edit session
DVD	DVD player	Before edit session
Slides	Graphics Station/scanner	Before edit session
1/4" audio tape	Reel to reel player	Before or during edit session
Audio cassette	Cassette player	Before or during edit session
DAT audio tape	DAT player	Before or during edit session
DA88 audio tape	DA88 player	Before or during edit session
CD	CD or DVD player	Before or during edit session
Mag (film audio)	Mag machine (make sure playback is at proper sound speed. Video can run at 30, 29.97, 24, and 25 frames per second)	Before edit session
Computer animation	Graphics station	Created before the session, then transferred before or during edit session
Title cards	Matte camera or Graphics station with scanner	Created before the session, then transferred before or during edit session
Electronic titles	Graphics station or character generator	Before session if they are complicated or during edit session if they are simple.

You should check with the edit facility to determine the availability of these machines. Usually there will be an additional charge for their use. All complicated graphics, credit rolls, animation, audio effects, etc., should be stored or transferred to tape before the session starts.

Figure 9-3 Routine methods of transferring non-video materials to video.

Many news stories, magazine shows, and industrial programs go directly on-line once an editing plan has been approved. More complicated programs may require a prebuild on-line session before the final on-line edit. A prebuild session is on-line because the video is being prepared for a final viewing. This footage will be used as a playback source when the entire program is edited together. The purpose of a prebuild on-line edit might be to create a complicated effects sequence or to edit segments that will be added to a studio show. This prebuild session may occur at a different facility from the one where the show is assembled. Sometimes a prebuild on-line edit is performed because a show requires so many expensive machines that it is cost-effective to do all the complicated editing at one time.

Dealing with Sources Not Originally on Video

Many picture and audio sources begin not on video but on 35 mm slides, CDs, DVDs, home movies, digital audio tapes (DATs), DA88s (another format of digital audiotape), 16 mm film, 35 mm film, photos from magazines and books, computer-generated images, physical title cards, and so on. These source materials must be transferred to video in order to be edited (see Figure 9-3). Some of these sources should be transferred to tape before the on-line edit, while others can be used during the edit session. The design of the particular edit bay will often determine whether the transfer occurs before or during the session.

SUMMARY

There are two types of editing sessions: off-line and on-line. The off-line edit is a creative session designed to create an EDL and an edited workprint. On-line refers to the final editing process of a production's picture and sound. An editing strategy must be determined before the editing begins.

An off-line edit results in (1) a copy of the off-line record master (also called a workprint), and (2) a record of the edits made (usually stored on a computer disk along with a physical printout of the edits).

An off-line editing session is considered if the program is even slightly complicated, because many different editing combinations can be tried.

Whether a show has been off-line edited or not, the most important aspect of a successful on-line edit is preparation.

In a prebuild on-line session, a master tape is made of a show segment or graphic. This tape will be used as a playback source when the whole program is edited together.

Many picture and audio sources do not begin on video and must be transferred to video before being edited.

10

Creating Video Effects

Video effects, when used properly, can improve the entire look of a show. However, the ease with which effects are created in nonlinear editors can lull the beginner into making every transition a complicated effect.

THE THREE TYPES OF VIDEO EFFECTS

Three types of effects are used in the video editing process:

1. Switcher effects—these are basically wipes, keys, and dissolves. Since the nonlinear editor has no switcher, we will still identify these effects as switcher effects for ease of description.
2. External effects—effects that use hi-cons or mattes that "hold" out the area used for the effect.
3. Computer digital effects—effects created in specialized effects computers.

SWITCHER EFFECTS

A videotape machine can only make a cut. It is the switcher that creates effects such as wipes, dissolves, and keys. The purpose of a switcher is to mix many sources of video into a single video signal, to which the record machine cuts. The number of inputs into the switcher determines the number of video signals that the switcher can access.

For instance, a switcher can mix sources such as a tape machine, a camera, a digital effects generator, a character generator, a color bar generator, or a safe-title generator. (A safe-title generator is a white box placed in a monitor to indicate the acceptable areas where titles can be placed and still be seen on a home television. Since a portion of the video picture is not visible on many home receivers, this equipment sets boundaries for title placement.)

The switcher can create background colors and matte colors but not video images. The video images that the switcher mixes always come from a source other than the switcher itself. A magazine picture, for instance, must be trans-ferred to video by a camera before the switcher can deal with it.

A switcher can be a tiny box with only a few inputs, or it can be six feet long and require two operators. Figures 10-1a and 10-1b are only two examples of video switchers. Some switchers have a built-in computer that allows you to program the effects, and others must be operated by hand. However it is used, the switcher's purpose is the same: to mix sources of video into one signal.

Almost all the effects discussed in the following sections can be found in nonlinear editing systems, from wipes to keys.

Wipes

A *wipe* is a transition from one picture to another using a pattern, such as a ver-tical bar that moves across the screen. The pattern reveals the new picture as the old one is wiped away. Some switchers have options concerning these wipe pat-terns. The edges of the wipe can be hard or soft and the wipe can have a colored border.

A very soft-edged wipe looks almost like a dissolve. Wipes come in many shapes and sizes, from stars to squares to diamonds. Not all switchers produce the same patterns. Some switchers can modulate or electronically distort these wipe shapes (see Figure 10-2). Using modulation, a circle, for instance, can become an undulating, wavy line.

Dissolves

A *dissolve* is a fade from one source to another. A dissolve to or from black, or a dissolve to a key is called a *fade*. For instance, the director might instruct the editor to "dissolve to reel 2, fade in the end title, and then fade to black."

Keys

A *key* is an electronic hole cut into a picture and filled with a video source. One example of a key is in the credit sequence at the end of a television show. The switcher cuts a hole for the words using a video source (a character generator,

Figure 10-1a The Grass Valley Kalypso switcher. Note that linear editing requires various hardware which occupies physical space, whereas nonlinear requires basically a computer, component boards, and software. However, linear editing does not bring up the storage issues of nonlinear editing systems. Photo courtesy of the Grass Valley Group.

videotape, or artwork) and then fills the hole with the video signal. Another example of a key is the digital effects box over a newscaster's shoulder. In this case, the switcher cuts a hole in the studio camera's video signal and fills it with the video from the digital video effects generator.

The four types of keys are luminance keys, chroma keys, key cuts from external sources, and matte keys.

Figure 10-1b An Abekas A84 component digital switcher. Note the graphic display of the switcher's status in the top center portion of the device. Switchers such as the A84 prove the widespread acceptance of the digital formats. Photo courtesy of Abekas.

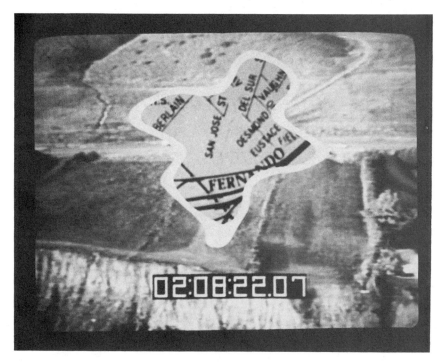

Figure 10-2 A modulated circle wipe with border. Photo by Sean Sterling.

Figure 10-3a   An art card under a matte camera.

Luminance Keys

Luminance keys are electronic holes cut by using the white or black portion of a source and then filling in with video (see Figures 10-3a, 10-3b, and 10-3c). An example is white letters on a black graphics card shot by a video camera. The luminance key cuts a hole in the background picture in the shape of the letters and then fills the hole with the same video signal.

Many times the video that fills the key can come from a source other than the key itself. The key could cut a hole using a graphics card, and then fill the hole with another image, perhaps a close-up of running water. This use of the luminance key can produce very interesting effects.

Chroma Keys

A *chroma key* is an electronic hole that cuts out a specific color in a video signal (see Figure 10-4). The hole is then filled with another video source. Chroma keys

Figure 10-3b A character generator and its monitor.

Figure 10-3c A luminance key from the character generator and matte camera over a beach scene. Photos by Sean Sterling.

Figure 10-4 A beach scene chroma keyed into color bars. A specific color was eliminated by the chroma key, and the beach scene was inserted in that opening. Photo by Sean Sterling.

are often used during the weather segment of news broadcasts. The weather reporter stands in front of a blue screen. The maps are then chroma keyed "behind" him or her. The reporter often seems to be looking off to the side of the screen because an off-screen monitor shows the switcher output of the chroma key. In reality, the reporter is pointing at an empty blue wall, and must coordinate his or her action with the map on the monitor.

Key Cuts from External Sources

In this case, the key is a separate video signal sent to the switcher by another machine, such as a character generator or a digital effects machine (see Figure 10-5). The switcher cuts a hole in the background video, using the key cut signal, and fills that hole with the video from the external source.

Again using the news as an example, the digital effects box over the announcer's shoulder is created by cutting the hole with the key cut signal from

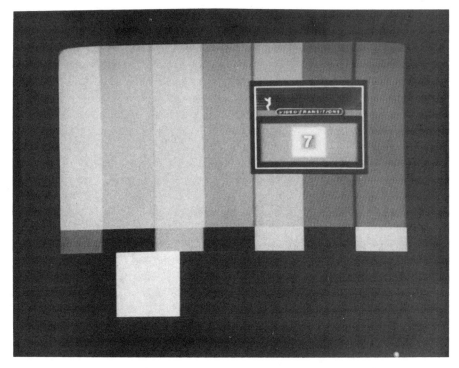

Figure 10-5 A key cut from a digital effects generator over color bars. Photo by Sean Sterling.

a digital effects machine, then filling the hole with the video from the digital effect. This creates a clean, defined cut in the background. If the video in the digital effects device contains both low and high luminance values, the switcher will not be able to cut an accurate hole in the background material using a luminance key or a chroma key. A high-contrast image can be used in the switcher or in a digital effects device to cut a clearly defined hole in the background. This is the most common use of the external key cut.

Matte Keys

Cutting a hole in the background source using a luminance key, a chroma key, or a key from an external source, and filling the hole with a switcher-generated color makes a *matte key*. For example, when shooting white letters on a black art card, a matte key could color the holes created by the white letters.

Figure 10-6 A spotlight effect. Photo by Sean Sterling.

Other Effects

The *nonadditive mix* allows two video sources to be combined with full video levels from each source at the mid-point of the transition. A normal mix (dissolve) allows only 50% of each video source at the mid-point of the transition. The spotlight (see Figure 10-6) is an option that lowers the intensity of a portion of the image while retaining the full video level in the remaining part of the picture. The spotlight is created with the switcher's wipe patterns.

Two Examples of Switcher Use

All switchers can create wipes, dissolves, and keys. Although these effects might seem limited, switchers can offer hundreds of ways to use them. Here is one example: A sportscaster is shown in a broadcasting booth. Keyed behind him is the stadium; in front of him, in the lower third of the picture, is his name. The background wipes to a blimp, the announcer fades out, and the game's statistics are dissolved in over the shot of the blimp. In this example, the character generator would be used twice to produce luminance or matte keys, the announcer would be chroma keyed over the stadium, and the stadium shot would use a wipe effect to transition to the blimp.

Another simple example is the end of a football play. The scores fly in, then as a block the scores rotate and fall below the screen. This effect uses a paint system or frame store to input the picture into a two-channel digital effects device. The digital effects device "flies" the score over the background, the switcher uses the effects device's external key cut to make the hole, and the video also comes from the digital effects device. The digital effects device (DVE) has to be two channels, because the side of the *slab* (a two-sided rectangular image) is another channel, moving in exact cadence with the front portion of the image.

EXTERNAL EFFECTS

The second type of effect is the *external effect*, which is created when another machine's video is fed into the switcher. External effects are often used in conjunction with switcher effects.

Character Generators

Character generators create video words. Most of these machines offer several fonts (boldface, roman, italic, etc.). In the more expensive models, words can be manipulated in much the same way that they are manipulated with a digital effects machine. Character generators can also create designs or capture images from a camera source and manipulate or store those images on a floppy disk. The character generator's signal is often keyed over other video sources. Many recent models of character generators are computer programs running on IBM or Apple computers.

Slow-Motion Devices

Most slow-motion effects are made using videotape machines, or in the case of film, an optical printer or high-speed camera. *Slow motion* is a generic term that indicates an alteration of the original speed of a moving image. Each slow-motion deck has its own limitations of the speed variation in both forward and reverse. As a general rule, the limitations of video decks are −100% in reverse, and +300% in forward motion. To make a 600% effect, you would have to record a tape going forward at 300%, and then play that recording back at 200%.

In a nonlinear editor, reversing or speeding up a shot is as simple as adjusting the clip's speed and then waiting a moment or two for the editor to render the effect. One must be careful to process slow motion effects in nonlinear editors. The interlacing needs to be removed before outputting motion effects to videotape.

Computer Digital Effects

The *computer digital effect* can be broken down into two categories: digital video effects, which are created by a digital effects generator, and computer-generated graphics.

Digital Video Effects

The *digital video effect* (DVE) is accomplished by taking an existing video source (a video image, a moving shot, a still shot from a camera, a wipe, or another effect created by a switcher) and manipulating its position within the video frame. This effect can be seen on almost any network newscast. The DVE can flip a picture upside-down or mirror-reverse the image; it can take a full-frame image and shrink it to infinity (nothing) or blow it up from infinity to full size. Most of these electronic devices can expand video past full frame, eliminating the possibility of a microphone's creeping into the shot or an accidental pan off the edge of the set.

Newer devices have the ability to bend the video frame into a ball or a cylinder, make a page turn, or create ripples and other distortions.

When a performer is shot in front of a blue screen and then chroma keyed into the scene, the digital video effects device is often used to position the performer and even move the artist during the shot.

One of the most effective uses of the digital video effect is to build a story from still pictures. Static, full-frame pictures are boring, but a picture that zooms out from a colored background, spinning until it reaches full frame, then slides off to reveal another picture, is much more interesting.

Digital video effects are created by a digital effects generator, which converts the video signal into digital form. Using complex mathematical formulas, the generator changes the image's size, aspect, and position, converts it back to video, and sends the new video signal, along with a high-contrast key signal, to the switcher.

Each channel of the digital effects generator can handle only one video signal. If, for example, an editor needed 10 digital effects on the screen at one time, he or she would need a 10-channel digital effects device, 2 five-channel devices, 5 two-channel devices, or 10 one-channel devices. Alternatively, the editor could build successive generations of effects by recording one group, then playing that tape back and adding another group, repeating the process until the job was completed. Some low-quality digital effects devices are extremely dirty or nontransparent. An experienced eye can see the degradation of the picture when such machines are used (see Figure 10-7).

Computer-Generated Graphics

Although there are several types of computer animation devices, all these machines have the same purpose: to create video images. Some have the ability to grab or capture a frame of video so that the animator can design a graphic to go over the picture, and some allow the animator to play or animate multiple frames of video. Others can animate the images they create. These devices are often used to create complicated openings. Computer-generated graphics are usually created before the editing session and recorded on videotape. These graphics devices are often divided into two categories: two-dimensional and three-dimensional graphics stations. The three-dimensional station can animate an object and show all sides, whereas two-dimensional graphics only have a front.

At the three-dimensional level, wire-frame models of each object are created in the computer and programmed for motion by an animator/programmer (see Figure 10-8). The computer can then throw light sources, textures, or other effects onto the landscape and/or the wire-framed object. This animation can then be recorded onto film or video.

COMPOSITING DIGITAL EFFECTS

Compositing a digital effect often uses several record tapes. As one layer of an effect is completed, the result is recorded onto the first record tape. This first record tape then becomes a source (playback) tape for the next layer or pass, which is recorded onto the second record tape. The second record tape then becomes a source tape to record back onto the first. This swapping of record tapes continues until the effect is complete. Simple in concept, compositing should be carefully planned. Many parts of an effect will be recorded separately, yet they must fit together precisely.

Compositing a video effect on tape usually requires four elements: the record tape, the playback of the previously created effect, the new video to be added this pass, and a hold out of the new material (see Figure 10-9). The exception to this rule is if you are prereading each effect. Although this puts the effect in jeopardy if you record a pass that is unacceptable (erasing the previous effect), it does eliminate the need for the fourth playback deck.

You can protect these effects by recording each successive layer onto another tape. Although time-consuming, this procedure will protect the effect if a mistake is made. A *hold out* is a high-contrast (black and white) image in which the white

a

b

Figure 10-7 A full-frame signal reduced in a digital effects generator (a), then reduced and keyed over a background color (b). Photo by Sean Sterling.

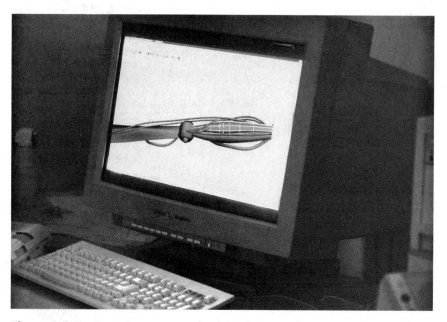

Figure 10-8 A computer-generated graphic image. Note the wire frame that will be filled in with a texture later on in the process. Photo courtesy of New Wave Entertainment.

portion of the signal is the exact shape of the image to be cut out of the background. There will be a matching video image to the hold out, which will be used to fill the hole created by the hold out. Although the human editor keeps track of each playback and record deck, someone or something (the off-line system or client) must carefully manage the new material and its placement, using the hold out.

Sometimes a fifth element is needed to composite an effect: a reverse hold out. For example, a cereal box might conceal a cartoon character. The reverse hold out would place the character between existing portions of the effect—in this case, in front of the background and behind the box in the foreground.

PREREAD

Several digital videotape machines have a video read head in front of the record head. This enables the recorder to use its own existing video as a source before recording over it. This enables you to perform a dissolve using a single playback and the record machine. The beginning of the dissolve comes from the record machine itself.

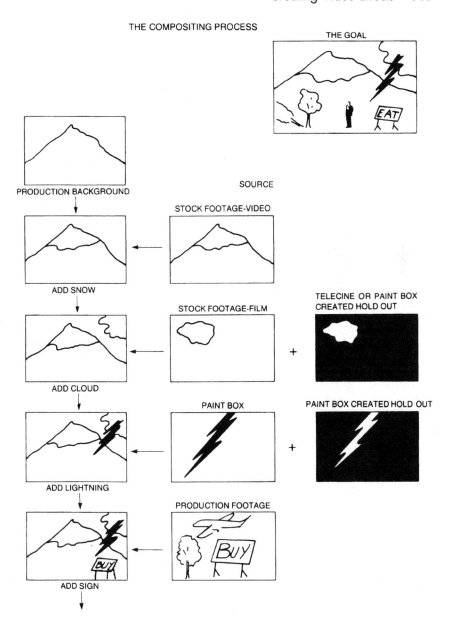

Figure 10-9a The compositing session must be planned. In this example, a nonexistent scene is created piece by piece. A producer, watching the author design this illustration, merely said, "It looks like someone didn't shoot the original footage correctly." In many instances, compositing can enhance a shot, but it is never inexpensive. Another point to note is that a DVE device was used in all layers to reposition the footage. If the money is available, this effect would be much easier to accomplish using a computer animation system instead of an edit bay.

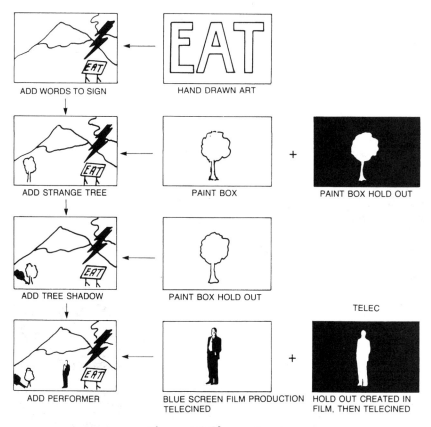

ADD WORDS TO SIGN   HAND DRAWN ART

ADD STRANGE TREE   PAINT BOX   +   PAINT BOX HOLD OUT

ADD TREE SHADOW   PAINT BOX HOLD OUT

TELEC

ADD PERFORMER   BLUE SCREEN FILM PRODUCTION   +   HOLD OUT CREATED IN
TELECINED   FILM, THEN TELECINED

Figure 10-9b *continued*

THE APPLE/IBM-COMPATIBLE VIDEO REVOLUTION

The accelerated power of home computers and the introduction of the digital transfer protocol called FireWire has brought video and audio editing into the home. Properly configured, these editing systems are very powerful and also have EDL support. At the very least they can provide the beginning editor with extensive experience in editing with a nonlinear system. Although each nonlinear system has its own method of operation, they are all very similar. Once you have mastered one, picking up another is not that difficult. There is a virtual explosion of software and hardware. Inexpensive, impressive effects are within the grasp of virtually every computer user.

SUMMARY

The three types of video effects are switcher effects, external effects, and computer digital effects.

The switcher creates wipes, dissolves, and keys. The purpose of a switcher is to mix the available sources of video and send one video signal to the record machine. The switcher only mixes video sources; it does not create images. Digital switchers come with frame stores and very intricate layering capabilities. The four types of keys are luminance keys, chroma keys, key cuts from external sources, and matte keys.

External effects come from other types of machines connected to the switcher. These machines include character generators and slow-motion devices.

Computer digital effects can be divided into two categories: digital video effects and computer-generated graphics. Digital effects are produced by a digital effects generator, which alters the direction and shape of the picture but cannot create video on its own. Each channel of a digital effects generator can handle only one video signal. Computer-generated graphics are normally created, or built, before the editing session and then recorded on videotape.

Digital video allows for many more video generations without the significant signal degradation of analog copying. Some digital tape machines allow the record machine to preread video before going into record mode.

PART III

Working with the Image

11

Shooting for Postproduction

Producing, directing, and shooting a visual program involves many more details than are discussed here, but paying attention to the following suggestions can help improve the overall quality of a show and make the postproduction process much easier and more creative (see Figure 11-1).

PREPRODUCTION

Preproduction planning should be done before any production work is started. Feature film directors often illustrate each shot of the production. This is especially important in animated or special effects movies. Even on a news shoot, the crew and cast need to know where they are going and what equipment they will have available. In producing dramatic shows, scripts must be written, locations chosen, actors cast, and a shooting schedule designed.

The Script

The script is the blueprint of a visual production. It takes less time to rewrite a scene than to shoot and/or edit a badly planned one. The production team should make sure that what is on paper can be accomplished.

Script Breakdown

Once the script is finished, a breakdown is performed. The script *breakdown* is a critical examination of the script that concerns all production aspects of the

Locations, studio rentals	Legal counsel
Costumes	Script breakdown
Make-up	Props
Additional sound effects	Equipment required for:
Power considerations on location	camera
Weather provisions	sound
Storyboards	lighting
Budget	set construction
Re-shoot days	Actor transportation
Script	Food for crew
Releases	Original production format
Petty cash	On-line format
Transportation	Editing facility
Stock footage	Special effects and their execution
Graphics	Music
Telephone and utilities	Mixing facility
Office location	Off-line editing choices
Insurance	Duplication choices

Figure 11-1 Preproduction considerations.

program. These items are details such as: How many and what kinds of sets, props, costumes, or locations need to be secured? Where will the shoot take place? Who in the cast and crew needs to be notified, how many days are they needed, and where do they report? How will the effects be created? Will the footage be shot on film or video? Will the effects elements be combined on film or video? At which facility will the effects compositing take place? All these questions and more should be answered before shooting begins.

There are several computer programs that help break down scripts, or you can do it by hand. Every nuance of the script, from weather, time of year, type and number of props, cast needed for each scene, types of costumes, to any other aspect of each scene, must be listed and acquired.

The Storyboard

Most productions should have some sort of storyboard (see Figure 11-2) prepared well in advance of the shoot. This shot-by-shot plan of the show helps avoid possible production and editing problems. It also helps the cast and crew see how the show will be put together. As much information as possible should be included in the storyboard—camera angles, dialogue, type of action—to keep potential production conflicts and problems to a minimum.

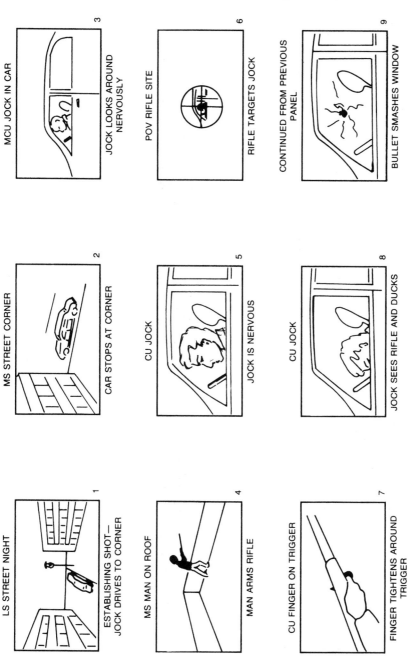

Figure 11-2 A sample storyboard. The storyboard helps identify editorial problems. For example, in this storyboard, panels 1 and 2 will not edit together correctly because the car's direction is reversed.

Production Schedule

The production schedule is a master plan for shooting a program and is the best way to keep all aspects of the shoot organized. There is no substitute for a detailed and accurate production schedule. As the script is broken down into its individual production demands, the production schedule translates this information into a plan of action. There are relatively inexpensive computer programs, such as Creative Planet's "Movie Magic Budgeting," that help automate some of those chores. A strip board can be used to keep all the pertinent information organized if money is not available for a computer program. Student productions may rely on detailed outlines. No matter how the plan is laid out, flexibility must be built into the schedule. Weather, personnel, equipment complications, or other changes can require alterations in originally scheduled production arrangements.

Even if a show is not scripted (for example, a documentary or news show), the production schedule keeps a crew on track and aware of each setup's location and technical requirements. Single-camera productions are usually shot out of sequence to avoid returning to the same location or set. In these cases, it is even more important to have a complete production schedule before the shooting starts.

One of the most critical aspects of the production phase is communication. The production schedule, crew and cast call sheets, and all other relevant information must be constantly communicated to everyone involved in the project. It is ironic that in a communication medium, most mistakes occur due to lack of communication.

Cast and Crew

A production comes to life through the coordinated efforts of the cast and crew. The casting of a show is an important function. Obviously, the most beautiful actress or most handsome actor is not always the best choice for a particular part; talent and attitude are often more critical factors. Arrogant, irresponsible, or lazy crew members or actors can cause more problems than their talent warrants. Likewise, all crew members should be chosen for their attitude as well as their abilities. An eager individual might be a great assistant to the director but a disaster as a lighting director. Similarly, a performance can be ruined by bad microphone placement or shaky camera operation. Making sure each crew member knows his or her job can make life a lot easier during production.

Equipment/Footage Check

Unless the production equipment has been used the day before or the equipment house has been checked out thoroughly, the equipment should be tested prior to a shoot. If possible, playback equipment should be available during the shoot to check each shot for dropouts, audio problems, tape damage, focus, continuity, and so on. Feature films almost always have a video feed from the film camera to check each shot. In the excitement of production, an errant boom mike or distracting background action can be overlooked. Take care to check the chosen take before proceeding to the next camera set up.

PRODUCTION

The production phase is probably the most thrilling aspect of putting a show together, but the cast and crew must not be carried away by emotion. During this phase, extreme caution and attention to detail must prevail. Production may be exciting, but the focus must be on shooting the best footage. Small errors, undetected in the shooting phase, become glaring mistakes in the editing room. A forgotten insert shot or overlooked action in the background can be harmful to the show's overall outcome.

Bars and Tone

Color bars (as discussed in Chapter 4) provide a visual reference signal that indicates how a particular camera is recording its images. Every production tape should have color bars recorded onto its head for at least 30 seconds, preferably one minute. If a tone generator is available, an audio tone should also be recorded at this time.

Slates

Slates should be recorded visually and on the audio track for every shot and every take. Information containing scene number, date, take, reel, location, and so on, should be at the head of each new recording. It does not matter whether these details are on a film-style slate or on a handwritten piece of paper; what is important is identifying each shot. These slates will be used often in the editing process, both in building the master log and in searching for particular takes during the editing session. Not slating a shot during production might save a few minutes during production, but will always cause delays in the editing room. Slate every shot, no matter how trivial or short. Also during this time, a record of each take along with director's notes is kept, and then included in the master log.

Ambient Sound

Often when editing visuals, the production dialogue track is altered, creating an artificial pause. These pauses must be filled with the natural sound of that

Figure 11-3 The Steadicam has been commonly used in the motion picture industry. Because small video formats are often employed, Steadicam adapted its ingenious device for lighter cameras. Photo courtesy of the Steadicam Corporation.

specific location. Finding 5 seconds of perfectly quiet ambience on a production reel is often quite difficult. To solve this problem, 11 to 30 seconds of ambient sound, or *room tone*, should be recorded at each location. This requires everyone on the set to be quiet, a feat not always easy to accomplish.

Clean Heads and Tails

The *head* and *tail* (the beginning and end) of every shot should have a few seconds of non-action so that the editor can make dissolves, L cuts, or subtle adjustments in pacing. All camera shots should also be steady, with the camera mounted securely on a tripod or a special handheld rig (see Figure 11-3). The director should try to wait a few moments at the tail end of a shot before calling "cut." This head and tail rule also applies to pans, tilts, and dollies (see the Glossary). The camera should hold steady for several seconds before beginning a move. Once the move has been completed, the camera should hold again. Even if the camera movement is imperfect, the head or tail of the take may be used by itself.

Reviewing Takes

At the end of each take, it is wise to check that the image was recorded, and that the action, for both the camera and cast, was acceptable. Pay careful attention to the delivery of lines. Were the actors stepping on each other's lines? Were unseen overhead planes or nearby cars creating noise during the dialogue? Is the take perfect? It pays to get it right on tape before continuing to the next camera setup.

If window dubs are being recorded at the same time as the original footage, do not check the window dub for these aspects of the shot. The master footage is what needs to be checked. On more than one occasion, a master record machine has not rolled, meaning that no original footage is produced; then after the take, the window dub is checked instead of the master footage. Because the window dub is available, yet there is no master footage, the take cannot be used because it does not exist.

Finally, one should make sure that the master footage is forwarded to the end of the last scene, to ensure that the original footage of the last take is not erased.

Multiple Takes

The recording medium, whether film or video, is relatively inexpensive compared to all other aspects of the production. Making a second, "insurance" take, if time permits, is a very cost-effective way of providing alternative readings and footage for the editor.

Releases

All performers in a program must sign releases, allowing the producer to use their likenesses in this particular show for all purposes (videocassette, broadcast, commercial use, etc.). Not obtaining a release (or not keeping it on file) can cause incredible headaches later, when a performer decides that he or she can hold up the sale of your program for a lot of money. A signed release must be in hand before the performer steps in front of the camera. There should be no exceptions. Even student productions must adhere to this rule. When an up-and-coming star performs in a program, the program can be sold if releases are on file. The possible windfall will be lost if a release is not in hand.

Short and Simple

Inexperienced directors and camera operators often plan complicated, difficult shots, such as capturing a reflection in a shiny hubcap, performing a 360-degree pan, or attempting a half-mile dolly for no reason other than to make a big impression. A critical look at a feature film or television show will illustrate the power of simplicity. Camera placement should tell the story, not distract from it. Complicated shots are all too often self-indulgent and pointless.

This simplicity also applies to the physical movement of the cast (blocking). Panning here and tilting there to follow a meandering actor can annoy the audience and limit editorial choices. Unnecessary movement within the frame is a sign that the director is either confused or not in control of the action.

If a camera move is justified, it should be made with ease, smoothness, and most important, purpose. The camera should stop on something that has visual impact and adds to the production. Handheld shots have the potential of eliciting powerful emotions, but most shots should be made with the camera securely placed on a tripod.

Overlapping Action and Dialogue

Overlapping action and dialogue is an extension of the clean head and tail concept. You should always try to overlap action and/or dialogue when changing the camera angle within a scene. The cast should repeat several lines of dialogue or the action that immediately precedes the new dialogue or action. If this overlap is not built into the shot, editing the two angles together will be difficult.

Toning Down Actors When in Close-Up

The close-up is an important aspect of any show. Inexperienced film actors tend to embellish emotional moments, and although this might work in a master shot, exactly the opposite approach is needed in a close-up. Since the actor's face fills the screen, even the slightest movement is exaggerated. When shooting a close-up, the director might have to tell the actor to tone down both movement and emotion.

Screen Direction

The screen direction of an action depends on how movement within the frame is shot. Action on the screen usually moves either left to right or right to left. If a woman rides a bike down a street and two shots are recorded—one from one side of the street and the other from the opposite side—when these two shots

PODUNK STADIUM

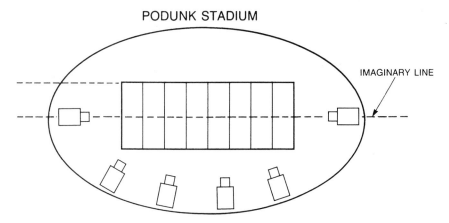

Figure 11-4 Generalized camera placement at a football stadium. In sports shows, cameras are usually positioned on only one side of the stadium to avoid changing the players' screen direction. Recently, the "reverse angle" shot has been used, but is clearly identified.

are edited together, it will *appear* that the woman has changed direction. She has not changed her direction, but she has changed screen direction.

In sports programs, most of the cameras are placed on one side of the playing field to avoid changing the screen direction of the players (see Figure 11-4). If the camera moves to the other side of the field ("crossing the line"), the players' screen direction will be reversed. However, not only has the increased sophistication of the viewing audience increased the number of cameras in sporting events, but the reverse angle is used more and more.

In situation comedies, though, all the cameras are on one side of the set. In dialogue sequences, the camera setups are on one side of the scene. In every scene, an invisible line dissects the action. If shots are not recorded in the proper order to make the transition from one direction to another, the audience will be very confused.

Consider this example: Two people are talking to each other. The camera is set up in front of the two actors (see Figure 11-5). Now imagine a line drawn straight through the people. If the camera crosses that line, essentially going behind the actors, the screen direction will be reversed. The same problem occurs if a car is filmed going down a street and the camera is placed first on one side of the street and then on the other. In the second shot, the car will appear to be going in the direction opposite to the way it was going in the first shot.

One method of changing the screen direction is to shoot a scene head-on. Placing the camera on the original imaginary line gives the viewer the opportunity to become oriented to a change in screen direction. Crossing the line without a proper transition (see Figure 11-6) results in tremendous editing problems.

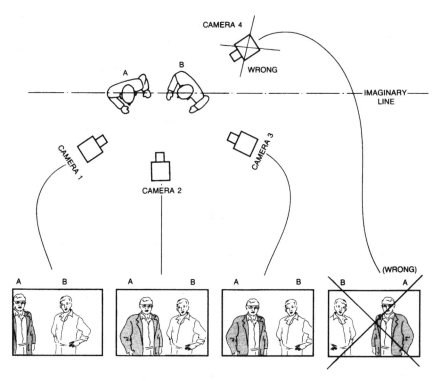

Figure 11-5 Camera placement in a two-person dialogue scene. Placing the camera on the wrong side of the imaginary line reverses screen direction. Note that the camera that has crossed the imaginary line shows character B on the left side of the screen, while the three other cameras have character B on the right.

Continuity

A program has a certain flow, and this flow, or *continuity*, must be maintained in every shot. For example, if a man picks up a cup with his right hand in the wide shot, audiences expect the cup to stay in his right hand in the medium shot. Continuity is not limited to the actions of the characters in a scene. A Boeing 757 parked behind a newscaster should not suddenly change to a twin-engine plane. Similarly, an actor in a historical production should not wear a watch.

Most feature films employ at least one person whose main concern is taking notes on every aspect of the show's continuity. Often this person uses a Polaroid camera to help in reconstructing how a scene was played, what type of makeup was used, how background actors were placed, and so on. If continuity is overlooked or ignored, all sorts of editing problems can occur, resulting in a very uneven-looking program.

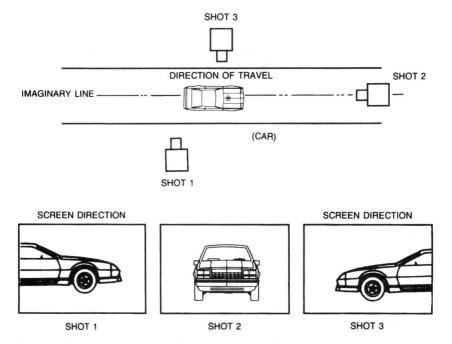

Figure 11-6 Crossing the imaginary line in a motion shot. A head-on shot can help reverse screen direction.

Cutaways

The *cutaway* is a shot of another location or object that is cut into a scene. For instance, a reporter might be talking about a crack in a local dam. The cutaway might be a close-up of the crack or an aerial shot of the dam, reservoir, and surrounding community. In dramatic shows, the cutaway could be a shot of the murder weapon hidden in a drawer or the clock ticking away precious seconds. The more cutaways that are available, the more freedom the editor has.

A Variety of Angles

Almost every scene starts on a wide shot. This sets the location and mood of the scene. The next shot is usually a medium shot, which is often framed to include one or more of the main characters of the scene from the waist up. In dialogue scenes, the medium shot is often over the shoulder of one of the characters. The close-up is used next. It usually shows the character from the neck or shoulders up.

Most dialogue scenes are played in close-ups and medium shots. Occasionally, the scene might return to a wide-angle shot if a lot of movement is required or to a high-angle shot if the director wants to show how small the character is in relation to his or her surroundings. A wide shot is often used in the same scene when a new character is introduced.

A scene can end in a close-up, medium shot, or wide shot. Nearly every soap opera scene closes on a distraught actor's face, but a medium or wide shot is appropriate for other types of shows.

The ideal scene is shot with a variety of angles. The camera can be raised or lowered to create a specific mood or emotion. Raising the camera in a high-angle shot tends to make an actor appear less powerful, while lowering the camera in a low-angle shot tends to make the actor appear powerful and strong. If the director uses a variety of angles and varies the position of the camera, the editor can control the pacing and visual content of a scene to produce a powerful visual experience.

Headroom

In shots where people are present, there should be plenty of headroom at the top of the screen (see Figure 11-7). It looks unnatural if the top of a person's head is cut off. The same holds true for any shot of a building or other object: There must be some space at the top of every frame.

The Lower Third

In a documentary or informational program, the on-camera speakers are usually identified through the use of a key in the lower third of the picture. If there is not enough room in the frame, the speaker's mouth will be covered by the lower-third graphic. It is a good idea to frame individuals in these types of programs so that identifying information can fit in the frame without covering the person's face.

Balance

An image's position within the frame has its own balance. For instance, a single shot of a girl running away from a pursuer requires lead room at the head of the picture. Putting the pursuer in the middle of the frame is considered bad framing. A camera operator with a sense of framing is invaluable. The professionals who work broadcast sports are just some of the camera operators who are excellent at framing and following action (see Figure 11-8).

A boat crossing a river has numerous possibilities in terms of balance within the frame. Is the boat participating in a celebration? Is the boat being left behind? Is the boat leading the procession? Each situation requires a different composition, or balance, within the frame.

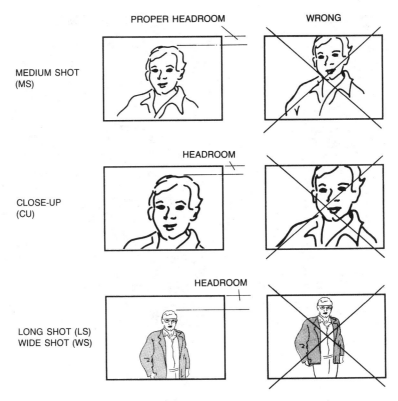

Figure 11-7 Examples of proper and improper headroom composition. Each shot should always have adequate headroom.

Safe Action/Safe Title

On a television screen, part of the picture is cut off; therefore, action should be positioned away from the edges of the frame and graphics should be placed in the center of the frame. If the graphic must appear on one side of the screen, use a crosshatch (Figure 11-9) to determine the point farthest from the center at which the graphic can be placed.

Controlling Background

Locations can provide wonderful and impressive visuals for a program, but unless careful attention is paid to the background, problems can occur. Just as in the earlier example of the 747 turning into a twin-engine plane, the background of an uncontrolled location can be troublesome. It is frustrating to have to redo a perfect reading of an important news story because the camera caught an

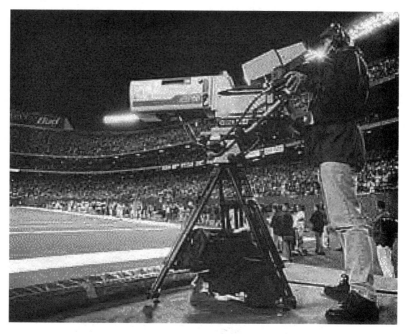

Figure 11-8 A Panasonic HD camera on location at a football HD broadcast. Photo courtesy of Panasonic Corporation.

obscene gesture made by an onlooker or because a microphone crept into the shot. To avoid serious problems, make sure at least one crew member keeps a close watch on the background during every shot. In addition, it is a good idea to check the footage before moving on to the next camera angle.

Labeling Original Footage

As soon as a reel is finished, a label must be applied to both the video case and the reel itself. The date, time code, and the names of the locations, production, camera operator, scenes, and performers must be written legibly or typed on the reel. Do not wait to get to a typewriter if one is not available. Label the reel before loading another. Memories are short in the heat and confusion of production.

Helpful Suggestions

The actor or sound engineer might have a suggestion about how a shot might be improved or a problem solved. It is always a good idea to listen to suggestions from the cast and crew, as a good production team can often get more out of a shoot than was originally thought possible.

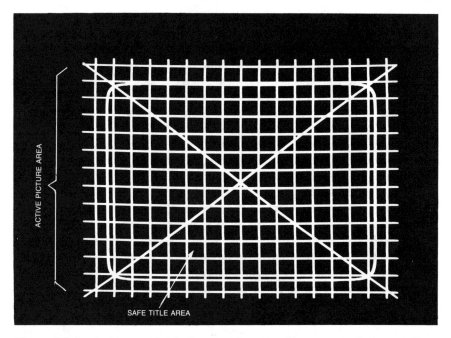

ACTIVE PICTURE AREA

SAFE TITLE AREA

Figure 11-9 A video crosshatch. One way to center a title on a screen is to use a video-generated design. The television-shaped screen is a *safe title area* (that portion of the screen where most televisions will be able to read a title). The center of the X is the screen center.

Storing Original Footage

Original videotapes should be stored in a safe, dry place. This might seem obvious, but tapes are often carelessly left on the back seat of a car on a 90-degree day or in a damp garage or basement over the weekend. It makes no sense to spend days on a shoot, and then leave the original masters in an unsuitable environment. In addition, you should always note where the originals are stored, as it could be months until they are needed for the on-line edit.

SUMMARY

Preproduction planning is crucial to the production process. The storyboard is a must for any planned production. It is also a good idea to build some extra time into the schedule to accommodate shooting overages. Testing production equipment before the actual shoot and reviewing all shots to make sure the technical and creative aspects are correct are also helpful in avoiding delays.

The production phase of a show requires extreme caution and attention to detail. Identifying slates should precede every shot, both in the picture and on the audio track. In addition, all shots, especially those involving camera moves, should have an ample head and tail. Keep all shots, camera movements, and action within the frame simple and motivated. To facilitate editing, always overlap action and dialogue when changing the angle of a shot.

When a close-up is being shot, the performer should tone down both movement and emotion. To ensure proper screen direction, avoid crossing the center line when moving the camera. If the line is crossed, make sure the proper transition angles are recorded.

In any show, pay careful attention to the details of each shot, including but not limited to the background, the lighting, and the actions and costumes of the extras and principal actors.

You should use a variety of angles in any scene, but always leave plenty of headroom at the top of the frame. Also, you should make sure to leave room for lower thirds, especially in close-up shots of speakers.

Balance is determined by the action within the frame. Action should be positioned away from the edges of the frame so that it is not cut off.

Check all takes for performance, irregularities, and flaws, both picture and audio. Get releases from all performers before they get in front of the camera.

Label all tapes as soon as they are finished with proper information, including date, locations, performers, time code, and scenes. Make sure to store original videotapes in a safe, dry place. Noting their location for future reference will save time later.

12

Editing Pictures

The essence of shooting, editing, and compositing can be appreciated by watching almost any network television commercial. A commercial must entertain and sell a product in 30 seconds. In addition, commercials are usually on the cutting edge of effects and graphics or reflect current editorial trends. Only the most necessary shots and audio are included in that half-minute. Days, sometimes weeks, will be spent making sure all 900 video frames are exactly the ones that should be shown.

Any visual program, whether a commercial, feature film, or documentary, is created by selecting a series of images and sounds. The editor, along with the director, chooses the specific images and audio that will be included in the show. This selection process makes an immense difference in how an audience reacts to a particular production.

In feature films, TV programs, and videos, the editor is awarded a single-card credit, just like the writer and director. Knowing the power of the editing process, the feature film director often negotiates for control of the final cut. Once the production phase of a program has been completed, whoever controls the editing process controls the program.

ORGANIZATION

The novice editor might think that the professional glances at the program script, then whips out a first cut that is brilliant, approved, and sent to on-line. Nothing could be further from the truth (see Figure 12-1). A high-caliber editor takes the time to log the available footage. Then, after consulting with the director, he or she begins the methodical process of cutting a program together.

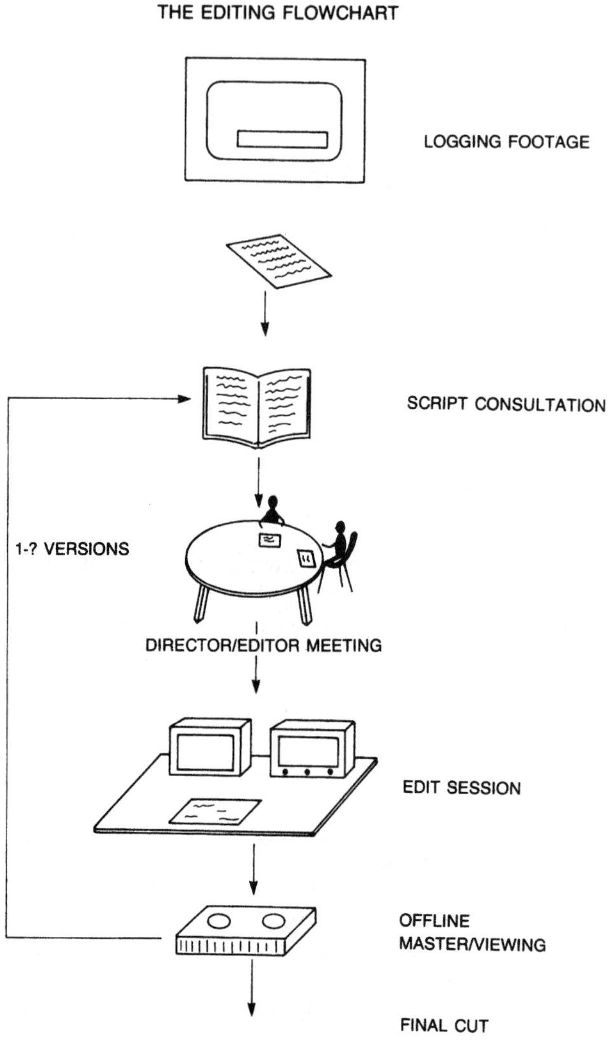

THE EDITING FLOWCHART

LOGGING FOOTAGE

SCRIPT CONSULTATION

1-? VERSIONS

DIRECTOR/EDITOR MEETING

EDIT SESSION

OFFLINE
MASTER/VIEWING

FINAL CUT

Figure 12-1 An overview of the editing process. The postproduction process is carefully planned and executed. Rarely does a show go through one simple, off-line edit. Changes often occur during the refining of a program, whether it is a 30-second commercial or a six-hour miniseries.

This is neither a quick nor an easy job. Knowing the available footage, understanding the show's purpose, and being familiar with the script are just the beginning of the task. Creating a show cannot be a haphazard affair, or the result will be equally haphazard. The master log, and the thought process that includes planning an editing approach, are as important as learning which button to push.

THE SHOW'S PURPOSE

Every show has a purpose. This might be to sell a product, to train or inform, to amuse, to frighten, or to excite. The show's purpose should be decided long before any footage is shot.

The editor places the images and audio in an order that supports the show's purpose. This is true in feature films as well as propaganda pieces, news, comedies, dramas, and documentaries. If the editor is confused about the show's purpose, then the audience will be confused.

THE INTENDED AUDIENCE

Each program has an intended audience, which may be broad or very limited. A training tape about the installation of car stereos would be geared toward technicians who will use the tape for instruction. Such a tape is edited very differently from a documentary on the life of a car stereo installer because the intended audience is different. The editor must know the intended audience of a program to satisfy that audience's expectations through the pacing and presentation of information.

CHOOSE, EDIT, AND TRIM

Shot by shot, a show evolves out of the images and dialogue chosen. In the first step, the editor views the footage and chooses the best images for the show's purpose and intended audience.

Viewing the footage involves building a master log. The master log indicates which shots have the proper delivery or performance and are technically acceptable. As the editor views the footage, he or she notes that one shot might connect well with another or that a particular length of footage might be appropriate for the opening titles, graphics background, or other purpose.

The editor then begins to piece the shots together in an editing session, using the master log as a guide. If the tape is for a news broadcast, the results of the first edit might end up on the air. In dramatic or documentary programs, however, the first cut is usually accomplished in an off-line editing session, and then refined.

Edits are often trimmed (occasionally lengthened, but usually shortened) even as a show is being cut for the first time. Most editors, once they have determined the IN points on the record and playback tapes, will let the edit run long on the OUT end. The extra footage at the end of the previous edit can be used to make sure the next edit comes in at exactly the right moment. Some editors come close to a fine cut if they examine each edit thoroughly. In larger shows that have the luxury of going through the off-line process, trimming takes more time. Edits are often cut in different sequences until the scene plays to everyone's satisfaction. When editing on a random-access editor, this trimming process can happen as soon as the following edit is placed, because the linearity of videotape is not a concern in random-access editing.

PACING

Each shot has its own pacing, and the connection of several shots creates the pacing or rhythm of one scene. The relationship of one scene to another creates the pacing of the entire show. Through the careful use of pacing within a shot, a scene, and the entire show, an editor can create tension, laughter, relaxation, arousal, or anger in the audience. The entire spectrum of human emotions is available to a sensitive editor with the proper footage. Maintaining the same pacing throughout any type of program will quickly bore the audience.

One of the most powerful tools an editor has is the ability to compress or expand time. With the proper editorial choices, a scene can affect the audience's perception of time. For example, a training tape about installing car stereos is intended to impart information about a technical process. The shots will be more than long enough to demonstrate the specific facts concerning the installation process. Some footage may be repeated.

The pacing of the program will be slow and methodical. This does not mean boring, but it will be paced for maximum content absorption. On the other hand, an action-adventure program will be cut quickly. The pacing will come from the action and movement within the frame as well as from rapidly occurring edits that accent that action. There will also be scenes within the program in which the pacing will slow to keep the audience members from being too shocked and let them catch their breath.

Controlling the Pacing

A program's pacing can be controlled in several ways. The first and most obvious way is the length of each cut. An edit can have extra time on the incoming and outgoing portions. This added time affects how the edit "plays." For instance, you may edit a close shot of a gun being raised, then fired, as in the sequence of Figures 12-2 through 12-8. An edit that uses the whole raising action and firing, including the moments after the firing, will be paced more slowly than the edit that starts just as the gun stops its upward motion and ends as soon as the shot is fired.

Another method of controlling the show's pace is with the number of cuts per minute. Again, referring to the raising of a loaded gun, the same real-time shot could be used to show the raising of the gun, but intercut with the intended

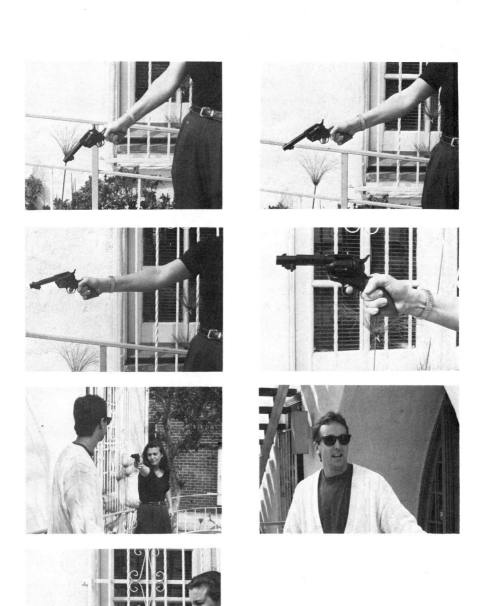

Figures 12-2 through 12-8 Time can be compressed or expanded, depending on how images are edited together. Using all of the images, the picture sequence elongates elapsed time by keeping all the shots of the gun being raised and cutting to different angles. Using only the fourth, fifth, and sixth images collapses the time in which the action takes place, providing a different pacing, yet still expressing the full action. Photos courtesy of Sterling Productions.

victim's face and the assailant's expression. The raising of the gun would take just as long, but the added footage would alter the scene's timing.

A scene may not have the same pacing throughout. The beginning might have quick cuts, with great tension, then the pace might slow down, only to speed up again as another threat or character is introduced. A show with no rhythmic change is boring. This is another reason to shoot several angles of a particular scene. The multiple angles allow for a flexible adjustment of pacing.

WHEN TO CUT

Cutting from one camera angle to another should be invisible to the audience. One of the best places to cut is during action. The eye is usually drawn to motion, so when a change in camera angle occurs during the motion, the mind automatically connects the action.

Another ideal time to cut is when the audience expects it. If two on-screen characters are having a discussion and another off-screen person is secretly listening at the door, a perfect time is when the on-screen characters discuss the eavesdropping friend. Similarly, if a narrator is describing Niagara Falls, this is a good time to cut to a shot of the falls.

In all cases, an edit must be motivated. Without motivation, either by concept, such as a narrator's line, or a physical action by an object or character, the edit will be jarring and obtrusive. When an edit occurs with motivation and on-screen action, the audience will be unaware of the shot change. Part of the editor's purpose is to mask the fact that an edit has taken place.

FOUR TYPES OF EDITS

A show that has been properly edited should appear not to have been edited at all. Viewing a program should be an uninterrupted visual experience. Edits appear to be natural or invisible when the cut follows one of four basic editorial concepts: action, screen position, form, and idea. One exception to this rule is an edit specifically made to jar the audience, a *shock cut;* another is in a music montage sequence, where edits are often made on the beat, making the cuts or effects obvious.

Action

Even a simple gesture, such as raising a hand, allows an editor to cut at numerous points during that action. An editor might choose to cut at the start of the move, in the middle, or toward the end, but cutting during the action is one of the best ways to change the camera angle within a scene.

Screen Position

If the eye is led to one side of the screen, the action or character in the next shot might be located on that side also. Again, the purpose of the cut is to allow the eye to follow the movement of the shot. In commercials, an image is often flipped to help an edit flow. Reversing screen position just to make an edit work better is a common practice. Of course, attention must be paid to any signs or other lettering in the shot, because they will be backwards.

Form

A cut from a porthole to a full moon is an example of an edit using form. Cutting from a Frisbee to the sun or dissolving from a burning match to a roaring fire are other examples. This type of edit often uses screen position to be most effective.

Ideas

Ideas are used to smooth the visual transition in edits. A dissolve from a crying woman to a rain-streaked window is an example of an idea edit.

The most powerful edits are those that combine two or more of these concepts. An example of a combination would be cutting from a high-angle shot of a diver leaping off a diving board to a side-angle shot of an ice cube landing in a glass. In this case, action, screen position, and idea are combined to create a transition.

THE SPLIT EDIT

The *split edit*, also called an *L cut*, is an edit in which the audio or picture leads a *both cut* (see Figure 12-9). This type of edit is extremely powerful, offering many possibilities for controlling dialogue and making shot transitions smoother.

The split edit can be used in any type of editing situation. An audio cut that precedes the picture can be used to prepare the audience for the next scene. For instance, the sound of waves might precede a picture of the stormy ocean. Alternatively, a picture leading into an audio split might be a close-up of a woman's lover as she finishes talking about him.

The split edit is most often used in static dialogue scenes (in soap operas or television dramas) where there is little variation in angles. For instance, one character's lines might be edited over the other person's picture.

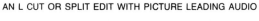

AN L CUT OR SPLIT EDIT WITH PICTURE LEADING AUDIO

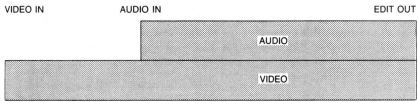

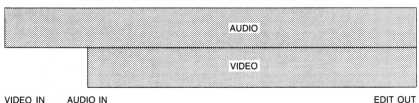

Figure 12-9 The L cut, or split edit.

AUDIO TRANSITIONS

Using audio can be an excellent method of creating a transition from one shot to the next. Although the most popular type of audio transition is the L cut, in which the incoming audio is edited into the outgoing scene, audio can also be used for shock cuts: a sudden scream occurs frames before the visual is introduced. Another use of audio is in a street scene that is enhanced by the sound of a police siren in the background, even though no squad car is ever shown.

Each edit should be examined in terms of its audio as well as its visual potential. Sounds that are not recorded during production can be taken from effects libraries or created later at a makeshift sound session. A door slam or a baby's cry can be enhanced, adding to the overall production value of a program. Many editors will go to audio experts for help and suggestions. Occasionally an off-line project will be roughly mixed for presentation. For example, senior audio mixer Arthur Payson has been called on to help the author on numerous occasions (Figure 12-10).

AUDIO INCREASES PRODUCTION VALUE

The motion picture industry recognizes the value of a carefully executed sound track. A multilayered audio track will always enhance the viewer's perception of a program. The final audio mix of a film contains hundreds of dialogue lines, special effects, music tracks, Foley effects, and ADR lines. Individuals create

Figure 12-10 Arthur Payson, an award-winning music producer and commercial mixer, works at a Fairlight digital audio workstation. Photo courtesy of New Wave Entertainment.

Foley audio effects on a sound stage as they watch a copy of the production footage. ADR (automatic dialogue replacement) tracks are created by performers as they listen to a loop of their own voices while watching the footage of themselves. Hearing themselves repeatedly helps the performers recreate the same inflections used during production.

FAST CUTTING EQUALS PERCEIVED ACTION

Editors of adventure films heighten the feeling of action by cutting often. Most shots last less than five seconds. In action sequences, an edit occurs at least every two seconds, if not quicker.

Even when cutting a lecture, the editor should use as many visuals as possible. The number of (motivated) edits will determine whether the production seems long or short to the audience. In the limited settings of television sitcoms, for example, camera angles and shots are constantly changing to give the shows their quick pacing.

Occupying the eye with new and different images that are consistent with the intent of the show will prevent the audience from becoming bored. Of course, a quick cut during a drawn-out funeral scene might be totally wrong, considering the scene's content.

USING SPECIAL EFFECTS

There is a time and place for special effects. In the early days of live television, every transition seemed to be a sawtooth wipe. In the 1980s, the digital video effect, usually flying boxes or flips, was seen over and over in every type of program. Digital effects are used to enhance programs as a compositing tool, to correct production errors, or to create subtle yet powerful frames. The feature film uses cuts for transitions; a film director will spend tens of thousands of dollars to create an illusion within the shot, but the transition between shots is almost always a cut. Effects should be used sparingly and with taste. Gratuitously flying images in and out, flipping graphics, or making every transition a new viewing experience does nothing to enhance the show's purpose. As each shot is selected for its contribution to the program, so should any effect be chosen to increase the overall impact of a program rather than to draw attention to the effect itself.

The overuse of effects is readily apparent in the productions of new users of nonlinear systems. It is so easy to put in a page turn or unusual wipe that novices use these effects far too much. The audience cares about people in the program and the show's intent. Unless an effect is unobtrusive or contributes to the transition, it is distracting and unnecessary.

Opens, Closes, and Bumpers

Some of the most important areas for effects are the show's open, close, and bumpers. *Bumpers* are three-to-five-second shots that identify a television program. Bumpers are usually placed before, after, and inside commercial breaks. They can be a single card with a voice-over announcer or costly multilayered effects created in a digital computer graphics station. These expensive bumpers can be seen on broadcast and cable networks. They are often bright, dazzling effects that end in a logo of the network. A carefully crafted open and close will make the viewer think the content of the show is important. Because these elements are crucial to the way in which the show is perceived, special care should be taken to make them unique and impressive.

SHOTS AND ANGLES

As discussed in the previous chapter, a scene usually starts with a wide or long shot, moves to a medium shot, then alternates between close-ups and medium shots. Most scenes are shot and edited in this manner for good reason: It works, as shown in Figures 12-11a and 12-11b.

a

Figure 12-11a A variety of angles keeps the pace flowing and the audience interested. The change in camera angle can also mask small continuity problems, such as hand placement. (See Figure 12-11b.) Photo courtesy of Sterling Productions.

b

Figure 12-11b Photo courtesy of Sterling Productions.

Occasionally, this rule can be broken. A new scene that cuts to a close-up of a knife can quickly build suspense. Cutting to a wide-eyed victim is also a powerful transition when coupled with the correct audio. As a rule, however, the audience wants to know where the action is taking place and what is happening at that location. Being obvious is better than being confusing.

A variety of angles will increase audience interest. Cutting back and forth to the same shots quickly becomes boring. Ideally, the director will provide the editor with enough editorial choices to allow him or her to incorporate a variety of different shots in the program.

DISSOLVES, WIPES, AND DIGITAL EFFECTS

The most important and powerful tool at the editor's disposal is the cut, but other effects are useful when editing a program.

Dissolves were introduced to indicate a time passage. Today, audiences are more sophisticated, and with the proper clues, they understand a cut to another time or location without the aid of a dissolve. However, the dissolve is still occasionally used as a time-passage device.

The DVE can stretch, expand, rotate, or reposition these elements to other areas of the frame. DVE repositioning is commonly used when combining elements in effects. Creating a mirror image is also a function of the DVE.

No matter what the effect, it should fit with the concept and feel of the program. It is also important to remember that any visual effect occupies the mind and, during the effect, the viewer usually does not recognize anything else. For instance, if audio information is given during an effect, the audience members might be distracted by what is happening on the screen. This "effect" time should not, therefore, be used to convey important information. Also, the editor must be sure that the images involved in the effect are on the screen long enough for the audience to really see them. Exceptions to this rule are the flash cuts like those used in music videos and some commercials. Flashes to white are acceptable ways to cover jump cuts from one take to another.

Planning Effects

When editing a complicated effect off-line, it is important to keep the various sources involved in that effect labeled and organized. When contemplating more than a wipe or dissolve, create a plan as to how to execute the effect. If there are more than a few effects to be accomplished, an edit session dedicated to effects building would probably be scheduled to complete the required effects without impeding the show's on-line session.

MORE INFORMATION EQUALS MORE INTEREST

The editor's purpose is to create a show in a cohesive, understandable, and orderly fashion. The more visual and aural experiences you can present (in context with the purpose and story), the better the show will be.

Often a production contains more than one story line. There are two methods of editing multiple story lines. The first is to tell one story, then go on to the next. This type of storytelling is called *continuity editing*. The second method is to tell the stories side by side, as they happen. This is called *parallel editing*.

For instance, if two brothers went to war and the editor wanted to show what happened during those years, she could tell the story of one brother, then focus on the other. That would be an example of continuity editing. If she took both brothers' experiences and intercut them, that would be an example of parallel editing.

Both methods of storytelling are effective. Parallel storytelling is inherently more interesting, but special care must be taken to make sure the audience knows which story is being told.

EDITORIAL PITFALLS

Shot Selection

A shot must have a specific purpose if it is to be included in a show. Ideally, each shot should have more than one purpose. For instance, a multipurpose shot might establish location, a character's mood, and climate all in one brief image. The audience will pick up on shots that do not belong in the program.

Once the shot's purpose has been fulfilled, the editor should make the next edit. The more visual information an editor can include in a production, the more interesting it will be to the audience.

Finishing the Action

One of the most annoying editorial flaws is not allowing a character or object to complete an action within a scene. If an action takes too long, time can be compressed through editing, but the action should be concluded. Cutting away from something in motion before the action is completed is as bad as lingering on a stagnant or slow-moving shot. An exception to this rule is in the editing of commercials or music videos. In these programs, the intent is to catch the audience's attention, not impart plot or pass along complicated information. The rapid edits and unfinished action are consistent with the program's purpose.

Similarly, it is important to remember that it takes a few moments for an image to register in the viewer's mind. The editor, having seen a shot over and over again, might cut away from an image before it has time to affect the viewer. The editor should let the viewer see what he is meant to see before cutting away. An editor must not let familiarity with a shot fool her into cutting too soon.

Continuity

As mentioned in the previous chapter, continuity is a major concern during production and is just as important during the editing process. A show should look seamless. In some cases, the editor might have to change the sequence of shots or even scenes to maintain the show's continuity. Having a character running in one direction in one shot and then suddenly going in the other direction in the next can ruin the best-edited scene and confuse the audience.

Jump Cuts and Cutaways

A *jump cut* occurs when two extremely similar shots are edited together. When a jump cut is viewed, everything in the frame seems to jump. This effect can be used to pop people or objects in or out of a frame, but in most instances, the jump cut is annoying.

In news editing, jump cuts are created as the audio bed of the piece is cut together. Once the story's narration has been built, cutaways are used to cover the jump cuts. Some interview shows and documentaries use soft-edged wipes or quick dissolves between similar shots to mask jump cuts.

Some videos and commercials purposely use the jump cut for effect. One of the easiest ways around mismatched action or dialogue mistakes is through the use of a cutaway. Although the cutaway is a powerful tool, it can be disruptive if used improperly (without audience expectation). An editor must choose cutaways carefully and with purpose. As with every edit, the cutaway should be motivated.

Respect for the Character

The audience is keenly aware of a character's expressions. Editors can forget that the audience most often reacts to people's expressions. Editors should treat screen characters as respectfully as possible. There are several specific rules about editing facial expressions and dialogue that are to be broken only for a specific effect.

Lip Flap

When using a close-up for a cutaway, the subject should not appear to be talking. This rule also applies to a character about to speak. If the edit requires cutting away from the person about to speak, the cut should happen before the speech, not as the talking begins.

No Closed Eyes or Open Mouths

An expansion of the previous concept: try not to cut to a character with his or her eyes closed or mouth open unless the shot is specifically designed to do so.

Careful Background Choices

Cuts to background characters should be made just as selectively as to those of the principals. Just throwing in a shot of people milling around can destroy the illusion of the program. When the editor is including shots that contain extras, the background actors should be dressed correctly and acting in character.

CONCLUSION

It really does make a difference how pictures are edited together. Through a combination of technical and creative skills, the editor can save a poorly shot program and make a good one even better. He or she can also change the focus or tone of a show, a fact that makes the editor's position very powerful.

SUMMARY

Editing determines the pacing of a show, the timing between dialogue lines, the expansion or compression of time, and the specific images that are placed against each other.

The concept of a show should be decided on before any editing begins. It is a good idea to know the intended audience and to be aware of that audience's expectations and limitations.

The process of editing is to choose, edit, and trim each shot to its minimum length while keeping its proper pacing and impact within the scene. Each shot has its own pacing. How these shots are connected creates the rhythm within a scene. How these scenes are connected determines the overall feel of the program.

There are four types of edits: action, screen position, form, and idea. The most effective edits are those that combine two or more of these concepts. The number of edits in a show will often determine whether the production seems long or short to the audience.

One of the most powerful tools in editing is the L cut. Each edit must be examined in terms of its audio potential as well as its visual impact. It is important to remember that audio can come from sources other than the production.

As a general rule, you should begin a scene using a wide shot, cut to a medium shot, and then edit the scene, alternating between medium and close shots. If it is possible and is within the context of the show's intent, a variety of angles should be used to increase the interest of the audience.

In almost every type of program, the cut is the most powerful and often the best method to change from one visual to another.

Effect time should not be considered content time.

Edits should fit with the concept and feel of the program.

There are two ways to edit multiple story lines: continuity editing and parallel editing.

A shot must have a specific purpose to be included in any show, and kept only long enough to fulfill its purpose.

Try to let characters complete their motion. Cutting away from a scene too soon also can confuse the audience.

Editing a program should create a seamless flow of information to the audience.

An editor should avoid breaks in continuity, such as jump cuts and improperly used cutaways.

Editing is one of the most powerful tools of the visual media.

PART IV

Working at the Keyboard

13

Machine-to-Machine Editing

Nonlinear editors are rapidly replacing time code editors. Yet there are still stations and production facilities that use machine-to-machine cuts-only editing to edit news segments and perform other postproduction chores.

In many postproduction situations, there is no edit controller between the record and playback decks. In some cases, recent editing advances have been built into the machines themselves.

There are edit IN and edit OUT indicators on the record deck. In most cases, the record deck will control the playback source deck. Trims are also available with machine-to-machine editing. The edit type (audio only, video only, etc.) is selected on the front panel.

This type of editing does not result in an EDL of any sort, but certainly makes edits quickly and efficiently and, in a pressure-filled environment, can be the difference between making the air in time and missing the deadline.

Figure 13-1 shows a Sony Betacam SP videotape recorder front panel that can be used as an edit controller. Attaching this deck to another compatible machine (a Betacam or one-inch, for example) can offer excellent cuts-only capabilities without adding the cost of a controller between the two decks. Engaging the specific insert button(s) (center right) or the assemble buttons starts an edit. Many professional video decks now have built-in editors, including the Sony HD recorder seen in Figure 13-2.

When you press the buttons to the left of the shuttle knob (right side of the machine), the player or recorder is engaged. Record and playback INs and OUTs are selected through the entry buttons to the left of the center shuttle controls. Pressing the entry key along with the IN or OUT button will program the edit.

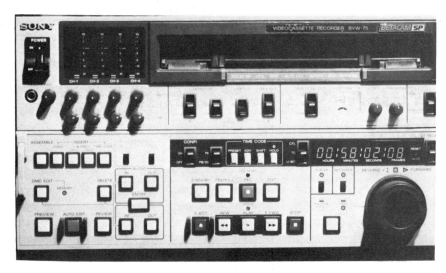

Figure 13-1 The front panel of a Sony Betacam SP. This sophisticated machine has a built-in editor; it can also sense the difference between SP tape and regular videotape. Note the four channels of audio displayed at the top left of the deck. Courtesy of Sony Corporation.

Figure 13-2 Sony HD video recorder. This machine is switchable from 1080i to 720p. Photo courtesy of American Production Services.

The machine is also capable of making split edits by programming audio separately from video INs. There are input levels for the four audio channels as well as an inboard VITC generator. The internal generator should be on when you are using VITC time code.

In addition, there is a dynamic motion control memory for the playback deck located on the left side of the control panel. This allows limited slow-motion programming of the playback deck. Like most simple editors, there is no memory on the deck, but it will lock to time code or control track.

Setting the edit INs and OUTs remains a constant in any editor. The record and playback INs are selected, and the OUT point determines the duration, whether it's the playback OUT or the record OUT. Preview and record (auto edit) are found at the bottom left of the deck. Many television stations use two Beta decks to accomplish their news editing chores.

AN EDITING EXAMPLE

News footage used to be shot and recorded on three-quarter-inch tape (see Figure 13-3). Now Betacam, BetaSX, and DV formats are making inroads to news editing.

"Courtesy of Sony Electronics Inc."

Figure 13-3 The Sony BVU-950 U-Matic® editing deck. This three-quarter-inch machine has a built-in editor similar to other decks. Note that this built-in editor does not have split capabilities, and has only two tracks of audio available.

A news reporter rushes into the editing bay. He has the story. It's only 20 minutes to airtime. The editor grabs a fresh, preblacked 10-minute cassette off the shelf for the edit master and puts it into the record machine. Luckily, she has just finished recording color bars and tone on the head of the tape.

"We've got two versions of the introduction and one close, a great interview that's too long, and some cutaways," the reporter says breathlessly. The editor puts the playback reel into the playback machine. She uses the playback controls to shuttle the tape at high speed until it reaches the beginning of the introduction. She presses Play and watches the two takes of the introduction. Both editor and reporter agree that the first take is better. The tape is then shuttled back to the head of the interview.

Now the editor works with the record machine. Thirty seconds past the end of the bars and tone, she puts the machine in pause. This will mark the IN point on the record machine. The source tape is paused three seconds before the reporter starts talking, marking the IN point on the source tape. Since this is the first edit, there is no need to worry about erasing any previous edit, and it is immediately recorded.

When the introduction has been completely recorded, the editor backs up the record tape to the end of the reporter's speech. The playback reel is shuttled to the interview, which the editor and reporter view in its entirety. They take notes during the viewing and discuss the selected segments when the viewing is over.

After they devise a plan, the editor shortens the interview by making a series of audio and video edits, thus eliminating unnecessary or unwanted sections of dialogue. This process results in a series of jump cuts. When the interview is finished, the reporter and editor play it back, listening with their eyes closed so that they are not distracted by the jump cuts and can concentrate on the audio, making sure the interview sounds natural.

Once the sound has been finalized, appropriate cutaways are used to cover the jump cuts. These edits will be recorded in the video-only mode.

The playback tape is shuttled to the reporter's close and put in pause. The record tape is paused at the end of the interview, and the close is edited onto that point. The editor rewinds the record tape, and she and the reporter view the story one more time to check for any mistakes or flaws that might have been overlooked.

"It's fine," the reporter says. "Let me have it."

The editor rewinds the record tape to the head, ejects it from the machine, and writes the name of the story, the date, and the reporter's and editor's names on the cassette.

"Thanks," the reporter says. "See you tomorrow."

"Sure," the editor replies. "About 20 minutes before airtime, right?"

There is no answer. The reporter and the tape are gone.

14

Reading the Computer Edit

Although computer editors offer greater control, using a highly accurate machine does not mean that all edits made on that machine will be brilliant or easy to reconstruct. A person must still decide which edit is to be recorded. What the computer editor offers is extreme accuracy and a set of standardized codes to note how an edit was accomplished.

AN EDITING EXAMPLE

The first edit on the record tape should begin at the most convenient time code number. To make the show's duration easy to calculate, we will start the program material at 01:00:00:00 (one o'clock). But several recordings must be made before the program itself begins.

We need to record one minute of bars and tone, 10 seconds of black, 10 seconds of slate information, and a 10-second countdown. This adds up to one minute and 30 seconds. To have the first edit of program material at 01:00:00:00, we must begin this series of preliminary edits at 00:58:30:00—one minute and 30 seconds before 01:00:00:00.

Preliminary Edits

Our first edit will be of color bars and audio tone. The color bars are a reference for calibrating the various video components. The tone is a reference for the audio record level.

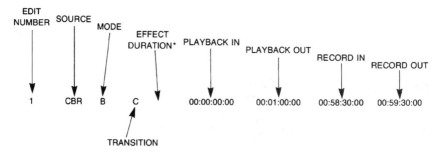

*Because a cut is an immediate transition, the cut has no effect duration.

Figure 14-1 Diagram of edit 1.

For this example, let's assume that we have two tracks of audio available on our record machine (many formats have four audio channels available). We will record the tone on both channels. Once the recording is completed, the computer will store the edit in memory. The computer listing of this format looks like Figure 14-1.

The first number we see, reading left to right, is our edit number, 1. The next piece of information is the source or reel from which the edit came. In this case, it is color bars (shortened to CBR). Then comes the mode description. Edit 1 was recorded on both tracks of the audio and video (V12), and the edit was a cut (C). Since there was no effect, no effect duration is listed. Four sets of eight-digit numbers follow. These numbers represent the playback IN point, the playback OUT point, the record IN point, and the record OUT point. Since color bars are not a moving source, as is a videotape machine, the playback IN time will be 00:00:00:00 and the OUT time will be the edit duration. The record IN number is the first frame in which the source will be copied to the record machine. The last number in the computer listing is the record OUT location.

The second edit accesses audio tracks one and two as well as recording video black for 10 seconds and is listed like this:

2 BLK   V12   C   00:00:00:00   00:00:10:00   00:59:30:00   00:59:40:00

The third edit is a video and audio track one and track two recording the video slate. The purpose of a video slate is to explain what is on the tape, including the date it was edited, the show name, the running time, the audio configuration, the production company, the director's credit, and any other important information about the show. Usually, the source of this information is an auxiliary input (AUX) on the switcher, often a character generator or video camera. It is listed like this:

3 AUX   V12   C   00:00:00:00   00:00:10:00   00:59:40:00   0:59:50:00

The fourth edit starts where edit 3 left off. This edit is a countdown with a duration of 10 seconds. The countdown's source is reel 50:

4   50   V12   C   00:10:00:00   00:10:10:00   00:59:00:00   1:00:00:00

Program Edits

The fifth edit of the computer list, and the first edit of program material, is from reel 7 and is a shot of a tree. The director checks the master log and finds that the tree shot is located at about "seven-o-one-even," or 7:01:00:00. Reel 7 is put into a playback machine and scanned at high speed. "It's the shot of the big tree," the director says. "You can't miss it." We do, and have to back up the tape until we locate the shot. The exact time code of the shot is 07:01:15:03 ("seven-o-one, fifteen-o-three").

The editor decides that a 30-frame fade-up from black should start the show. The computer listing for a fade is different from that for a cut. The dissolve or wipe has two lines of information. The first line identifies for the computer the point in the previous edit at which the new effect will take place. The second line represents the incoming material that will be subjected to a dissolve or wipe:

5   BLK   V1   C   00:00:00:00   00:00:00:00   01:00:00:00   01:00:00:00

5   007   V1   D   30   07:01:15:03   07:01:27:03   01:00:00:00   01:00:12:00

In edit 5, we made a cut (C) to black at 01:00:00:00 on the record tape and then immediately dissolved to reel 7. (An effect occurs immediately if the record IN points of a two-line event are the same.) The edit involved both audio and video, but audio was recorded only on channel 1 of the record tape. The second line of the edit indicates that the effect was a dissolve (D) with a duration of 30 frames. The edit ended at 01:00:12:00 on the record tape (see Figure 14-2).

The director informs us that the second edit of the show (the sixth edit on the record tape) will be a video-only edit from reel 10. It will begin at the end of a zoom out from a close-up of a flower and will stop when the flower is out of focus. Reel 10 is loaded into a playback machine. With some searching, we find that the zoom stops at 03:41:15:02. This is the playback IN. The flower is out of focus at 03:41:25:12. This is the playback OUT. If we subtract the IN from the OUT, we find that the duration of this edit is 10 seconds and 10 frames.

Suddenly, the director changes his mind and wants to end the shot half a second before the flower is out of focus. If the flower is out of focus at 03:41:25:12, we must subtract 15 frames (half a second) from the OUT point so that the edit will end half a second earlier. We now have a new playback OUT point of 03:41:24:27. As a result, the edit duration is changed to nine seconds and 25 frames.

RECORD TIME CODE

	00:58:30:00	00:59:30:00	00:59:40:00	00:59:50:00	01:00:00:00	00:01:12:00
AUDIO TRACK 1	TONE	SILENCE	SILENCE	COUNTDOWN AUDIO	30 FRAME FADE UP ON	
AUDIO TRACK 2	TONE	SILENCE	SILENCE	COUNTDOWN AUDIO	30 FRAME FADE UP ON	

VIDEO	COLOR BARS	SILENCE	SILENCE	COUNTDOWN VIDEO	FADE UP ON FIRST PICTURE

PLAYBACK TIME CODE ⟶ 07:01:15:03   07:01:27:03

EDIT	REEL	MODE	TYPE	DURATION	PLAYBACK IN	PLAYBACK OUT	RECORD IN	RECORD OUT
1	CBR	V12	C		00:00:00:00	00:00:00:00	00:58:30:00	00:59:30:00
2	BLK	V12	C		00:00:00:00	00:00:00:00	00:59:30:00	00:59:40:00
3	AUX	V12	C		00:00:00:00	00:00:00:00	00:59:40:00	00:59:50:00
4	050	V12	C		00:10:00:00	00:10:10:00	00:59:50:00	01:00:00:00
5	BLK	V12	C		00:00:00:00	00:00:00:00	01:00:00:00	01:00:12:00
5	007	V12	D	30	07:01:15:00	07:01:27:03	01:00:00:00	01:00:12:00

Figure 14-2 Diagram of edits 1 through 5.

Now that the edit is defined, we can go to the record tape. The director indicates where he wants the flower shot to cut into the image of the tree. We discover by pressing a key on the computer editor (see Chapter 15) that the time code at this point on the record machine is 01:00:06:00. If we record the edit at this point, we will erase the last six seconds of the tree shot, since the tree edit lasted until 01:00:12:00. The edit listing from the computer after the recording looks like this:

6   010   V   C   03:41:15:02   03:41:24:27   01:00:06:00   01:00:15:25

This edit listing indicates that edit 6 came from reel 10; the edit was a video-only cut; playback IN was 3 hours, 41 minutes, 15 seconds, 2 frames; playback OUT was 3 hours, 41 minutes, 24 seconds, 27 frames; record IN was 1 hour, 0 minutes, 6 seconds, 0 frames; and record OUT was 1 hour, 0 minutes, 15 seconds, and 25 frames.

There are several ways to communicate time code verbally. One way is to list the numbers followed by hours, minutes, seconds, and frames, as above. Another is to list just the numbers with no designations. In a case where there are no leading hours, such as with our video slate at 00:59:40:00, this time code number would be said without the leading zeros: 59, 40, 00, or 59 minutes and 40 seconds.

The third edit of our program, and the seventh to be recorded, is an audio-only edit—the sound of a bee buzzing—found near the end of reel 13. Reel 13 is loaded into a playback machine, and we find the buzzing at 13:55:05:10. On the record machine, we have decided to start the audio of the bee just before the beginning of the flower shot. The video edit of the flower starts at 01:00:06:00 on the record tape, so we start this audio a third of a second (10 frames) earlier

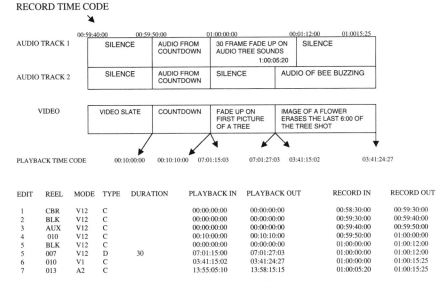

Figure 14-3 Diagram of edits 1 through 7.

than the picture. That puts the record IN at time code 01:00:05:20. The director instructs us that the bee noise should end where the flower shot ends and that the bee noise will be on the other audio track, track 2 (the background audio from the tree shot was recorded on track 1 in edit 5).

After we record the edit, the computer listing looks like this:

7   13   A2   C   13:55:05:10   13:58:15:15   01:00:05:20   01:00:15:25

Edit 7 is from playback reel 13; it is an audio-only edit onto track 2; record IN is 1, 00, 05, 20, and record OUT is 1, 00, 15, 25 (see Figure 14-3).

Now that we have looked at several edits, let's examine the dissolve and wipe listings more closely. The director decides that he wants to dissolve from the flower to a shot of the sky. The sky is found on reel 25 at 11:11:12:00. We keep reel 10 in a playback machine because we will be dissolving from it, then load reel 25 into another playback machine and find the shot. The edit duration is to be 15 seconds and the dissolve rate 3 seconds.

Fortunately, the computer editor is able to make edits on the exact frame. This is called a *match cut* or *in-frame edit*. We make a match cut edit where we left off on the flower shot and dissolve to the sky shot. The edit listing looks like this:

8   10   V   C   03:41:24:27   03:41:24:27   01:00:15:25   01:00:15:25

8   25   V   D   90   11:11:12:00   11:11:27:00   01:00:15:25   01:00:30:25

The first line of the listing is the continuation of the video that will be dissolved out (the flower shot). The second line is a continuation of edit 8, the sky shot. (The second line of a two-line event always indicates the beginning of the effect.) Note that in this example, the duration of the top line is zero frames. This indicates that the effect will start immediately. The new incoming video, from reel 25, starts at the same record IN time, 01:00:15:25. The edit is a video-only, and the dissolve rate is 90 frames.

The dissolve starts at 01:00:15:25 on the record machine and ends 90 frames, or 3 seconds, later. From 01:00:15:25 to 01:00:18:25, video from reels 10 and 25 is involved in the transition. The video from reel 25 at 11:11:12:00 will not be seen, however, because it is the beginning of the dissolve. Ninety frames later (the duration of the effect), the video from reel 25 will be full, and there will be no trace of reel 10 (the outgoing video). Nevertheless, there must be usable video on reel 10 up until 03:41:27:27. Even though the list does not show it, those additional 90 frames are used in the dissolve.

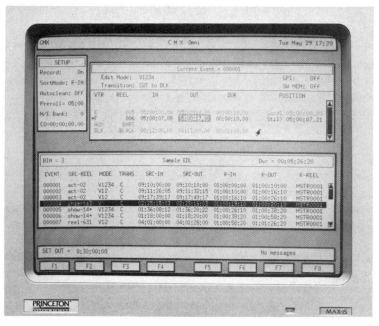

Figure 14-4 This display of a CMX Omni edit controller shows an actual EDL. Note that the edits displayed in the large center rectangle are accessing either channel 1 and 2 or all four channels of the record deck. Other available information includes the status of the machines in the top rectangle. The setup function on the top left indicates other parameters, such as whether the record function is active, or whether the automatic list cleaning function is on, and the length of preroll. Photo courtesy of CMX.

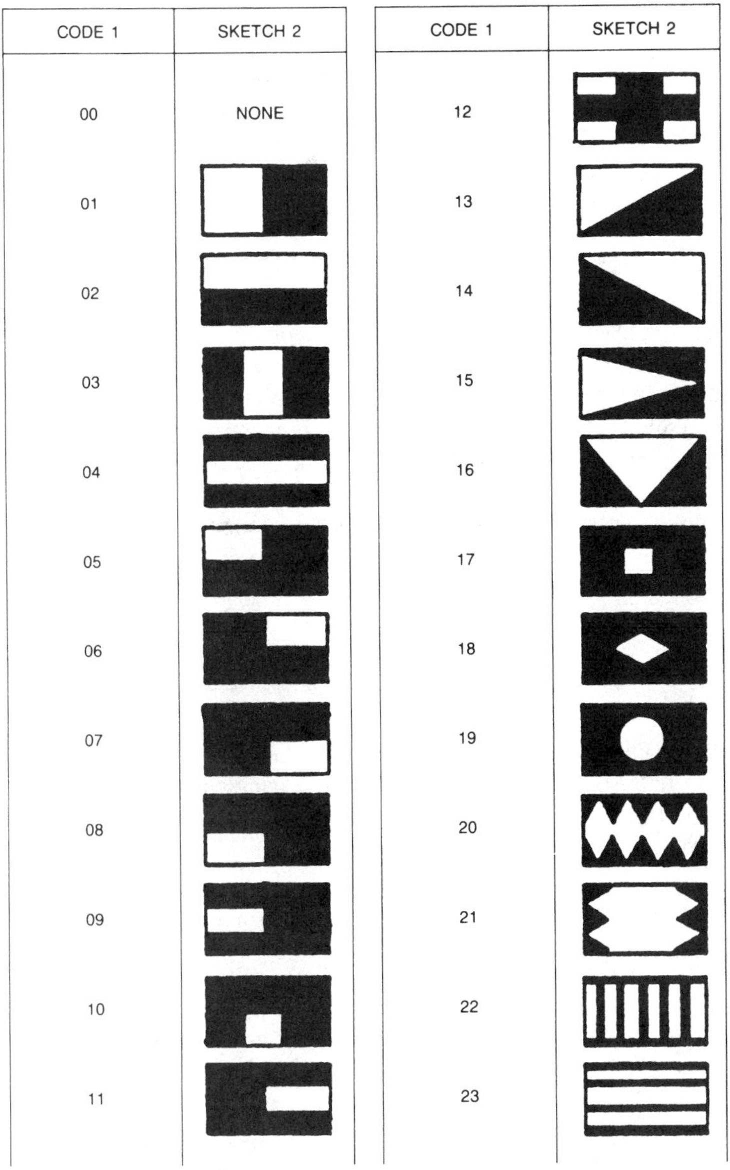

CODE 1	SKETCH 2	CODE 1	SKETCH 2
00	NONE	12	
01		13	
02		14	
03		15	
04		16	
05		17	
06		18	
07		19	
08		20	
09		21	
10		22	
11		23	

WIPE PATTERNS

NOTES: 1 WIPE CODE IS FOR NORMAL-DIRECTION WIPE. ADD 100 FOR REVERSE-DIRECTION WIPE.

2 SKETCH SHOWS EFFECT. NORMAL DIRECTION OF CHANGE IS TOWARD INCREASING WHITE AREA.

WIPE CODES FROM 24 TO 85 HAVE NOT YET BEEN STANDARDIZED SINCE EXPANDED WIPES ARE ONLY AVAILABLE ON NEWER MODEL SWITCHERS.

Figure 14-5 Common wipe pattern designations. The numbers under the code are generally accepted wipe patterns, although some switchers use other numbers for the same patterns.

For a match cut to work properly, all the video components of the outgoing scene must be matched exactly to where they were when the first part of the edit was made. With digital video decks this matching process is automatic. With older formats, a human sets up the video parameters and if these elements do not match exactly, the picture will shift in color, video level, or position on the screen.

One way to help ensure the match cut's success is to keep the playback reel on the same machine and make no adjustments until you are sure that it is not needed for an effect. In this way, all the aspects of the video (video, setup, chroma, luminance, and vertical and horizontal alignment) will be the same.

Sometimes, depending on the machines involved, it is impossible to make an in-frame edit at a later date. In this case, you must rerecord the video prior to the effect. This might not be a problem in a single dissolve sequence, but if 15 dissolves occur in a row, changing one could be very time-consuming.

In our case, since edit 6 is a cut and the OUT point of the second part of the dissolve is also a cut, the edit could be listed and performed in the following way:

8   10   V   C   03:41:15:02   03:41:24:27   01:00:06:00   01:00:15:25

8   25   V   D   90   11:11:12:00   11:11:27:00   01:00:15:25   01:00:30:25

The top line of the new edit is identical to edit 6. The computer editing system will perform the dissolve as one continuous edit, eliminating the match cut.

If the director decided to change the dissolve to a circle wipe, the listing would look like this:

8   10   V   C   03:41:15:02   03:41:24:27   01:00:06:00   01:00:15:25

8   25   V   W19   90   11:11:12:00   11:11:27:00   01:00:15:25   01:00:30:25

The W stands for a wipe, and the 19 refers to a computer code for a circle wipe. The computer wipe code indicates certain wipe patterns (see Figure 14-5) and does not have any way to note the softness of the wipe border, the color of the border, the position of the wipe, or the pattern modulation.

SUMMARY

The listing that results from a computer edit represents most of the information required to re-create the edit. One of the most important tasks for the newcomer to time code editing is to become accustomed to reading and interpreting the computer listing.

15

The Computer Keyboard

Numerous types of computerized time code editing systems are available, each with different keyboard layouts and functions (see Figure 15-1). Despite these differences, there are many similarities between brands. This chapter briefly explains some of the more common computer editing keys and typical keyboard layouts.

Keyboards that differ radically still have similar function keys. Other editing systems have additional keys that enhance the system's edit and list management capabilities. (List management refers to the ability to alter edits once they have been recorded.) See Figure 15-2 for an example of a computer editing keyboard.

SOURCE KEYS

Source keys access particular machines and other switcher inputs, such as color bars, matte cameras, color cameras, character generators, and digital effects generators. Once the machine has been selected by pressing a source key, other functions can be applied to that machine.

TRANSPORT KEYS

Transport keys move or stop a selected machine. Normal keyboard functions are Rewind, Fast Forward (FFWD), Slow (usually 25% of normal play), Stop (or Still),

Figure 15-1 An on-line editing console. Photo by Sean Sterling.

Figure 15-2 A computer editing keyboard. Photo courtesy of Editing Technologies Corporation.

and Play. Most keyboards also have a Cue, or "go to" key, which sends a tape to a specific time code number. Some computer editors have joysticks, others have circular knobs; both the joystick and knob are used to shuttle the selected tape machine at various speeds.

TIME CODE KEYS

Time code keys are used to enter time code from a selected machine into the computer.

SET IN/OUT KEYS

Set In and Set Out are used to enter known time code numbers into the computer. These numbers are known because someone has already noted them during an off-line edit or viewing session.

MARK KEYS

Mark In and Mark Out enter time code while playing a selected machine. When either the Mark In or the Mark Out key is pressed, the machine's time code is marked and loaded into the computer.

Mark In enters the time code into an IN position on the CRT; Mark Out enters the time code into an OUT position on the CRT. In some editing systems, the mark keys must have the VTR in motion to access the correct time code number. The exception occurs when vertical interval time code is being used, because VITC is accurate whether or not the tape is moving.

TRIM KEYS

Trim In and Trim Out alter time code numbers already entered into the computer. The time code numbers in the IN or OUT positions, and the duration of the edit can be altered by either a plus or a minus. If an IN point was marked 10 frames too late, it can be changed by trimming it by 10 frames.

EFFECTS KEYS

Effects keys instruct the computer to cut, dissolve, wipe, or key. The following paragraphs explain how these effects are programmed on each keyboard.

Cut

Pressing the Cut key will change a dissolve, wipe, or key to a cut. Then a source machine will have to be defined by setting the appropriate source key.

Dissolve

Pressing the DIS (dissolve) key initiates a dialogue between the operator and the computer. Usually the computer asks, "Dissolve from?" The operator then presses the source select key of the deck from which the dissolve originates. The computer then asks, "To?" The operator again presses the source select key of the machine from which the incoming picture or audio originates. Finally, the computer asks, "Duration?" The operator types in the number of frames the dissolve entails, then presses the Enter or Return key.

Wipe

Wipes are programmed like dissolves. When the operator presses the Wipe key, the computer starts a dialogue. Usually the computer asks, "Wipe from?" The operator presses the source select key of the deck from which the wipe originates and the computer asks, "To?" Again, the operator presses the source select key of the machine from which the picture or audio originates. Then the computer asks, "Duration?" The operator types in the number of frames the wipe entails, then presses the Enter or Return key. Finally, the computer asks, "Wipe number?" As discussed in Chapter 14, wipes are programmed by number. Most switchers have various patterns available.

Multiple-Source Effects

Effects requiring multiple-source machines to be rolling at the same time can be accomplished in different ways depending on the edit system. One of the most common commands is "Master/Slave." When this key is pressed, the computer asks which machines will be linked together; multiple machines can be put into play during the edit. For simple two-machine effects, a dissolve with a duration rate of 0 can be used to roll two playback sources. The Master/Slave key can also be used to enable editing to multiple record machines.

AUDIO/VIDEO KEYS

Audio/video keys are used to tell the computer whether the edit is to be an audio-only edit, a video-only edit, or both an audio and a video edit. Some systems also have keys that determine on which track the audio is to be recorded. Various keyboards have different key names for these functions. For instance, an audio-only key might be labeled A, AUD, or A Only. A video-only key might be labeled VID, VID Only, or V. A key for both an audio and video edit might be labeled B, Both, AUD/VID, or Audio/Video. In advanced editors, there are additional selections that can be made, depending on the editor and number of audio tracks available on the record tape.

PREVIEW KEYS

Preview keys are used to rehearse edits without actually recording them. Each video edit comprises three sections: (1) the picture and audio on the record tape located just before the edit, (2) the edit material that has been chosen for the preview, and (3) the material located just after the edit. Three types of standard previews are described in the following paragraphs and illustrated in Figures 15-3, 15-4, and 15-5. Figure 15-6 compares the three types.

Video-Video-Video

The video-video-video (VVV) preview (see Figure 15-3) is the most common preview. It shows a portion of the outgoing edit, the incoming edit, and a portion of the next edit.

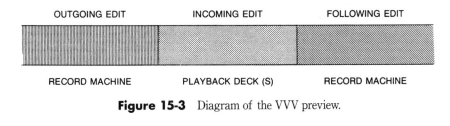

Figure 15-3 Diagram of the VVV preview.

Figure 15-4 Diagram of the VBV preview.

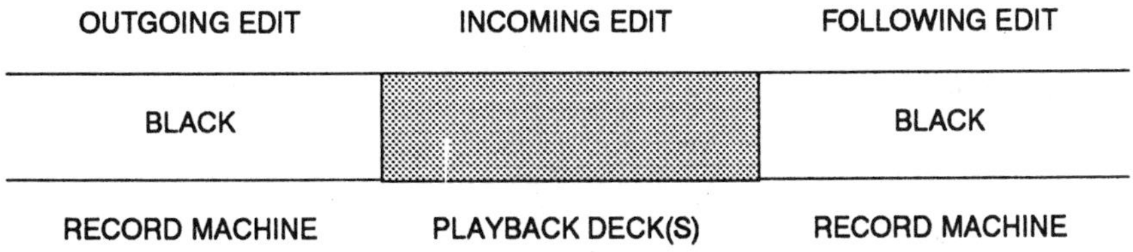

Figure 15-5 Diagram of the BVB preview.

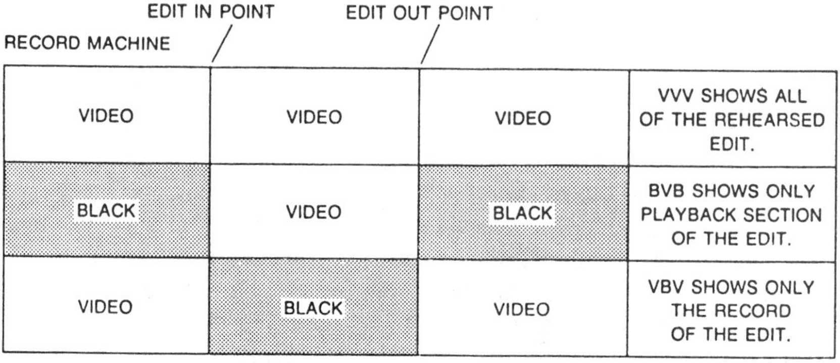

EDIT IN POINT   EDIT OUT POINT

RECORD MACHINE

VIDEO	VIDEO	VIDEO	VVV SHOWS ALL OF THE REHEARSED EDIT.
BLACK	VIDEO	BLACK	BVB SHOWS ONLY PLAYBACK SECTION OF THE EDIT.
VIDEO	BLACK	VIDEO	VBV SHOWS ONLY THE RECORD OF THE EDIT.

Figure 15-6   Diagram of the three types of previews.

Video-Black-Video

The video-black-video (VBV) preview (see Figure 15-4) shows only the record machine material. At the edit IN point, black is shown on the monitor. When the edit ends, the picture returns to the record master. This preview is often used to examine exactly what is on the record machine at the beginning and end of the edit.

Black-Video-Black

The black-video-black (BVB) preview (see Figure 15-5) shows only the playback portion of the edit.

Other Previews

Advanced edit controllers may have additional previews available. These previews may include a switcher preview, which will trigger the switcher to perform any effect that has been programmed in a particular edit, or a multiple event preview, which can preview several edits at once.

REPLAY KEY

The Replay key rewinds the record machine and shows the last edit that was recorded. Most editors do not bother with this key and instead manually rewind the tape to review the edit.

RECORD KEY

The Record key instructs the computer to record the video and/or audio information indicated on the CRT onto the record tape. Many editors require the operator to press the CTRL (control) key and the Record key simultaneously to perform the record function.

EXIT KEY

All computer editors have some sort of Exit key. Pressing this key aborts any dialogue between the operator and the computer and returns the menu to a non-interactive status. This is the key to use to cancel whatever is currently on the screen.

MASTER/SLAVE KEY

Depending on the controller used, there is a function on computer editors that will tie multiple playbacks and/or record decks together. Once the relationship is established, a trim on one of the decks will change the others equally. In addition, all decks involved in the master/slave setup will roll when the edit is performed.

The master/slave option is used to create multiple playback effects. The basic dissolve function can drive only three decks (the record machine and two playbacks), but the master/slave function can roll as many sources as are available.

PERIPHERAL CONTROL

Again, specific to individual controllers, a series of keystrokes can trigger peripheral devices. Usually these triggers are grouped into three basic categories.

Switcher Operation

Advanced switchers can often have their complicated effects setups stored in memory or even within the EDL. Depending on the edit controller, effects may be loaded into the switcher or merely triggered.

General-Purpose Interface (GPI)

The GPI is a single pulse sent to an external device, such as a character genera-tor or DVE. This pulse indicates that the device is to perform a prearranged event (run forward, stop, freeze, run backward, etc.).

Playback Speed Control

The third type of external triggering apparatus controls the playback speed of one or more decks. Each controller creates this command differently, but all con-trollers require two vital pieces of information: what speed the deck is to travel and when it is to begin its variable-speed function. Some computer controllers cannot preroll at variable speeds, preventing a slow-motion effect from entering an edit at its exact, predetermined frame. Other controllers, CMX and Sony con-trollers, for instance, can preroll at the variable speed and enter an edit at the exact frame desired.

ALL STOP KEY

The All Stop Key on most computer systems is the space bar at the bottom of the keyboard. Pressing this key aborts any action that is being performed by the system, including recording.

You must be careful when aborting a recording in progress. If the All Stop Key is pressed while you are recording an edit, there will be no evidence of that edit in the EDL, even though there will be video and/or audio placed on the record tape. There is always a different key that cancels the recording process, but main-tains an accurate edit record. In most computer editors, you simply press the Record key again; however, you should check the editor's operating manual first.

EDL KEYS

The computer editor creates an EDL as it edits. The EDL keys enable the com-puter to store and make copies of the EDL in different formats. The operator can also load an EDL into the computer by using these keys.

MISCELLANEOUS (POWER) KEYS

The following advanced function keys are often found on computer editors. Occa-sionally they are not readily apparent or are not on dedicated keys, but must be accessed by a series of keystrokes.

BINS—Moves the display into one of several separate files of EDLs, all of which are active within the computer editor.

CONSTANTS—Maintains offsets for reference in a computer file so that commonly used numbers can be recalled and used in list management.

EJECT—Remotely ejects a tape from a machine.

ENABLE/DISABLE—Indicates to the computer editor whether or not an edit has been recorded. Enabling an edit essentially tells the computer that the edit needs to be recorded.

FILL—A calculation key that, when given record and playback durations, computes the speed of the playback needed to fill the record duration.

LEARN (MACRO) KEYS—Saves a series of commonly used keystrokes.

LOOK AHEAD—An option by which the computer looks ahead in the EDL for edits and then precues machines not involved in the current event.

MATCH—Causes the computer to look back in the EDL for a time code match to a previously recorded edit. This facilitates finding an edit in an EDL.

MULTIPLE RECORD OPTION—Allows two tapes to record a program at the same time, producing two same-generation edited masters.

PAGE—Scrolls up or down an EDL a page (one full screen's worth) at a time.

REC START—Tells the computer at what time code on the record tape a program begins. The computer can thus display the running time of the show.

REEDIT—Recalls a previously recorded edit. Changes can be made to the edit, and it can be reinserted into the EDL, or it can be recorded as a new event.

SPLIT EDIT—Allows for starting audio or video later than the IN point of the edit. Some editors allow for both split in and split out edits at the same time.

SYNC ROLL—Rolls numerous VTRs and allows for editing on the fly. Every time you touch a new source machine, the switcher changes sources and an edit is noted in the EDL.

TEXT EDITING—Changes reel assignments, modes, or other information globally within an EDL.

Compatibility

Each editing system encodes information in separate ways. Sony, CMX, Grass Valley, Ampex, and other manufacturers are trying to keep up with exploding technology and still stay somewhat compatible. You should investigate the conversion of EDLs if you are going from an off-line to on-line system and changing brands.

SUMMARY

The computer is neither friend nor foe. Learning computer editing is not easy, but using a computer editor can be a very rewarding and remunerative experience.

16

Off-Line and On-Line Random-Access Editing

The limitation of linearity in videotape editing is an annoying reality. If three video edits are recorded and you want to change the duration of the middle edit, you must rerecord the third or the first edit. In the past, several attempts were made to rectify this problem. The first random-access editor was the CMX 600, described in Chapter 1. The technology at that time was not reliable enough to support a true random-access editor. At its best, the CMX 600 held only 35 minutes of video. This is barely enough to cut a half-hour sitcom. Today's random-access editors are capable of holding hours worth of video and audio.

Hundreds of random-access editors are employed in the film industry, the commercial arena, broadcast television, and the nonbroadcast video industry. Not only are there hundreds of off-line random-access editors, there are hundreds of on-line random-access editors. The linear tape editing bay still exists, but new bays are being built around the nonlinear editors. The exception to this rule is that high-definition bays are mostly tape-to-tape linear bays because of the huge storage needs that an HD signal requires. There are even very affordable low-end editors that can output industry-standard EDLs or even perform on-line chores.

The speed with which changes can be effected and the easy output of a clean, accurate EDL and/or negative cut list has brought random-access editing from the research and development stages into mainstream postproduction use (see Figure 16-1). Besides making editorial changes quickly, random-access editors eliminate the time consumed by shuttling tapes back and forth.

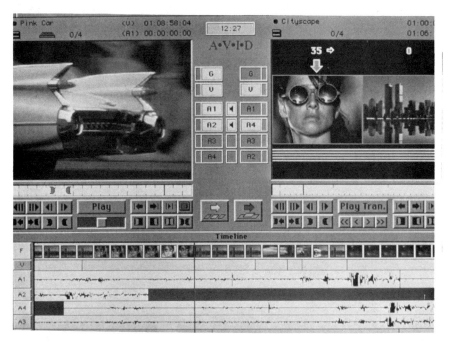

Figure 16-1 The display screen of an Avid random-access editor. Note that the time code is completely absent from the screen. In its place, graphic symbols indicate the edit mode. Photo courtesy of Avid Technologies.

Let's review exactly what a random-access editor is. Editing videotape is a linear process. Each edit is physically recorded onto a record tape. These images occupy a firmly defined space on that tape. To change the length of any edit and maintain the content of the remainder of the show, the edits following must be recorded one by one, or the segment recorded onto another tape, then placed back into program. A random-access system is not constrained by this linearity. Because the entire program is stored in the computer it has no physical length. The show is essentially a preview; any change in length is immediately taken into account by the computer. The edits following the change are instantaneously adjusted to accommodate the change.

A videotape editor is to a random-access editor as a typewriter is to a word processor. The typewritten page needs to be retyped to include new words or to delete words. The word processor, like a random-access editor, just makes room to accommodate the changes. The display of a word processor is only a preview of what the page will look like when printed on paper; similarly, the random-access editor only previews what all the edits of the show will look like when

Figure 16-2 A screen display of Final Cut Pro, an Apple Computer product. This random-access editor has already found many users at home and professionally. Its low cost and ease of use explain its rapid acceptance. Photo courtesy of Apple Computer Inc.

output to videotape. Conventional editing systems can only preview one or two edits at a time.

When a random-access editing session is over, the show is recorded on tape for viewing. The program on that tape is now a finite length because it exists in physical space.

The appeal of a digital computer random-access editor is obvious. Changes can be made easily; the computer, not the editor, manipulates time code; there are no tapes to shuttle, and the linearity of tape is a nonissue. Most nonlinear systems also have the ability to create a myriad of effects. Icon-based computer screen interfaces are also employed to eliminate the dependency on time code manipulation.

As the cost of computers and their associated memory has continued to drop, "prosumer" editing systems became more powerful. Apple's "Final Cut Pro" and Adobe's "Premiere" began to incorporate many of the features that dedicated editing systems promoted as unique (see Figures 16-2 and 16-3). Because these editing systems cost a fraction of the professional systems, more post-production companies began to explore their use in off-line and nonbroadcast applications.

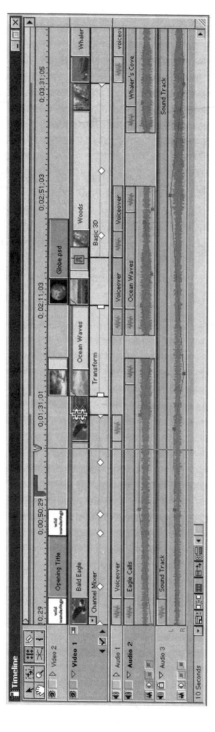

Figure 16-3 A screen display of an Adobe Premier Timeline. This random-access editor has also found a large user base. With effects and compatibility with other products (Photoshop, After Effects, Boris, etc.), it too has been embraced by home and professional users alike. Photo courtesy of Adobe, Inc.

Figure 16-4 A working on-line nonlinear editor. This system, called a Discrete "Smoke," produces hundreds of commercials and broadcast specials each year. Photo courtesy of New Wave Entertainment, a leader in motion picture promotion.

Garbage In/Garbage Out

Though a random-access editor is fast, reliable, and flexible, if erroneous information is put into the system, erroneous information will flow out. Inputting footage with the wrong reel number, or losing the original master footage is just as inefficient and costly as in a linear videotape system. It is extremely frustrating to have a supposedly immaculate EDL delivered to on-line with incorrect reel assignments. This causes a massive search for the correct reel, costing time and money. Tapes without time code that are input into the random-access editor will create an EDL with inaccurate time code references. Organization and attention to detail are required for every edit situation, no matter what system is being used. An error during the labeling of a reel will cause problems later.

Creativity versus Speed

Every year some major motion picture is cited in terms of how quickly it was brought through the postproduction process to the screen. Editors and other postproduction professionals read these press releases and sigh. Hundreds of people worked long hours into the night to accomplish the impossible. Random-access editors have not created more time for editing. On the contrary, because more options are available, there are more editorial choices; thus the creative process takes longer with more versions. The word processor does not make the creative process of writing any quicker, but it makes revisions easier and faster. When projects were cut on film, there were fewer changes. Linear video off-line editing sped the process up, but executives saw the ability to make alterations closer to the program's deadline. With nonlinear editing, the time between a "locked" off-line and delivery has shortened even further.

THE POWER OF RANDOM-ACCESS EDITING

Random-access editing is unlike traditional tape editing. Search and preview times are dramatically reduced or virtually eliminated. All successful random-access editing systems maintain accurate, clean edit decisions lists. Many also convert video footage to film key numbers for finishing projects on film.

ISSUES INTRODUCED BY RANDOM-ACCESS ON-LINE EDITING FIELD DOMINANCE

A frame of standard definition 525-line video comprises two fields. When video-tape is played backwards, the dominance of the video reverses automatically. A nonlinear editor does not automatically reverse field dominance. If this issue is not addressed, the result may be a jitter when reversing footage.

Deinterlacing Video Effects

Because each frame of standard definition video is also interlaced, slow-motion effects and other video effects need to be deinterlaced. This process combines the two video fields into one field, which will not include the artifacts of the interlaced frame.

Hidden Tracks

The nonlinear editor often uses video tracks on a timeline. These tracks can be turned on and off by the operator in order to view the project without effects. The operator might need to see specific issues in the footage without dealing with the video effect. If a project is being output to tape, with a track inadvertently turned off, an effect can be missing from the project. It is a good idea to examine a tape once it has been recorded from a nonlinear editor to make sure everything has been included.

Storage

Storage is always a concern in a nonlinear editor. Because storage is expensive, projects are edited and then offloaded once they have been completed, because there is only so much information that can be held on any system's disks. This offloading process, called *archiving*, stores all the program's footage in a special order on videotape. On a separate storage medium, the information about how this footage is put together is recorded. The archiving process takes time, and is one of the "housekeeping" items that takes the nonlinear editor out of service.

AN EXAMPLE OF A RANDOM-ACCESS EDIT SESSION

The commercial has to be on the air tomorrow morning. Broadcast airtime has been bought and paid for. The client is waiting. The spot has to be created and on-lined today, dubbed overnight for the broadcast. The production crew has returned from their grueling shoot. A three-quarter-inch window dub has been made of the original material. It is time to edit.

The three-quarter-inch videotape is transferred (digitized) into the random-access editor, like the one in Figure 16-5. During this process, time code, picture,

Figure 16-5 The off-line edit bay—a working random-access edit bay. The three-quarter videotape deck is to load audio, video, and time code into the computer as well as to record the output. A mixer controls the output of the computer to the three-quarter tape.

and audio are recorded by the editing computer. The three-quarter-inch tape, the original footage, and now the digitized footage all contain the same label information. The original footage is sent to the on-line facility. Other footage and support material (graphics, logs, and prebuilt effects) have also been loaded in the editor.

The off-line edit session begins. Narration and sync sound bites are placed onto tracks one and two, creating the framework of the commercial. Picture is carried along on the video track as sync sound is placed. Several music segments are cut into a music bed that builds to a climax. Since we input the audio at maximum quality, it will be output onto a DAT (digital audio tape) and used in the final commercial mix.

Now picture edits are made. Cutaways are placed over the narrator's lines and the jump cuts that were created by cutting the performers' narration together. The editor works frantically, trying different combinations of edits, saving each version that she likes. Finally, she has two similar but different versions of the commercial. The in-house producer cannot make up his mind on which one he likes best. Luckily, the facility has a fiber-optic line that feeds directly to the client's office. The two spots are played over the fiber and viewed in the client's office across town. The client makes several changes in the alternate version. The changes are accomplished in a matter of 15 minutes. Remember, so far no video-tape has been used in the editing process, except the three-quarter-inch tape that was used to put into the random-access computer.

Another fiber session results in another series of requests. These too are incorporated into the commercial. Two three-quarter-inch dubs are made of the approved spot. A DAT of all audio tracks (narrator, dialogue, effects, and both tracks of the stereo music) is made. The EDL is output to a floppy disk and a paper copy is printed.

Now comes the amazing part. The commercial could be sent on to a linear bay, or a disk of the edits could be put into an on-line random-access editor, like the one in Figure 16-6. The on-line editor only digitizes the needed material, along with graphics and other visual material. Once the footage has been input, the spot is essentially complete. There may be some minor adjustments made, as not all the parameters of the off-line spot are totally transferred to the on-line editor. The off-line copy of the commercial is compared to the finished one, and then the picture is recorded onto delivery videotape for audio to be placed and dubs to be made.

Another copy is made onto a separate tape and sent on to the audio facility. This copy will have three passes of the commercial on it. The first is the copy that was delivered for broadcast with mixed audio on tracks one and two. The second copy will be textless (no graphics) and will contain a split audio config-uration of narration, dialogue, music, and effects, each on separate audio chan-nels. However, this pass will only have a mono music track. On the third pass, the spot will be either texted or textless with narration on channel 1, dialogue and effects combined on channel 2, and stereo music on tracks 3 and 4. This

Figure 16-6 A working on-line Avid "Symphony." This system is compatible with the Avid off-line system and can immediately incorporate many of the effects performed off-line.

would allow for foreign delivery. The textless version can be used for foreign language graphics, and the narration can be replaced with the appropriate language.

The finishing process of this example could be accomplished on a linear system. The speed in finishing the spot is dependent on operator experience. However, when it comes to changes, a nonlinear editor is extremely quick. Edits can be adjusted without re-editing. The downside of nonlinear editors is that the cost of hard drives, though becoming more affordable, is still expensive for broadcast-quality images. To finish a one-hour program might require the archiving of other projects to make room for the longer program. This can take time, too. In other words, there are additional time considerations that are connected with nonlinear on-line systems besides re-editing.

In terms of audio finishing, nonlinear editors and digital audio workstations are standard equipment in most mixing houses. The digital material that is used in the off-line process can be used for the final product if the material is properly recorded and digitized.

Returning to the commercial edit example, a dub of the finished visual is sent to the sound facility as a final check for sync. When the audio is laid back to the video master, the commercial is again fibered to the client in his office across town. Picture is approved. The video master is dubbed for protection. The original tape is sent to the audio facility and laid back with final audio.

Another fiber session results in final approval. This final version is cloned (a digital copy of the original is created in a digital-to-digital edit). This clone is delivered to an uplink facility and satellited to a dubbing facility in the Midwest. At the dubbing facility the commercial is copied to many delivery formats (one-inch, D2, Betacam, etc.) and overnighted to over 400 stations for broadcast the next morning.

Dozens of shows have been on-lined within the random-access computer. Random access will be the standard method of video on-line; it is just a matter of time. The tools of the editor will continue to change, but the task will not. Organization, conceptualization, and selection of shots and audio that serve the show's audience and purpose will continue to be the editor's ultimate goal no matter what machines are used.

SUMMARY

The speed of the random-access editor has only increased the versions and complexity of off-line editing. Though revisions on a nonlinear editor are quicker, there are other time-consuming processes that the machine requires, such as clearing the disks of unneeded materials, called archiving.

A powerful nonlinear editing system does not necessarily make powerful or creative programs. Only a talented human can accomplish this task.

The cost of nonlinear as well as linear editing will go up as high-definition formats enter the mainstream of postproduction.

17

The Linear On-Line Edit Session

An on-line edit session can be as simple as performing a single cut or it can involve thousands of edits. In this chapter, we will look at the linear on-line session from an operational standpoint and explain what happens during the session. Most of these considerations, other than multiple generations, are of concern whether the edit session is linear or nonlinear.

BEFORE THE SESSION

Before starting the editing process, the editor must make sure that the audio levels are properly aligned. A 0 dB tone (−20 for digital displays) sent from the mixer or playback tape should read 0 dB on the record deck during a test record. The audio test tone should also read 0 dB on the record machine playback VU meter. Finally, audio monitors and mixer should be properly balanced before the session begins.

Also check that all the necessary equipment is in the editing room and that the editing system can access all those machines. The editor should have a list of what the client needs, to help make sure that all equipment ordered is operating.

THE SESSION

Once the record tape is loaded into the record machine, like the one in Figure 17-1, and the room has been properly set up, the on-line session can begin. The

Figure 17-1 A DVW-500 Digital Betacam recorder. The Betacam is an extremely popular small-format recording and editing medium.

first edit is usually bars and tone, the reference for later playback of the tape. A black space is then recorded so that a video slate can be inserted later.

During the on-line session, the editor must attend to many details. The following sections explore common areas of concern for an editor during a typical on-line session.

The Audience

Each program has an intended audience, and the on-line editor must be aware of both the audience and the client's expectations of the finished product from the beginning. A simple show on tax preparation does not have to be a dazzling display of digital effects, but another type of presentation might require careful use of such effects.

Slates

One of an editor's most important tasks is making sure that every videotape created during the on-line session has video identification (a slate) and that paper labels are affixed to each box and reel. This simple attention to organization makes keeping track of jobs much easier.

Audio Levels

Audio is a very important aspect of any visual project. Audio levels should be carefully monitored, and each audio edit should flow smoothly into the next. If a show is to be viewed on a television with small speakers, it is a good idea to listen to the edited master through that type of speaker, rather than the large studio speakers often found in on-line rooms. Smaller speakers often mask annoying hisses and hums that originate at location shooting. If the show will be broadcast over a large speaker system, careful attention should be paid to the audio quality of all edits.

If the show will be sent to a professional sweetening facility (see Chapter 18), audio should be recorded without equalization, at full volume, and with at least one-second heads and tails if possible. This gives the sweetening engineer ample room to cross-fade the audio.

Color Balance

Studio productions require few, if any, adjustments once the color bars have been properly set up. A good way to align color bars on a playback tape is to create a hard-edged horizontal wipe at the switcher between the switcher's color bars and the color bars on the playback tape. The playback bars are then adjusted at the TBC to match the switcher's color bars. Location shoots, however, usually require extensive adjustments because of fluctuations in natural lighting. The on-line editor should pay close attention to the video levels indicated on the scopes. An improperly recorded signal might look great on the video monitor but actually be beyond the recording capability of the videotape machine.

Each shot should be balanced with the next. Facial tones and the video and chroma values of the sky and background should match as well as possible, allowing for an easy transition for the eye.

List Management

It pays to keep a clean EDL while performing the on-line edit. If a shot must be changed later, a clean EDL makes this change much easier. Having a simple video-only insert erase part of an expensive and time-consuming effect because a record OUT point was not cleaned can be very discouraging, both for the editor and for the client.

To avoid potential trouble, an editor should make sure that the on-line EDL accurately reflects the edits on the record master. Editors working with control track systems often forget that there might be changes, even after the editing session is over. These changes might require that the on-line edit be repeated.

Without proper notes about where the original edits came from, reconstructing an editing sequence can be extremely difficult.

Spelling

An editor should double-check all titles and credits with either the client or a dictionary. It is frustrating to have to re-edit a section of a show because a name was misspelled or a location was keyed in with a typographical error. The editor should check anything that he or she is not absolutely sure is spelled correctly. Editors often create textless portions of programs, which are then used as a playback source. Then changes in graphics do not require extensive re-editing. Many factual checks can be made using a computer with Internet access. The author will do a search to verify spelling or correct movie credits.

Record Inhibits

On the bottom of three-quarter-inch cassettes is a little red button, or at least a hole where there used to be one. If this button is removed from the cassette, the cassette is protected from accidental erasure by a record machine. The cassette can still be erased by a strong magnetic field, such as that generated by a bulk eraser. The red button must be in place to record on the cassette and should be removed when the edit session is completed.

Record-inhibit tabs can be found on the back of VHS tapes. There are also record-inhibit switches on professional cassette-style videotapes. Take the time to enable the record-inhibit device on any video master to protect from accidental erasure.

Time Considerations

Fast editors are always in demand, as the ability to complete a project in a short amount of time is a plus when you consider the cost of an on-line session. But completing a session quickly at the cost of increased errors does not save time or money. Speed comes with experience, but speed for speed's sake is worthless if the product is flawed.

Although many editors are capable of editing efficiently for hours at a stretch, errors can occur when an editor becomes fatigued. Some companies frown on their editors taking regularly scheduled breaks, but a walk around the block or simply getting up for a drink of water can make a big difference in editing quality.

All machines can and will fail. When something goes wrong, a professional editor usually tries to help the engineer in any way possible. The editor might also be able to work on other parts of the show while waiting for a particular piece of equipment to be repaired.

Chroma Levels

When the final product will be distributed on three-quarter-inch tape or consumer-quality half-inch tape, the editor should be careful to keep chroma levels down. Too much chroma can cause electronic tearing (where the chroma appears to smear) on half-inch formats. Red is the first color to show signs of deterioration in multiple tape generations.

Editing into Existing Masters

When you are editing into a video master that was created on a different machine, you must match video and audio levels to the old recording. Some machines are not compatible with others. An engineer should be consulted about using a tape that was originally edited on a different machine.

Glitches

Glitches (see the Glossary), video hits (any abnormal flaw in an image), and bad edits come from a variety of sources, including a large dropout, irregularity in a tape's control track, a power fluctuation during a recording, poorly recorded time code, or a machine that was not locked up when the record machine went into edit. The glitch also could be recorded into the video on the playback material. If an editor spots a glitch during an on-line edit, he or she should stop immediately and find out whether the problem can be corrected before continuing. If the editor spots a glitch during an off-line edit, he or she should check the master footage as soon as possible to see whether the glitch is on the original. If the glitch is on the master and cannot be viewed, a cutaway or other footage might be used in the problem area.

If the glitch is on a source tape, and the record tape is capable of prereading, you might be able to freeze the previous frame from the record tape in the switcher, and if the glitch is not too big, in a preread edit, use the frozen frame and damaged frame, combine the two in the switcher, and possibly repair the damage.

Multiple Generations

With the commercial acceptance of various digital formats, the number of times a program can be duplicated has increased dramatically. The digital video signal, when contained within a digital path, can be duplicated hundreds of times, while three-quarter-inch tape can only withstand a few copies. The complexity and budget of a project often determine the format of choice. A 30-second commercial with many effects may be edited for weeks on a nonlinear system, but a syndicated game show may be recorded on one-inch and the broadcast copy may be only one generation away from the camera original.

Television network video is usually crisp and clear because a great deal of money is spent to keep the equipment in prime condition and the original footage is obtained with quality equipment. The following table indicates the number of generations an editor can go without seeing too much of a loss, assuming he or she starts out with network-quality video.

Number of Generations

Format	Average	Maximum
One-inch type C	4–6	5–7
Three-quarter-inch	2–3	4–6
D1*	40–60	250+
DCT*	40–60	250+
Digi Betacam	40–60	250+
D2*	10–20	100–120
D3*	10–20	100–120

*Assume digital-to-digital dub or edit.

Audio Sync

Several commonly used video devices can delay the video, which can result in a lip sync problem. Frame stores, for example, are electronic devices that synchronize video signals by storing one or more frames of video. The stored frames are then fed out to a system. This is the result when video is processed through a DVE. A one-frame delay is usually not noticeable, but if several generations are made through these devices, the lip sync should be checked carefully.

AFTER THE SESSION

It is always a good idea to watch a show after the editing process has been completed. While in the throes of an editing session, the editor can easily miss errors in content and technical problems. Duplicating a faultily edited master wastes everyone's time, so an editor should always make a final check of the tape before making copies.

THE EDITOR–CLIENT RELATIONSHIP

The client is often present during the on-line edit, and the editor should do every-thing possible to establish a good working relationship. The first meeting with the client is probably the most important. How the editor reacts to the client makes a lasting impression. Certainly the editor should not have to baby-sit the client during a session, but a brief description of the bay might be in order before the session begins. If the client understands what is going on, he or she can usually be more helpful during the session.

What if the client insists on making a terrible edit? Some editors try to offer an acceptable compromise, while others either make the edit and then modify it after the client leaves, or refuse to go any further. The editor should remember that he or she is being employed by the client and must weigh the consequences of being obstinate.

The client has responsibilities, too. Nothing is more frustrating to an editor than having to search reels for shots that do not exist or not having all the reels at hand. The client should make sure the editor has everything he or she needs for the session.

The client should also watch for missed edits and watch the master monitor closely for edits that look wrong or off-color. The on-line session is the last chance to correct or improve a show. The client should take this opportunity to do so if a change is warranted.

SUMMARY

The on-line edit is a demanding process that requires the editor's eyes, ears, and brain to be at peak performance. It requires that everyone work together to produce the most entertaining and/or informative program possible.

18

The Student Editor

Student editors bring new ideas and fresh concepts to the postproduction world. However, there are several common situations that the student editor can avoid.

OVERCUTTING

The student editor usually feels the need to make many edits. Often these are edits that include effects. There are programs that require numerous effects and some scenes that require extensive cutting. Many scenes, however, need breathing room where characters take over. Occasionally in feature films a scene will play in a two shot without any edits, if the performances are outstanding.

Keep in mind that the audience wants to watch the characters, not the editor's handiwork, and that the best editor is the one whose work is not noticed.

THINKING THE COMPLETION OF A PROJECT IS EASY

Organizing, cutting, and finishing a visual production is never easy. Production mistakes, changes, deadlines, political considerations, and technical problems are just some of the challenges the editor faces. Always assume there will be delays in the post process and that the editing of a project will take longer than expected.

The individual who can finish a project is a special and talented person. There are many people, professionals as well as novices, who talk a great line, get a production together, and even manage to get some semblance of quality on tape, but the person who can organize, edit, and finish a project is a unique individual.

LACK OF AUDIO IN THE PROGRAM

The student editor all too often thinks that audio work is unnecessary or unimportant. Audio effects, mixing, and careful attention to the program's sound track are vital to the audience's perception of a program. Picking the right music, editing it well, using the best possible narrator with proper microphone (see Figure 18-1), using on-camera and off-screen effects, and picking the best possible take both for visual and aural content are necessary considerations for any visual project.

Even the adjustments of individual tracks (mixing) is so important that there are professionals who just mix tracks. These individuals do not cut, choose,

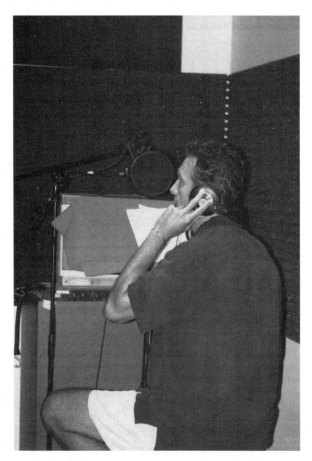

Figure 18-1 Hiring professional voice-over talent and using professional microphones and announce booths is just one of the ways to utilize audio to its fullest potential. Jeff Myers (*above*) has been the voice of thousands of commercials.

place, or create audio tracks. Their only purpose is to combine the tracks at their optimum levels for any particular moment in the program. Similar concerns for audio should be in the student editor's mind.

WAITING UNTIL PRODUCTION IS OVER BEFORE DEALING WITH THE PROGRAM

The student editor will sometimes forget that being involved in the entire production process can make the editing process much easier. Understanding the director's goals and observing the footage are ways to spot editorial mistakes that can be fixed with an extra cutaway or camera setup before shooting wraps. Perhaps, if there is time, the editor could read the script and spend some time with the production crew to get a feel for the show.

LOGGING AND ORGANIZATION

The need for careful logging and organization cannot be emphasized enough. Keeping accurate records and master logbooks keeps the cutting room clean and footage easy to find. Unfortunately for most student productions, this organization does not occur, and footage is either misplaced or editorial opportunities are lost.

Recently I had a discussion with a commercial producer. She was complaining that a client had called with changes to a spot she had cut a month ago. The changes were simple, but the media (picture and audio) had long ago been deleted from the edit system hard drives. When another editor attempted to redigitize the material, they found that the reels had been mislabeled and it was nearly impossible to retrace the steps that were made to create the commercial. The original three-quarter-inch dub was input into the nonlinear editor, and the original spot had to be recreated, edit by edit.

Searching for that one shot that you saw three days ago could be frustrating and time consuming. The effort spent labeling the tapes associated with a project can be minimal compared to the time spent trying to locate something a client knows you have and cannot find (see Figure 18-2). Organization is the key to success for every creative individual and every visual production.

NONLINEAR EFFECTS

The nonlinear editor poses a trap for new editors. The ease with which effects can be used in a program can mask an editor's creativity. The story or message

Figure 18-2 The video vault is a daunting, challenging, dark hole where tapes can disappear forever. Make sure that each tape is properly labeled, filed, and input into the nonlinear editor properly. A lost tape is a lost edit, if not more.

is of primary concern to the producer, director, writer, client, and audience. Creating a spectacular effect that does not involve the program's message or intended audience is of little value. Preprogrammed effects can be jarring and obtrusive. If you are going to use that special wipe or DVE move, it might be a good idea to soften the edges and movement to match a camera pan or motion within the frame. Modifying an effect to the show's needs can not only be creative, but add to the program's visual impact.

If multimillion-dollar feature films use cuts as their primary transitions, maybe this is an acceptable way to transition from one angle to another, and change from one scene to the next. In the "old days," to accomplish a special effect was a feat itself. Nonlinear editors make creating effects extremely easy. Try not

Figure 18-3 Veteran audio mixer David Cantu sits in front of the automated faders of his digital audio workstation. Just above his shoulder is the master monitor for the DAW. David's hand is holding a light pen. Bottom right is a DAT machine. Photo courtesy of New Wave Entertainment.

to be fooled into thinking that because an effect looks great it is needed in every project.

TOO MUCH EGO, NOT ENOUGH REALITY

Unfortunately, editing and even overseeing the finishing of a student project is not enough experience to qualify one for editing a major motion picture. There are many qualified people who know the players and can do the job. Of course a level of confidence is necessary in any technical endeavor, but do not be fooled that years of college or technical school productions will open doors to the post-production industry.

Make friends, make contacts, and remember that you may already have the tools to do the job. As was said in the brilliant film *Joe versus the Volcano*, "I know he can get the job, but can he *do* the job." Getting the job is the hard part. Make sure you can do the job, without the ego. There are more than enough proud (warranted or not) people in the visual industry.

THE REAL WORLD

The real world is not like school. There are wonderful people who want to help others move up in this industry. There are also insecure people who will try to stop younger people from taking their job. Technology will change and the players will change. Your friend may end up being the head of a network, a studio, or a postproduction firm. There is no end to the distance you can travel or the number of challenges you may face. It is a good idea to keep a list of what you have accomplished in school and use it sparingly. The real world is interested in real results.

SUMMARY

The ability to segue from school to the real world of postproduction is not so much a technical challenge, but a mental one. The professional deals with personalities as well as machines. After a few years, you will find yourself doing the same chores over and over, with different footage and clients. Once this challenge is met, the difficulty will be to make each new day and each new client a positive experience.

PART V

Other Editing Processes

19

Audio Postproduction

All too often, the audio portion of a show is limited to what was recorded during production. In this type of program, the only sounds added during postproduction are likely to be laughter, audience reactions, or perhaps a short piece of music to connect scenes (often called a *sting*).

The use of stereo and surround sound audio for television has emphasized the need for greater care and planning of audio in postproduction. Many people listen to television through their home theater systems. Film producers are keenly aware of the emotional impact that audio can have. Most filmed television programs have extensive music tracks. These shows also add effects in the background sound tracks. Feature films go to even greater lengths to heighten, enhance, and improve their audio.

SWEETENING

Sweetening is the placement and mixing of audio on a digital audio workstation (DAW). DAWs store audio information on computer hard disks and are then able to perform mixes within the computer without rolling tape until output is required. The DAW controls equalization, compression, volume, echo, and track slippage.

The first step in sweetening is to edit the program onto a video master in a normal video on-line session. The edited master could be on any standard video format. The digital formats have the added advantage of four available channels for recording audio. These allow for recording overlapping dialogue, music, or effects on different channels, giving the audio mixer *handles* (additional material at the beginning and end of each edit) for creating audio fades or for multiple audio cues.

All audio is recorded at full level without fades or equalization and with ample heads and tails to allow the sweetening engineer to crossfade the audio tracks. The audio edited onto the master includes all production sound, as well as other effects that are available on source videotapes. Often dialogue is recorded on one of the audio tracks and effects and music on the other.

The edited master is then brought to the sweetening facility, where the audio from the edited master is transferred from the videotape to the digital audio workstation. During this process, called a *layover*, the time code from the edited master is also copied into the computer. Some DAWs have video recorders that store the visual reference for mixing. Others can control videotape machines to view the program's video.

Once these preparations have been made, prerecorded music, prerecorded or live voice-over narration, effects, and background sounds are input into the mixer. The process of transferring all of the necessary original elements and other audio information into the digital audio mixer is called a *prelay*. Once the elements have been put into the computer, they are placed in their proper relation to the picture (edited). When the bulk of the audio has been received and loaded into the mixer (DAW) the mixing process begins (see Figure 19-1).

There are usually five final audio tracks in a project: dialogue, effects, narration, and two for the stereo music. These elements are mixed together to get a balance, depending on the show's purpose and intended audience. A musical special will be mixed differently than a situational comedy.

The audio sources on the workstation are mixed down to their individual tracks. In many cases, shows are also sold internationally. A *split track master* is often created to facilitate international programming. Using a split track master, foreign languages can be dubbed into a program because the narration and dialogue have been separated out of the show.

The process of recording the mixed stereo audio onto the final videotape is called a *layback*. The layback is accomplished by locking the time code of the record master to the audio mixer and performing an audio-only edit on the edited master.

AUDIO ON NONLINEAR EDITORS

As a general rule, audio mixing has been separated from video editing. The reason for this is that audio cutting and mixing takes a different talent than does editing visuals.

Nonlinear editors have the ability to adjust and manipulate audio. These editors are capable of making reasonable mixes, if time and care are taken with the input and mixing of the sources.

Using nonlinear editors as a final mixing tool can be an excellent way to keep costs down on industrial and nonbroadcast programs. Figure 19-2 shows the overview of the audio mixing process. However, it may prove more cost effi-

Figure 19-1 A video sweetening suite. Note the large mixing console in front of the two men as well as the window dub being projected in front of the room. Photo by Gil Smith, Courtesy of Compact Video Services, Burbank, California.

cient to have a professional audio mixer combine the final audio tracks. A poorly mixed show can ruin even the best picture.

DIGITAL AUDIO TAPE (DAT)

Digital audio tape (DAT) stores audio on tape using digital encoding rather than analog encoding. As with other digital recording media, DAT can be copied over multiple generations with little effect on the original recording quality.

Because of DAT's small physical size and high quality, it was quickly accepted in the audio world. DAT is used for recording and transferring

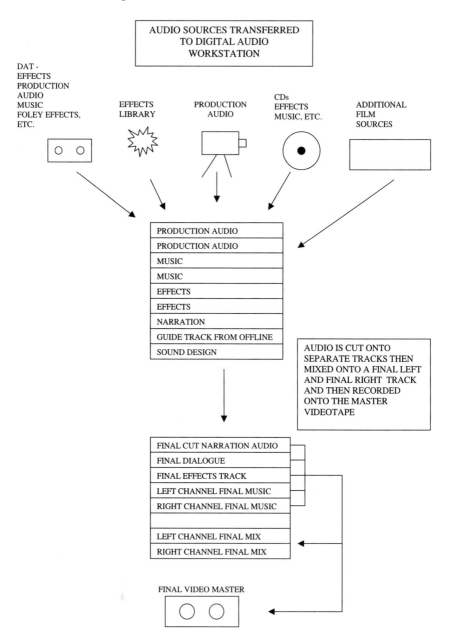

Figure 19-2 The audio path for digital audio mixing. Various audio sources are input into the hard drives, edited, then mixed onto five separate tracks: narration, dialogue, effects, and two tracks of stereo music.

Figure 19-3 A DA88 audio recorder/player. This digital device has eight tracks. It is one of the standard audio devices used along with the DAT audio player.

material from one audio facility to another. Broadcast-quality DAT machines use time (sweetening). The original tracks are transferred to final tracks, but not mixed together. This process allows the mixer to return to his or her original audio and make changes. Saving the four separate audio tracks (production dialogue, music, effects, and narration) allows for foreign distribution, as well as other audio functions, such as remixing for syndication or revisions. Another digital tape format is called DA88 (see Figure 19-3). This format has eight tracks available.

AUDIO COMPRESSION, LIMITERS, AND EQUALIZATION

There are three major areas of audio manipulation beyond the obvious adjustments of placement and relative volume. The first area, *equalization*, is the selective alteration of a specific frequency within a given sound. For instance, if a sound had a hiss, proper equalization could isolate, then reduce or eliminate the hiss. At the other end of the audio spectrum, a thin voice could be made stronger by increasing the low-end or bass frequencies.

The other areas of audio manipulation—compression and limiting—are similar, yet different concepts. *Compression* has two elements: the threshold and the ratio of compression. A *threshold* is a level at which compression is to take place. The *ratio* is the amount of compression that will take place above the threshold. A 4:1 ratio will reduce a sound that is 4 dB above the threshold to 1 dB above it. The limiter also has a threshold, but *limiting*, unlike compressing, just cuts off any sounds above a certain volume level.

LIP SYNCING

Lip syncing to playback audio can cause problems in the editing bay. The speed of an audio cassette machine or reel-to-reel machine will fluctuate.

If lip-syncing is planned, you should use a CD for playback. A CD, being digital, will always play at the same speed. When the piece is edited, that same CD could be used for the audio source on the record master.

SUMMARY

Audio is probably the most ignored or forgotten aspect of a video production. With a little work, audio can add more excitement and interest to a program than you would have believed possible.

20

Editing Film on Video

From video assist (an on-set video recording of what the film camera exposes on the negative), random-access editors, mixing on digital audio workstations, to creating effects on high-end paint systems, the film business is working less and less with actual film.

HIGH-DEFINITION 24P

Many television productions use film for original production. Even if the program was originally edited on video, another version of the show would be created on film so that overseas markets could use the film's high-quality images for broadcast. The transfer process from NTSC video to PAL or SECAM was not acceptable.

Now, with high-definition video, a program can be shot on film, transferred to HD 24p, edited in HD 24p, and then the video master can easily transfer to any other video format.

Although high-definition 24p edit bays are not as common as standard definition NTSC bays, eventually the postproduction community will embrace this new format as more shows need to be edited in HD.

THE STANDARD DEFINITION TELECINE PROCESS

Before any film can be edited electronically, the film image and audio must be transferred to an electronic medium. In most applications, this medium is videotape. Even if the footage is to be edited on a random-access editor, tape is used as an intermediate step. Telecine machines transfer film to tape (see Figure 20-1).

. igure 20-1 An Ursa® film-to-tape telecine manufactured by the Rank Cintel Corpo-ration. This high-end transfer machine can feed and color-correct a video signal from a film element. Note that the left side of the film reel, the supply reel, is nearly full. Photo by Sean Sterling.

Top-of-the-line telecine machines can perform numerous tasks. They usually employ a CRT to expose the film onto three video pick-up tubes or charge-coupled devices (CCDs—see the Glossary). Mirror images, reverse plays, zooms, and image reductions are commonly accomplished in the telecine session.

Several considerations within the telecine environment should be addressed. The first is key code. *Key code* is the Kodak bar-code system that records key numbers on film. An additional piece of equipment is needed to read key code during the telecine transfer, but it is an ideal way to encode video footage with visual key numbers. If key code is unavailable, key numbers can still be burned into the video picture. Inserting key numbers into the footage enables film negative cutters or other personnel to quickly determine the original source of the visual footage.

Time code is a second consideration. At the time of the telecine transfer, time code is recorded onto the videotape. If a film workprint is being transferred, a log correlates the videotape's time code with the original negative's key numbers. A sync point, usually the closing of the clapboard, is used as a common reference point. These key numbers are then entered into the random-access computers. In addition to key numbers and time code, the final medium is another vital concern. The medium determines the level at which all film-to-tape transfers will be made. If the final product will be film finish, the film-to-tape transfer will not be a critical process because the final film timing and color balance will be determined at the film lab. If the video footage is to be used for a video finish, the color and brightness of the film transfer merit careful attention. The best telecine operators (called *colorists*) maintain an extremely high standard. However, every client has his or her own look. Music videos are transferred with a different color style than a wildlife documentary.

Other issues also affect the telecine process. On widescreen footage, which area of the screen should be shown, or should the footage be letterboxed? What type of audio is to be transferred to tape? Does music or dialogue need to be transferred? Should the tracks be mixed or recorded onto separate tracks (narration, dialogue, music, and effects)?

THREE-TWO PULLDOWN

NTSC television runs at 30 frames per second. Film is shot at 24 frames per second. Repeating fields of visual information, a process called *three-two pulldown*, resolves this six-frame difference. For every other frame of film, one field of video is repeated. Over the course of one second, the six frames are filled. Some producers, knowing that they will edit and finish on videotape, shoot the film at 30 frames per second to eliminate three-two pulldown (see Figure 20-2).

When you are converting time code back to film key numbers, occasionally the three-two pulldown process creates edits on frames that do not exist in film.

THREE-TWO PULL DOWN

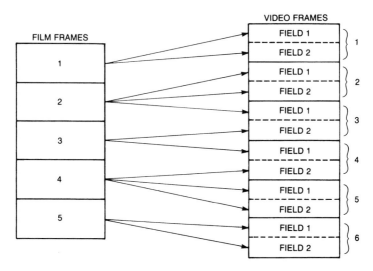

Figure 20-2 In three-two pulldown, the 24-frame-per-second film footage is transferred to 30-frame-per-second videotape. This is accomplished by repeating a field of picture every other film frame. Four frames of film are converted to five frames of video: 24 film frames result in 30 video frames.

In this case, the negative cutter has to adjust the film edits to accommodate the duplicated fields (see Figure 20-3).

An error may occur when using 30-frame videotape to edit 24-frame film. For every other film frame, an extra frame of video is created through the three-two pulldown process. If both the beginning and ending frames contain a manufactured field, there are now two video fields of nonexistent footage, the equivalent of one frame (see Figure 20-3). In a video finish, these extra frames are of no concern. But in a film finish, the negative cutter will have to add one film frame during the negative process to keep proper sync.

FILM TRANSFERRED TO HIGH-DEFINITION 24P

Since HD 24p is running at the same frame rate as film, there is no conversion. The HD 24p signal is frame-for-frame accurate to the film frame. The program can be edited electronically on a linear or random-access editor entirely in the HD environment (see Figure 20-4). Titles, graphics, effects, and credits can be composed in the 24p world. Then the final program could go to any other necessary

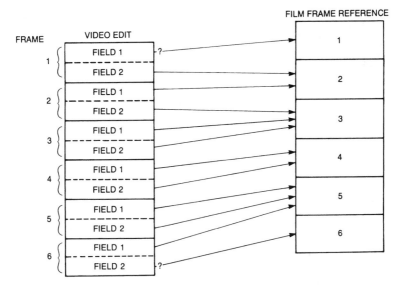

Figure 20-3 Considering the three-two pulldown that occurs during film-to-tape transfer, there is the possibility of missing a frame when conforming the film to the off-line work print. In the example from Figure 20-2, if key numbers displayed in the window dub are used to cut the film negative without physically checking the edit, the cut negative will be one frame (2 video fields) short. In many video-to-film conversions, a kinescope (video-to-film transfer) is created to ensure that edits follow the video precisely.

broadcast format, including the NTSC standard definition format that we currently watch.

The issue today is that high-definition off-line effects and finishing equipment are not very common. However, when the broadcast industry embraces a format or concept, the rush to acquire that equipment is amazing.

ADVANTAGES AND DISADVANTAGES OF ELECTRONIC EDITING

Editing a film project on a random-access system is fast and exciting. There are no *trims* (remainders of shots that are not cut into the workprint). Random-access editing is visual rather than character oriented; pictures are cut, not time code numbers (see Figure 20-5). There are some drawbacks to the electronic process, however. For example, feature films require previews in movie houses, yet the electronic image cannot withstand expansion to a full screen. Often, feature film editors have to keep a current film workprint ready for screenings. Yet even with these drawbacks, electronic editing has become a common method of editing feature films.

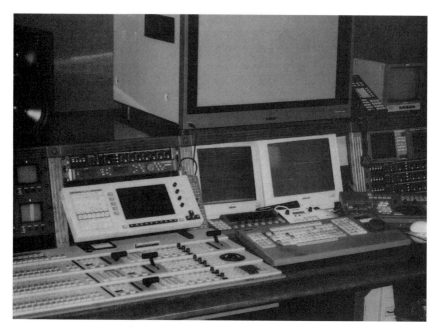

Figure 20-4 A high-definition edit bay. This linear bay is one of several in the Los Angeles area. Photo courtesy of American Production Services, located in North Hollywood and Seattle.

Figure 20-5 A working Discrete "Inferno" bay. This high-end video compositing workstation is ideal for film imaging work. This particular device is utilized in many film trailers (coming attractions). The film is transferred to electronic files, manipulated, and when approved, output to a file, which is scanned onto film negative. The device is the equivalent to an optical printer, but makes changes quickly and very cost-effectively. Photo courtesy of New Wave Entertainment, a leading motion picture and television production and promotion corporation.

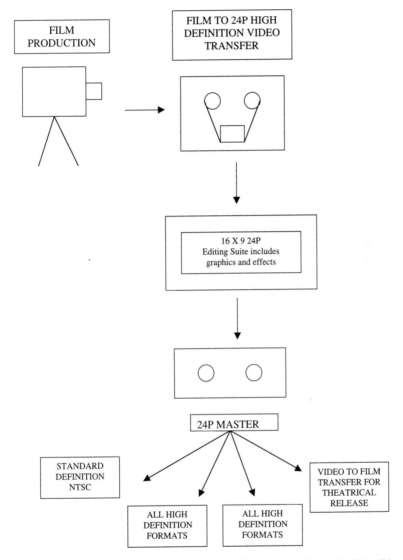

Figure 20-6 The film to 24p postproduction route. Note that without the 2/3 pulldown or other video artifacts, the transfer, editing, and delivery of the 24p product is simple, high definition, and easy to convert between standards, either back to film or any other video format, high definition or standard definition.

TWO STANDARD PATHS

Several standard paths use electronic editing to finish a project shot on film. The first method finishes the program on video and the second finishes on film. When HD 24p production and postproduction is widely accepted (see Figure 20-6), the few programs that use film labs to complete projects will probably switch to high definition.

FILM-TO-VIDEO FINISH

The first path, in which a program is finished on video, has two generally accepted finishing processes (see Figures 20-7 and 20-8). One uses film-editing equipment; the other employs electronic editors.

Using Film-Editing Equipment

Conforming video to film keeps the creative editing tasks within the film process. Some producers and film companies are still comfortable with film editing, and this method retains an established system. The film editor cuts the show on film using a film copy of the camera original. This workprint is created in a film laboratory. The editor cuts this workprint and *mag* (the accompanying sound that has been transferred to audiotape in the shape of film). Once the workprint picture has been approved, the many audio tracks are mixed. The audio mix is accomplished using either electronic or film-style procedures (see Chapter 19). The combination of film workprint and final audio is often then transferred to video for intermediate reference viewing.

After the workprint picture has been approved (often called *locked*), the original film negative image is transferred to video. There are two methods to accomplish this transfer: either only selected takes are telecined, or a negative cutter cuts the negative. The cut negative, which represents the entire final picture, is transferred to video.

Cutting the Negative

Cutting the film negative retains the film-finishing aspect of editing, so that only color timing, effects, and titling are added in the video environment. Image manipulation and chroma keys are generally done during telecine.

Titles, fades, wipes, and dissolves are created in an edit bay. If the negative has been cut to conform to the (film) workprint, this film negative is transferred to video and synchronized with the transfer of the video workprint and audio track. The audio portion of the program is finished at a sound facility, once the workprint is approved, in a standard dubbing process (that is, film style).

When there is more than one reel to edit, as with an hour-long drama, the several reels of cut negative are transferred to video and edited together to match the workprint. Titles may be added on a second pass, using the edited video master as a playback to preserve an untitled version of the show for later use in syndication. (The running time of a show is altered for syndication, usually requiring the original show to be shortened. Having an untitled master facilitates this editing process.)

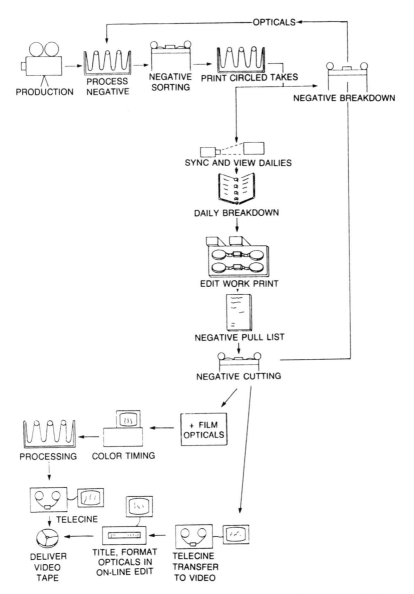

Figure 20-7 The film edit-to-tape finish route. Note that there are two choices once the workprint is approved: pursue the film process all the way through opticals or, alternatively, do the final picture conforming on-line. If there are many edits, an off-line edit is performed to locate all footage before going on-line.

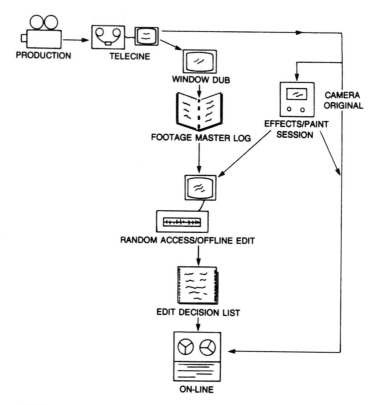

Figure 20-8 Electronic editing with a video finish. The window dubs refer to the telecine original footage for an auto assembly. Any effects created in on-line or graphics sessions are window-dubbed in the off-line session.

Using Select Shots for On-Line Editing

Instead of cutting the negative, the production staff may choose to edit the program on-line in a video bay. In this case, an off-line editing session typically precedes the on-line edit.

The selected camera negative is transferred to videotape. Instead of color correcting all the footage, the film-to-tape transfer process is shortened by making a quick, one-shot run at the film footage with one generic setting. This single pass of color correction is called a *one-lite*. The one-lite footage is transferred to an on-line format videotape and a window dub of the footage is made. Unusually, the window dub is recorded onto three-quarter-inch videotape.

An off-line edit, either with a linear or nonlinear system, is performed using the dub of the one-lite. The results of this edit session are an edit decision list (EDL) and a viewing cassette for approvals.

Next the EDL is given to the telecine operator who color corrects only the portions of the footage that are used in the program and rerecords the color-corrected images on the on-line format, erasing the one-lite image with final color-corrected video. The show is on-lined using either a linear or nonlinear edit bay. The audio portion of the program is finalized, using either digital or analog procedures at a video sweetening facility.

ELECTRONIC EDIT-TO-FILM FINISH

Finishing a program on film allows for projection in movie houses or a return to video in a telecine session. This film-finish process, again, allows for transfers to PAL or other formats through telecine transfer (see Figure 20-9).

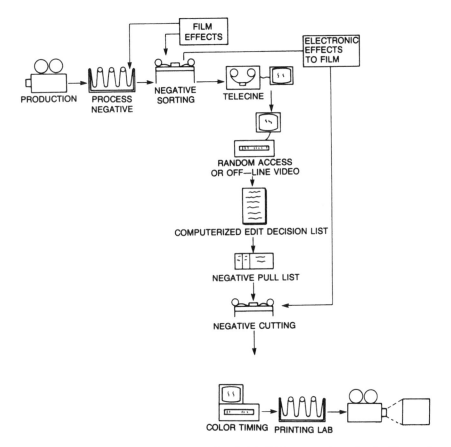

Figure 20-9 Electronic editing with a film finish. With a properly maintained key code or time code reference, film can be edited on video. The time code listing is then converted to key numbers for film conforming.

The film *dailies* (daily footage) are transferred to video with key numbers and time code correlation logged at the telecine session and visually burned into the picture of the video. The transfer is edited either linearly or on a random-access editing system. If possible, especially for single-camera productions, production footage should be transferred to video in scenes. This approach ensures a logical place to record each new day's footage as it is brought in to be transferred. If the transfers are made randomly, it becomes difficult to locate scenes during the editing process.

Once the program is cut and locked (approved), the editing system can produce an EDL and viewing copy. Some random-access editing systems can produce both a time code edit list and a key number list for conforming the film negative. A *kinescope* (a film copy of the video program) is often created for the negative cutter so he or she can have a film reference of the program.

Audio can be finished in either film (dubbing) or video (sweetening) style. Dubbing completes audio for most projects edited in a film style, but the DAW (digital audio workstation) has become the standard in film postproduction.

ELECTRONIC FILM EFFECTS

Until the 1990s, film effects were created using an optical printer. This machine is capable of exposing the same film negative multiple times, and uses mattes to hold out areas of the negative from being exposed to a particular image. Video and electronic effects did not have the image quality for movie projection. Now there are several high-resolution effects computers that are used to create film-quality effects, titles, trailers, and other image manipulation.

The process is to transfer production footage, one frame a time, to an electronic storage medium similar to a huge floppy disk (usually a storage device called an *exobite*). These frames are then input into a computer that has the power to manipulate and store large amounts of data.

Everything from the elimination of rigging wires and telephone poles to building entire cities within the computer is now commonplace. There are even movies that have been created almost entirely within the computer. Examples of these types of effects exist in almost every movie released today, especially action-adventure movies.

THE FUTURE

With the advent of high definition, the choice of shooting on video or film is becoming a matter of "look" rather than image quality. At least one prominent director has proclaimed that he will never shoot a feature film on film again. The choice may be to shoot on film and finish electronically for broadcast or cut negative for theatrical release or shoot on high definition, edit electronically and create a film negative master, project the project electronically, or broadcast the high-definition master.

SUMMARY

There are several ways to use electronics in the film postproduction process, all of which require transferring the film to video or to another electronic storage medium:

1. Video finish—Film is edited and cut using traditional film-editing methods. Cut negative is transferred to video. Effects and titles are added during a video on-line edit session or in an optical printer.
2. Video finish—Camera-original film negative is transferred to video for editing on an electronic system (linear or random access). The resulting EDL is used to edit the program in a video on-line edit session. Effects and titling are created on-line.
3. Film finish—In this process film dailies are transferred to video for editing on an electronic system (linear or random access). The resulting EDL is given to a negative cutter and the program is finished on film. Effects are created electronically or in an optical house.

In any of these situations, audio postproduction can be accomplished by sweetening (video-type audio finishing) or dubbing (film-style audio finishing).

21

Special Circumstances

TELEVISION'S 4 × 3 RATIO

The NTSC 525-line television picture is in a 4 × 3 ratio. Transferring feature films to video often requires special care because movies are usually shot in a widescreen format. That is why some movies shown on television often have a black mask at the top and bottom of the frame during the title sequences. A technique called pan-and-scan (see Figure 21-1) is used in the body of the film to keep the essential portion in the center of the screen, but the sides of the image have been cut off.

High-definition television, in its 16 × 9 ratio, will easily accept film's widescreen images. As an original production medium, high definition will appear like film, too. However, during the several years that high def is broadcast simultaneously with standard definition, the same issues will occur. The 16 × 9 image is wider and narrower than the 4 × 3 image. The question is, how will broadcasters deal with the widescreen format? Will they shoot with the important action in center screen and inconsequential action on the sides of the image? The other option would be to have the 16 × 9 image panned and scanned like a film. The most likely answer will be that both of these possibilities will be used, depending on how a program is shot and how much the show's budget is.

USING STILL PHOTOGRAPHS

Adjustments need to be made when still pictures are transferred to video. A tall, narrow picture or a thin, wide photo may not fit the format that is needed (remember that there will be two broadcast formats, 16 × 9 and 4 × 3). Decisions about the proper format will have to be made about including photography. One method

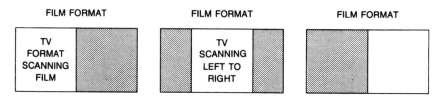

Figure 21-1 Diagram of the pan-and-scan concept used in transferring wide-format film to videotape. Because the television screen ratio differs from most feature film screens, the essential portions of the picture are scanned by the film-to-tape machine.

used to present the photo is to pan up or down. Another method is to shoot the whole picture and make a box wipe around the edge. A background color is often used in this instance to enhance the presentation of the picture.

With so many cable documentaries using still pictures, specialized cameras mounted on computer-controlled tracks have been developed that can pan and zoom into specific areas of a photograph. One of these cameras can transfer all sorts of different types of images from a single photo. You can pan, zoom, and go into a specific area of a photo or several areas of a photo. Then the video of the photo session can be transferred to a workprint and included in the off-line of the program.

DUPLICATION

Misunderstandings in communicating video duplication orders can be costly. When making dubs of master material, the editor must make sure that there is a *submaster* (also called a *protection* or *safety master*) to back up the edited master in the event something happens to the duplication master. In addition, the editor or producer must provide explicit instructions for the duplication company.

Making a submaster for duplication or protection is common practice. Too much money is spent on the production and editing to risk damage to the master, either in duplication or in additional editing. A protection copy is very inexpensive insurance.

Duplication runs of 100, 1,000 or even 2,500 copies of videotape projects are not unheard of, but there have been examples of people who have ordered 100,000 copies of the wrong tape. To avoid such disasters, every aspect of the duplication process must be clearly explained to the duplication facility in writing. Constant communication with duplication facilities and production companies will help avoid potentially costly misunderstandings.

TAPE CONSIDERATIONS

What happens when a shot is on a tape that has no code or is at the head of the tape and there is not enough pre-roll to edit the shot? What if the tape just in front of the shot is damaged and cannot be played? You can transfer the section to another time-coded tape. In this way, enough code can be recorded at the head of the shot to allow for editing, every frame of the good portion can be accessed, and any damaged tape will be played only once.

HOME COMPUTERS

Home computers have permeated video postproduction. Computer-controlled effects devices, editing systems, and animation programs can create or edit material on videotape.

Logging/List Manipulation Programs

These computer programs can manipulate simple VTR functions and mark time code locations for logging and building EDLs. Such off-line screening can result in a rough EDL that can be brought to off-line or on-line editing sessions. Log creation is simplified, and with detailed logging, a word processor or log program can search for specific lines or locations. Databases and word processors can be designed as logging tools for pre-edit lists. Databases can be extremely helpful in documentary shows because a single shot can be logged for a variety of aspects, such as dialogue, audio effects, characters, location, and reel number.

PCs and Macs both have sophisticated editing systems available. The key to any editing system is hard drive space and processor speed. The programs available do nonlinear dissolves, wipes, titling, two- and three-dimensional effects, but differ in the speed with which they operate and how much video can be stored.

NONLINEAR AND SPECIAL DIGITAL EFFECTS

Nonlinear editors have the ability to import effects programs. These can be used to render finished programs. To finish a program using a different facility or different computer, that particular effects program may have to be purchased, or an effect that looks like the original will have to be created. Check to make sure that the effects program is available in the on-line facility.

GRAPHICS

Most visual programs use graphics of some sort. Graphics come from one of several sources: an art card, computer output, or a graphics computer. No matter what the source of the graphic, there is a difference between a video-quality graphic and a graphic made for film projection. The amount of visual information required for projection or high definition is much greater than for the current NTSC television standard.

An *art card* comes from an artist or graphics company. Sometimes it is as simple as a block-lettered card, or it can be a colored drawing. These elements are placed under a video camera and recorded on tape.

Computer-originated elements must be recorded onto an editor-compatible format. Proper computer-to-video conversion must take place for the graphic to be included in a typical editing situation. Usually, computer files are converted to video and then either included in a linear editing situation, or imported into a nonlinear editor.

Extremely powerful graphics computers often create complicated animated images that have many elements and seem to be three-dimensional. Movies-of-the-week and some prime-time news shows have elaborate graphics openings. Most of these are created in the rarefied environment of high-end graphics computers. These computers can process multiple layers of graphics and holdouts. The advantage to creating complicated effects is that each layer is usually accessible. The disadvantage is that using this type of equipment is not inexpensive.

A consideration when using computers to build graphics is that a complicated graphic or opening takes disk space, which is always limited. Usually if you create a project, then leave the facility for any amount of time, the project is archived onto videotape. If you return or want changes, it usually takes some time to restore the project into the computer, as that drive space is limited and is quickly occupied by the next client.

THE EDITING ROOM

When in an actual edit session, keep track of the time spent in the room, along with the equipment used and how long it was in operation. If you need only three playback machines, you should not pay for four. Although comfortable editing bays often lull producers into complacency, this is no time to let your guard down.

SYNC MODE

To understand sync mode editing, imagine a concert recorded with six cameras, each with its own record machine. When the concert is over, the tapes are brought to an editing facility. Using sync mode (called *real time* in some systems), all source tapes are run in sync during each edit. While the six playback machines are rolling, the editor can switch from one tape to another as if the show were being cut live. This method of editing is also described as *on-the-fly editing*. (Some random-access editors are also capable of editing in sync mode.)

The advantage of this type of editing is the ability to edit using all sources at once, yet still have the option to make corrections and changes. If a mistake is made or sections of the show must be deleted, normal editing is performed until the correction or pull-up has been made, and then all playbacks are put back into sync and editing resumes in sync mode.

The disadvantages of this method are that (1) more edits tend to be made and (2) more playback machines mean higher costs for the edit session.

ADDING VIDEO

An editor finishes the on-line editing of an hour-long show. Now someone (the star, the director, the network, the editor's mother) wants to add a shot in the middle of it. This presents a challenge with tape because you cannot just cut the tape in half to insert a new slot.

The show has been on-line edited but not sweetened. There are three ways to add this new shot to the existing show:

1. Go down one generation of video on the whole show, except the new shot. The easiest way to approach this problem is to rerecord the show in an editing session. The edited master is now the playback. A new piece of record stock is placed on the record machine. A (very long) edit is made until the scene change. The new shot is added and another edit performed, copying the rest of the show onto the new master video stock.
2. Do another on-line edit of the show, adding the new shot. This option is not usually considered. On-line editing of a video show is costly to begin with, so doing it again is almost unheard of. Nevertheless, this might be an option for shorter shows or commercials.
3. Save the longest portion of the show and go down two generations on the shortest part. This approach is used to fix credits or when the change is in the first or last few minutes of a program.

    The first step is to copy the shortest portion of the show, either from the beginning of the show to the new shot or from the new shot to the end. The new shot is then added, which erases a portion of the original show; however, that section has been preserved on the dub.

    If the end of the show was the shortest section, the dub of that portion is added to the end of the tape after the new shot.

    If the front end of the show has been dubbed, it is backtimed to end at the same point as the beginning of the added video.

    The editor must make sure that there is enough videotape to make this correction. Adding 10 minutes to a 60-minute show on a one-hour tape cannot be accomplished.

This procedure must be approached cautiously. Editing a show takes time and patience. Erasing a portion of the video is a big move and must be done only when the editor has backed up the video and protected the tape as much as possible.

PERSONNEL

Any piece of equipment, from an expensive film-to-tape transfer machine to an inexpensive off-line system or character generator, is only as good as its operator. Good equipment in bad hands is worthless. A good editor, a clever machine operator, and a reputable on-line facility can make the difference between a high-quality, profitable venture and a dud. Unqualified or sloppy personnel can do irreparable damage to a production.

SUMMARY

The professional use of video facilities and their equipment can be a pleasant experience or a nightmare. To get the most out of a commercial company, an editor must be familiar with the editing requirements of the show and the company's capabilities. Then the editor must be aware of the special circumstances discussed in this chapter.

22

Examples of Professional Video Editing

With any show, there are probably a half-dozen correct ways to edit and finish the program, five other methods that would be considered acceptable, and many, many methods that are just plain wrong. Each show tends to find its own path through the postproduction maze, depending on its technical and political (whose brother owns the editing company) needs. The following examples reflect the varied approaches to video postproduction in the real world.

NEWS

News editing is accomplished at an incredibly fast pace. This rush has been exacerbated by the competition between cable news stations, independent television stations, live broadcasts, the networks, and local broadcasters.

Much of a news show consists of clips that are shot in the field, edited, then played back during the broadcast. Most of these clips are shot with a single camera and one record machine. The footage is edited with a machine-to-machine editor. What is now coming to market is a series of editors that combine digital processing with hard drives (see Figure 22-1). These editors can operate quickly and can transfer edited material or raw footage at up to four times sound speed.

When editing a news story, especially one that is *breaking*, or happening now, there is no time to experiment. The editor, along with the producer or on-camera talent, views the original camera footage, records the narration, then

Figure 22-1 A Sony field editing station. This device has slow-motion capability, playback and record monitors, jog knobs, and audio playback and record controls. This editor is ideal for field use.

starts cutting. In some cases, the editing system is transported with the camera crew, and the clip is edited and then broadcast from the location.

Most news editors tell a similar story: They perform pre-editing preparation (coding tapes, organizing labels, recording bars and tone, and making sure the equipment is operating properly) for the first part of the shift. Then, one or two hours before the broadcast, the reporters show up with their footage and there is a mad rush to edit the stories before airtime. Editing the news is not for the faint of heart. It is a pressure-filled job, and the bigger the news operation, the greater the pressure.

There are editing systems in some remote trucks. Here the reporter helps the editor put the piece together on location and the live reporting and the edited piece are broadcast from the truck.

If the production crew and reporter have done their job, the heart of the story will appear at the front and middle of the reel, often with the reporter talking on camera. Action footage available on location should be cutaway footage that can be used to cover jump cuts. The editor often works in conjunction with the producer or on-air talent, madly throwing cassettes into the machines, hoping there is enough time to go back and cover the jump cuts and perhaps include that special shot. There is a very funny, and somewhat accurate, news editing scene in the movie *Broadcast News*.

Larger news operations spend time and money on the production of feature news stories. These edited pieces take longer to put together because they use computer-generated graphics and digital video effects. Many news specials are off-line edited on a computer editing system before the on-line session.

MULTIPLE-CAMERA VIDEO PRODUCTION

Many television shows, especially *sitcoms* (situational comedies) are shot with multiple cameras. Each camera is recorded on a separate video machine. Usually two complete performances are taped. The first is often called the "dress rehearsal." The second can be the "air taping" or "final performance." Some sitcoms tape their shows in front of a live audience, while others work on closed sets. But even a closed set has some people in the audience. It is extremely hard to perform in a comedy without some kind of reaction, even if it is friends and family who are watching.

After the two shows have been completed, the director often asks for *pick-ups*. These are scenes or lines that did not work or had flaws in both of the earlier performances. These pick-up lines and scenes are recorded using the same multiple-camera setup as the performances.

When the production is complete, window dubs are made of all the original tapes (occasionally the window dubs are recorded simultaneously with the camera originals). Often an additional window dub is made of all four camera angles on one tape. With this tape, the editor can see what each camera is recording at any particular time. This makes the shot selection somewhat easier. In the off-line editing suite, the editor and the director choose the best angles and takes for each performance from the two performances and the pick-up scenes/lines. During the off-line session, usually on a nonlinear editor, the show is edited to a specific running time with the proper breaks for commercials. Once the director, executive staff, and occasionally the talent have approved the off-line cut, the show is finished either in a linear or nonlinear editing system. A sweetening process follows, and the program is often color corrected as well. The finished show is delivered to the network or station for broadcast.

SEGMENT SHOWS

With the demand for less-expensive programming, more and more reality shows are being broadcast. The "best of," dating games, survival shows, nature shows, home video shows, rescue, and police programs are particularly common

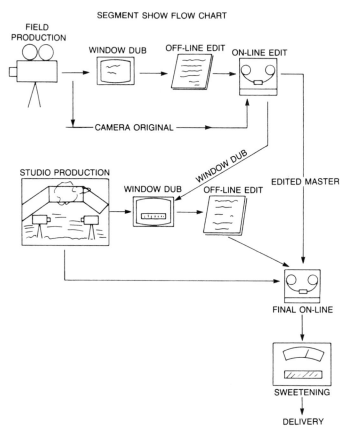

Figure 22-2 A segment show flow chart.

shows that are edited in segments. These shows use pre-edited segments that are combined with studio footage to make the program. The segments are often shot on location or in studio using single-camera or multiple-camera techniques. The segments are off-lined using window dubs. Once the segments are approved and on-lined, the remainder of the show is recorded. These wraparounds are combined with the segments in an on-line session. The final master is sweetened before being broadcast. Figure 22-2 illustrates the steps of a segment show.

COMMERCIALS

Commercials go through many revisions. The corporate representatives, director, lawyers, and advertising agency representatives are involved in the postproduction process. Obviously, this becomes a political juggling act as each of the players tries to take creative control. However, there is a great deal of money in editing commercials and the people in demand live very well. A combination of graphics and editorial sense is most important in commercial editing. There are a number of ways that a commercial can be cut. Most large commercial editing companies use random-access editors to the exclusion of all other types of editing.

INFOMERCIALS

Infomercials have become a common broadcast product. These shows are scripted and shot like other studio programs. They are usually shot with multiple cameras, but budgets can restrict the number of recorders. Higher-budgeted shows will have each camera's feed recorded, or a director can be live-switching the program. If a mistake is made, the performers back up and pick up where the error occurred. Again, the number of special effects, complexity of the show's graphics, and amount of audio work done on the program are directly related to the show's budget.

LIVE SHOWS

Live shows, such as sporting events or award ceremonies, often have edited segments played back during the broadcast. These segments may include interviews, promotional pieces on specific colleges, a brief biography of an individual who is playing in a sporting event, a clip from a music video, or a scene from a motion picture. Often these clips are edited weeks ahead of the broadcast.

SUMMARY

There is no ideal editing process. Each show has its own requirements in terms of look, speed of completion, equipment, budget, and personal preferences. With the tremendous flexibility of video, there are usually several right (and many wrong) ways to fulfill a show's postproduction needs.

23

Finding a Job in Postproduction

Video editing can provide a challenging, lucrative, and enjoyable career. Every show is different, the footage is never the same, and the demands of each program vary. Video editing is creative, challenging, and always new. Given identical footage, 10 editors will come up with 10 different versions of the same show.

There are many types of editing: show editing, commercial editing, motion picture promotion, sports and comedy editing, cable editing, and documentary editing. There is off-line, on-line, linear, and nonlinear editing.

The video editing job market continues to grow, even outside the broadcast community; hospitals have extensive video departments, as do department stores and car and electronics manufacturers. Large corporations and smaller companies offer management jobs overseeing video productions. Small video companies, larger network production companies, cable companies, local television stations, and nationwide television networks offer thousands of editing opportunities. Although off-line and on-line editing facilities hire numerous editors, some people choose to go it alone, earning some or all of their living taping Little League baseball games and weddings.

NARROWING DOWN THE FIELD

The first step in finding a job in postproduction is deciding where you want to work and what type of program you want to edit. Should you work in a big city or small town? Which is preferable: working with home videos, corporate videos, or television programs? How about a career in editing instructional programs or documentaries?

Competition and Cash

Video has become a popular field, and more and more schools are offering video courses. As people graduate from these schools and enter the marketplace, competition increases in all areas of the industry. Landing a good job requires talent, expertise, and a certain degree of politicking. Résumés and reels demonstrating your talent and experience are important tools to use in the search for employment.

As a general rule, you should begin a career in the type of company that reflects your ultimate goals. Starting out in a small town and hoping to someday move to New York does not work as well as going to the city, getting a feel for the environment, and meeting the people who can help advance your career. Knowing the right people is often half the challenge of getting a job. This is true not only for the political connections, but because desirable jobs are often filled by word of mouth. There are no ads in the papers for a nonlinear off-line sitcom editor. Your friends in that small town cannot always help you land a job in the big city.

The pay scale for well-trained, professional video editors, tape operators, film transfer technicians, and postproduction coordinators is wide. One point to remember is that more money usually means more responsibility. In addition, jobs in larger cities usually pay more, but the cost of living is higher and the competition tougher. Corporate video editing usually does not pay as well as editing network television programs. However, the pay scale is rising at some of the larger corporations, especially as the powers-that-be recognize the vast influence a video department can have.

Employment Opportunities

More and more companies are installing their own video equipment. Some corporate installations have only two video machines, while others have multiple on-line editing bays that run several shifts (see Figure 23-1). With the cost of video production and postproduction still dropping, the video boom has crept into every conceivable type of company.

Some of the ways in which individuals earn income from video editing are not always readily apparent. Artists have received grants for video projects as well as video documentaries. There are also internships available in many production, advertising, and postproduction companies. Certain educational facilities hire videotape editors, as do companies that teach professional editing.

Real estate companies show houses on videotape in the office, saving both the agent and the prospective buyer the time and expense of traveling to a location. Point-of-purchase advertising (tapes played in stores to promote a special item of sale) is often edited by a store's in-house video department, and corporate video newsletters are sent through a video network.

Figure 23-1 An on-line studio editing room.

One company makes videotapes that play at a well-known resort hotel and describe the surrounding places of interest. These tapes are hour-long commercials for nearby tourist attractions and are set up so that segments can be easily added or deleted. Other enterprising individuals traveled to Hawaii to shoot exotic footage. After editing, the tapes were sold to distributors for home video rental or were marketed directly to consumers by mail. One individual shot large bulldozers and earthmovers at work. That home videotape made the producer a millionaire.

Editing for television is also a growing field. If network and local broadcasting seem voracious in their demands for programming, cable is insatiable. All these shows must be edited somewhere (usually at a well-known editing company in a large city), and editors are needed to staff these facilities (see Figures 23-2 and 23-3).

PLAN OF ACTION

Once you have determined an area of employment, it is probably best to move close to a facility that offers those specific opportunities. For instance, if you wish to work on hospital-type programs, you should contact some of the leading hospitals in your location of choice and find out what types of positions are available.

Assistant director
Assistant editor
Audio cutter
Audio mixer
Graphics operator
Client representative
Computer animator
Editor
Effects coordinator
Effects creator
Effects supervisor
Facilities scheduler
Facilities owner
Foley artist
Gopher
Graphics
Graphics manager
Graphics creator
Offline editor
Online editor
Postproduction coordinator
Postproduction supervisor
Production assistant
Sales
Script assistant
Sound designer
Tape room assistant
Telecine assistant
Telecine operator
Vault personnel

Figure 23-2 Potential jobs in postproduction.

If you want to edit network shows, then New York and Los Angeles are the places to go. You should seek an entry-level position at a production company if you are interested in the management aspect of postproduction, or an entry-level position at an editing company if that is your area of interest. As with any job, there is no one way to secure the perfect position. But no matter what your ultimate goal may be, it is best to go right to the production source and get some kind of job inside the business. Making personal contacts is an excellent way to move up the professional ladder.

THE POLITICAL ARENA

People hire people they know, especially in the entertainment industry. Even in corporate situations, if a person knows one applicant and does not know another,

Animal comedy
Cartoons
Clip shows
Corporate videos
Daily network news
Documentary
Drama
Fashion show
Feature film
Game shows
Home improvement
Home video
How-to videos
Industrials
Informational programs
Local news
Move behind the scenes
Movie promotion
Movies of the week
Music videos
National commercials
Network news specials
Network specials
News
Public service announcements
Reality shows
Regional commercials
Sitcoms
Sports
Sports promos

Figure 23-3   Some types of shows that are edited electronically.

with all other things being equal, the known individual will be hired. If you decide to pursue a network editing job, contacts are vital. The best method in any industry is to become known to those in power or those who do the hiring.

Being the best editor in the world is a good calling card, but unless the people hiring know who is the best and who is available, the editor probably will not be hired. One way to meet those who are hiring is to work as a freelance editor. Rather than being a staff editor, the freelancer works one job at a time, sometimes one day at a time, for a variety of clients. In this way, the editor finds out about the facilities as well as the people in each location. It also allows the people at the facilities to get to know the freelance editor.

The premise always remains the same: The editor needs clients and a facility. The only way to meet these people is to get close to the individuals who work in your chosen field and make friends with them. Friends will hire a friend before they will hire a stranger; it is as simple as that.

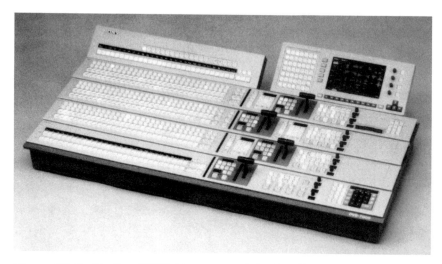

Figure 23-4 The Sony DVS 7000, a master switcher found in broadcast control centers. This on-air switcher is operated by quick-moving technical directors (TDs) who control which signal (of up to 100) is going to be broadcast from the network.

THE EXPANDING NUMBER OF JOBS IN POSTPRODUCTION

There are more and more jobs in video postproduction, and also more types of editing controllers, tape formats, and editing jobs. This fractionalization of the market requires more training and more knowledge of different types of editing. A good editor can cut any type of show, but editors are paid for their experience.

The previously mentioned plan of action should always be in the editor's mind. For example, if you want to cut sitcoms, random-access editors and program formats are items that you should thoroughly understand.

SUMMARY

The video revolution has invaded the home and the corporate world, opening new avenues of employment and offering new challenges. Whatever aspect of video postproduction appeals to the new editor, employment opportunities are here to stay and will undoubtedly continue to grow as the video field expands even further.

24

A Look into the Future

Video is an electronic medium, and the electronic world is constantly changing. The video reality that exists today will change. High definition is already altering how we shoot, edit, and watch all the visual media. Equipment is changing (see Figure 24-1). Television and movies are already being shot in this new format. Surround sound will probably become a standard in all high-definition broadcasts. The 4 × 3 picture will gradually disappear. Reruns of *Gilligan's Island* and *The Dick Van Dyke Show* may not stay in their original 4 × 3 format when broadcast in high definition.

As more technological improvements are implemented, more sophisticated, high-paying jobs will be created. The difference between random-access off-line editing and random-access on-line will probably disappear. What you edit will be the final program.

Most movies will continue to be shot on film, but the postproduction chores will enter the domain of electronic editing. Most of the feature film effects are now being created on computers and then output onto film.

DESKTOP EDITING SYSTEMS

One of the fastest-growing areas of postproduction will continue to be desktop editing systems. These systems, which have made three-quarter-inch editing obsolete, will drive the price of on-line editing into affordable off-line/on-line systems. Already, home editing systems are very powerful. Learning "Final Cut Pro," or Adobe's "Premier," or any of the other systems is a great training ground for entry into the professional postproduction field.

Ultimately, film dailies will be delivered to editors on DV or password-protected DVDs. Then low-cost editors will be used to cut features and promos,

Figure 24-1 A Sony high-definition switcher. With switchable HD formats, sophisticated color correction, and computer controllability, it is in operation at a Hollywood hi-def postproduction facility. Photo courtesy of American Production Center, North Hollywood, California.

with the output of these systems used to on-line (either linear or nonlinear) the programs.

RANDOM-ACCESS NEWS EDITING

Random-access invaded the television and motion picture world and now it is headed for the newsroom. Special cameras will record digital images that can then be transmitted to the station and loaded directly into huge memory systems at the station. The day's footage will be available immediately to the entire station and/or network. Editing will be incredibly fast. There will be no dubs because the station can air the finished piece from the same file server that is storing the field footage.

VIDEO PROJECTION AND EDITING

Theaters will probably install huge video screens that can project satellite transmissions based on a single print of a motion picture. This process would eliminate thousands of film prints that are now physically transported from theater to theater around the world. As for editing, random-access editors will continue to drop in price and become more powerful and more accessible to the general public.

SUMMARY

No matter what changes, editors will still be cutting pictures and making edits. The machines might change and the technical process might be different, but people will still be required to choose the right shots and place them in a logical, creative order.

And if all these amazing changes do come about, there will only be more employment opportunities in the postproduction world.

Appendix:
Compatibility

The video editing environment comprises many types of computers and machines. Each machine has its limitations in addition to its compatibility with other, similar machines.

VIDEO RECORD MACHINE COMPATIBILITY

Any video machine can, if not properly maintained, make a recording that only it can play back. To avoid this situation, a videotape record machine must be regularly checked and maintained.

Editing into a tape that was created on another video machine will often require some adjustment. You should pay careful attention to the chroma and video record levels, tension, and skew, and should also look for potential whips.

COMPUTER EDIT DECISION LIST COMPATIBILITY

In the early days of editing, there was neither a standard format EDL nor a standard technical method for recording an EDL on a computer diskette or paper punch tape. Today, although the CMX and Grass Valley (GVG) formats have been recognized as the industry standards, a number of editing systems have been marketed, and there is no guarantee that floppy disks will be compatible.

Most disks created by editing systems of the same company are compatible, but when planning to use the floppy disk of an EDL from one type of computer editor on another, you should first check their compatibility. Also, most linear editing systems are on IBM-compatible or RT11 hardware. Avid random-access editors run on Apple computers. Sony Linear editors use IBM-compatible disks. Older Grass Valley editing systems use RT11. It is a good idea to have your EDLs put on both an Apple-formatted disk and an IBM-type disk to save any confusion during the on-line session. Many computer editing companies will either convert or accept other machines' EDLs. You should discuss the disk requirements and limitations with any facility that you are intending to use. Another good idea is to input a short EDL to see everything is working correctly. There are also computer programs that will convert one EDL format to another ("Phoenix" and prereader! are two such programs).

VIDEOTAPE

Within the United States, VHS is a standard video format, as are digi Beta, Beta SP, and three-quarter-inch. Some machines are backward compatible, that is, they can play earlier versions of recordings in the same format. For instance, some digital Betacams have an option that allows them to play back analogue Beta SP recordings. One cannot assume, however, that this compatibility is always available. One should always check to see if the proposed on-line facility has the capability to play back the proposed video format without the time-consuming and expensive process of dubbing the footage from one format to another and then editing.

CHARACTER GENERATOR FLOPPY DISKS

Generally speaking, each type of character generator writes its storage diskettes in a different format. There is no industry standard for character generators.

INTERNATIONAL STANDARDS

Each country has its own broadcast standard. The NTSC recommendations were accepted by the FCC as a national standard for the United States. This standard consists of a 525-line, 29.97-frames-per-second scanning system, which is also used in Japan and South America (countries using alternating current of 60 cycles per second).

PAL is another standard, which is a modified form of NTSC. PAL uses 625 lines and 25-frames-per-second scanning.

A third major video standard, SECAM, varies significantly from NTSC and PAL. Though incompatible, SECAM also uses 625 lines, scanned at 25 frames per second.

None of these systems is compatible; an NTSC recording cannot be played back on a SECAM tape machine. Following is a list of the different formats and the countries that use them:

NTSC—Antilles, Bahamas, Barbados, Bermuda, Bolivia, Burma, Canada, Cayman Islands, Chile, Colombia, Costa Rica, Cuba, Curaçao, Dominican

Republic, Ecuador, El Salvador, Greenland, Guam, Guatemala, Honduras, Jamaica, Japan, Mexico, Nicaragua, North America, Panama, Peru, Philippines, Puerto Rico, Sri Lanka, North Korea, South Korea, Surinam, Taiwan, Trinidad, Venezuela, Vietnam, Virgin Islands

SECAM—Bulgaria, Congo, Czechoslovakia, Egypt, East Germany, France, French Guyana, Gabon, Greece, Guadeloupe, Haiti, Hungary, Iran, Iraq, Ivory Coast, Luxembourg, Madagascar, Martinique, Monaco, Morocco, New Caledonia, Niger, Poland, Rumania, Russia, Saudi Arabia, Senegal, Syria, Tahiti, Tunisia, Zaire

PAL—Afghanistan, Algeria, Argentina, Australia, Austria, Bahrain, Bangladesh, Belgium, Brazil, Brunei, Canary Islands, China, Cyprus, Denmark, Ethiopia, Fiji, Finland, Ghana, Gibraltar, Great Britain, Hong Kong, Iceland, India, Indonesia, Ireland, Israel, Italy, Jordan, Kenya, Kuwait, Liberia, Malaysia, Malta, Mongolia, Mozambique, The Netherlands, New Zealand, Nigeria, Norway, Oman, Pakistan, Paraguay, Portugal, Qatar, Sierra Leone, Singapore, Spain, Sudan, Swaziland, Sweden, Switzerland, Tanzania, Thailand, Turkey, Uganda, United Arab Emirates, United Kingdom, Uruguay, West Germany, Yemen, Zambia, Zanzibar, Zimbabwe

PAL and SECAM—Burundi

Bibliography

INTERNET SOURCES

http://www.ashtabuladigital.com/p4deals.html
http://www.atsc.org/Standards/A54/a_54.pdf
http://www.cybertheater.com/Tech_Reports/HD_Projectors/hd_projector.html
http://www.digitalvideosolutions.com/articles/tapeformats.htm
http://www.dtvcity.com/resources/dtvchart.html
http://www.dvgear.com/videoformats.html
http://www.henninger.com/library/hdtvfilm/
http://www.highdef.org/
http://www.hut.fi/~iisakkil/videoformats.html
http://www.laserpacific.com/high_definition.html
http://www.panasonic.com/pbds/production.html
http://www.usa.quantel.com/dfb/
http://www.videoexpert.home.att.net/artic3/262hdvr.htm
http://www.videofonics.com/videofonics/glossary.html

MAGAZINES

Digital Television, October 1999, Vol. 2, No. 10, Cahners Business Information, New York, NY

DV Magazine, April 2000, CMP Media, San Francisco, CA

Editors Guild Magazine, July/August 2001, Vol. 22, No. 3, Motion Picture Editors Guild, Hollywood, CA

Editors Guild Magazine, September/October 2001, Vol. 22, No. 4, Motion Picture Editors Guild, Hollywood, CA

Editors Guild Magazine, May/June 2001, Vol. 21, No. 3, Motion Picture Editors Guild, Hollywood, CA

Film & Video, June 2001, Vol. 18, Issue 6, PBI Media, Los Angeles, CA

Hollywood Reporter, New Media IV: Digital Filmmaker Special Issue, Vol. CCCLXIII, No. 32, June 23, 2000, Los Angeles, CA

In Camera, January 2001, Kodak Limited and Eastman Kodak Company, Rochester, NY

In Camera, October 2001, Kodak Limited and Eastman Kodak Company, Rochester, NY

Millimeter, April 2000, Intertec Publishing, Skokie IL

Millimeter, May 2001, Vol. 29, No. 5, New York, NY

Video Systems, August 2001, Primedia Business Magazine, Overland Park, KS
Video Systems, May 2001, Primedia Business Magazine, Overland Park, KS
Video Systems, April 2000, Primedia Business Magazine, Overland Park, KS
Video Systems, March 2000, Primedia Business Magazine, Overland Park, KS

TEXTBOOKS

Anderson, Gary H. *Video Editing.* 2nd ed. White Plains, NY: Knowledge Industry Publications, Inc., 1988.

Anderson, Gary H. *Electronic Post-Production: The Film-to-Video Guide.* White Plains, NY: Knowledge Industry Publications, Inc., 1986.

Avid Media Composer User's Guide. Tewksbury, MA: Avid Technologies, Inc., 1994.

Browne, Steven E. *Film-Video Terms and Concepts.* Boston: Focal Press, 1992.

Browne, Steven E. *The Video Tape Post-Production Primer.* Burbank, CA: Wilton Place Communications, 1982.

EECO. *The Time Code Book.* Santa Ana, CA: EECO Inc., 1984.

Fuller, Barry J., Steve Kanaba, and Janyce Kanaba-Brisch. *Single Camera Video Production.* Englewood Cliffs, NJ: Prentice-Hall, Inc., 1982.

Harwood, Don. *Everything You Always Wanted to Know About Videotape Recording.* Syosset, NY: VTR Publishing, 1983.

Millerson, Gerald. *Video Production Handbook.* 2nd ed. Boston: Focal Press, 1992.

Ohanian, Thomas. *Digital Nonlinear Editing: New Approaches to Editing Film and Video.* Boston: Focal Press, 1993.

Paulson, C. Robert. *BM/E's ENG/EFP/EPP Handbook.* New York: Broadband Information Services, Inc., 1981.

Roberts, Kenneth H., and Win Sharples, Jr. *A Primer for Filmmaking.* New York: Pegasus, 1972.

Schetter, Michael D. *Videotape Editing.* Elk Grove, IL: Swiderski Electronics, 1982.

Weise, Marcus. *Videotape Operations.* Woodland Hills, CA: Weynand and Associates, 1984.

Weynand, Diana. *Computerized Videotape Editing.* Woodland Hills, CA: Weynand and Associates, 1983.

Glossary

4×3   The aspect ratio (width : height) of conventional (NTSC) TV and computer displays.

16 × 9 (16 by 9)   A widescreen television format in which the aspect ratio of the screen is 16 units wide by 9 high as opposed to the 4 × 3 of normal TV. 16 × 9 can be a high-definition image or a 16 × 9 image displayed on a 4 × 3 screen, which would leave black stripes on the top and bottom of the image.

A & B rolls   Two separate reels of video or film on which scenes are alternately placed to perform special effects.

A-frame edit   A video edit that starts on the first frame of the 5 video frame (4 film frame) sequence created when 24-frame film is transferred to 30-frame video (see 3:2 pull-down). The A-frame is the only frame in the sequence where a film frame is completely reproduced on one and only one complete video frame. Here is the full sequence. (The letters correspond to film frames.) A-frame = video fields 1&2, B-frame = video fields 1&2&1, C-frame = video fields 2&1, D-frame = video fields 2&1&2.

A mode   A description of a computer on-line procedure in which the edits are recorded sequentially starting with the first edit, then the second, and so on. Also referred to as an A mode assembly or assemble 1. See also **B mode**.

Address track time code   Time code that has been recorded onto the address track of a three-quarter-inch format videocassette. Address track time code must be recorded at the same time as the video signal. Only certain machines can record this type of time code, and not all brands or models are compatible.

ADR   The abbreviation for automatic dialogue replacement. Process in which a loop of video or film is created so that a performer can repeatedly deliver a line while watching the footage.

AGC   The abbreviation for automatic gain control.

All stop   The abort command on a computer editor, usually activated by pressing the space bar.

Ambient audio   See **Room tone**.

Ampex   The company that invented the quad videotape machine and markets many video products, from videotape to one-inch machines to editors.

Analog   The storage or encoding of a signal through the use of continuously varying voltages representing signal characteristics. See also **Digital**.

253

Animatic A test of a commercial. By using several drawings and a video camera with a zoom lens, a commercial is simulated using the artwork, the camera work, and the editing (including simple effects) to demonstrate how the spot might look.

Animation The drawing (either electronically or in a physical medium) of motion. Usually animation is completed in a frame-by-frame process.

Aspect ratio The ratio of a picture or display's width to its height. A standard definition NTSC TV has a 4 × 3 (1.33:1) aspect ratio. HDTV and 16:9 Enhanced DVD has a 16 × 9 (1.78:1) aspect ratio. Many films have a 1.85:1 aspect ratio, while some (e.g., CinemaScope or Panavision) have 2.35:1 aspect ratios. Other ratios are also used.

Assemble recording A technical method of recording video. An assemble recording replaces all existing video, audio, and control track with new signals. See also **Insert recording**.

Audio The sound portion of any show.

Audio-only An edit that records only audio, not affecting the picture portion of the record tape. The only way that an audio-only edit can be performed is by making an insert recording.

Audio/video keys The keys or switches on editing keyboards that designate whether an edit will record audio, video, or both.

Auto assembly An automatic on-line edit in which an EDL is loaded into a computer editor and the computer performs edits as the human editor watches for technical problems in the video. In almost all cases, these assemblies use an insert recording, not an assemble recording.

Automatic gain control (AGC) An electronic device in an audio circuit that automatically raises and lowers the record volume. This type of circuit should be used with caution because of its tendency to raise and lower background sounds between words or other sounds that are meant to be recorded. Video cameras also have an AGC circuit. This device opens and closes the aperture on the camera, depending on the amount of light available. Most professional camera operators do not use the AGC.

AVRxx The designation of digital recording level used in Avid® random-access editors. AVR1 is the lowest quality level of picture representation; AVR77 is one of the highest. AVR77 is on-line picture quality, but it is not anywhere near the same quality of a digital Betacam.

Avid® One of the established random-access editing systems using digitized video and audio to store information.

B mode Also called a checkerboard assembly. An on-line procedure in which all edits from the available playback reel are performed, skipping edits that require different reels. Then another group of playback reels is loaded, and the edits from those reels are performed, until the show is completed. This method requires that the entire EDL be loaded into the computer editor and that the EDL be perfect. See also **C mode**.

Background (1) The source of video over which other video sources are keyed. See also **Key cut**. (2) The area behind the main action in a visual frame.

Back porch   That portion of the blanking interval from the end of the color burst to the beginning of the picture signal.

Backtiming   The process of placing a particular point in an edit by calculating the distance from the designated point to the end of the edit.

Bars   A reference signal recorded on the beginning of a videotape for the purpose of aligning the playback of that tape. Most often, an audio reference (tone) is recorded at the same time as the bars.

Bay   Another word for an editing room.

Betacam   The brand name of Sony broadcast-quality half-inch videotape and recorders. A standard in news and low- to medium-budget video productions, the camera and recorder are contained in one lightweight unit. The recorder also has a Dolby encoder, an audio limiter, and the ability to record address track time code. Slow-motion playback of this format is available. This format is also available in a metal tape format (Betacam SP®) and a digital format that can play back analog or digital recordings. This format is being replaced by Betacam SX and DVCPRO.

Bins   (1) Electronic storage areas where edit decision lists are kept. (2) Metal containers with hanging devices where strips of film are stored during the film editing process.

Black   In NTSC video, this level of white is also called pedestal or setup level. On a waveform monitor, black is measured at 7.5 IRE units (see Chapter 4 on time base correctors and video scopes). Anything below this level is considered part of the horizontal blanking and is unacceptable as part of the video broadcast signal according to FCC definitions. Blank tape is not black tape. Blank tape is blank, devoid of any video signal. Consider video black as a video signal. In some editing systems, black (BLK) is used in the EDL to indicate that the source of the edit is black.

Black and coded tape   A videotape onto which a video signal of black (7.5 IRE units) and time code has been recorded.

Black-video-black preview   See **BVB**.

Blanking   A portion of the video signal that is not displayed by normal television sets. The technical information for making the picture (the horizontal blanking) and information such as automatic color tuning and vertical interval time code (the vertical blanking) are recorded in this area. During the blanking interval, the electron beam that scans the picture tube is blanked to retrace to the beginning of the next line of video or to the start of the next video field. Blanking is created by the original video source, which can be a camera or a film-to-tape transfer. Vertical blanking is 20 to 21.5 lines. Horizontal blanking is to be 10.3 to 11.4 microseconds.

BLK   In an EDL, an indication that the source of the edit is black.

Blocking   The planned movement of performers or the camera.

Bosch-Fernseh   The inventors and manufacturers of the Type B videotape format.

Both cut   A cut that records both audio and video.

Breezeway   That portion of the horizontal blanking interval from the end of the sync pulse to the beginning of the color burst.

Broadcast   To modulate a signal onto a radio frequency and beam that signal into the atmosphere for the purpose of being received and decoded (demodulated).

Broadcast quality   A term that refers to the technical specifications of the video signal and the actual look of that signal. A technically perfect video signal might look terrible. For instance, a VHS tape, properly doctored through a digital effects generator, might meet a station's technical requirements but be rejected because it is not a broadcast-quality picture. Each broadcast company, network, or station has its own level of quality.

Bulk eraser   A machine that creates a limited but very strong magnetic field. Placing a videotape on this machine will disorganize the magnetic particles on the tape, effectively erasing any signal on that tape. There is no protection for any tape placed on a bulk eraser once the machine is turned on.

Bump   A term used in reference to transferring video from one format to another. For instance, three-quarter-inch tape could be bumped to one-inch, or a two-inch tape to Betacam.

Burned-in time code   Another way to describe the window in a window dub.

Buzzing   See **Ringing**.

BVB   An acronym for black-video-black. A preview that shows black, the incoming edit portion, then black again.

C   In an EDL, an indication that the edit is a cut (as opposed to a dissolve, wipe, or key).

C mode   Another form of checkerboard assembly. An on-line procedure in which all edits from the available playback reel are performed in ascending order. All edits from one reel are accomplished first, shuffling the record machine back and forth, while the playback reel moves forward to the next edit, saving shuttle time and therefore edit time. This method requires that the EDL be clean and accurate, because the entire show cannot be viewed until the on-line is completed. See also **B mode**.

Camera   See **Video camera** and **Film camera**.

Camera original   The first-generation videotape that has the original camera signal recorded on it. If there were two tape machines recording a signal from one particular camera, there would be two camera originals of that footage.

Cartridge machine   Also known as a cart machine. A machine used at television stations to roll commercials automatically. For instance, 20 commercials in separate quad cartridges might be loaded into a tractor-like mechanism. A master computer would then tell each cartridge when to play. An audio cart machine performs a similar function at automated ratio stations.

Cassette   A videotape or audio tape contained in its own housing.

CCD   The abbreviation for charge-coupled device, an electronic chip that converts light into electrical impulses. The CCD has replaced pick-up tubes in most video cameras.

CCIR 601   The standard for digitizing component video. For NTSC, this standard calls for an image of 720 by 486 pixels sampled at 4:2:2 with a depth of either 8 or 10 bits.

Character generator An electronic device that creates letters and symbols in video. The top-of-the-line models can store video frames and create effects similar to wipes, dissolves, and digital effects.

Checkerboard assembly See **B mode**, **C mode**, **D mode**, and **E mode**.

Chroma key A key that electronically cuts a specific color out of a background picture and inserts another video source in that hole.

Client The person directly responsible for booking, paying for, and/or supervising a session.

Clip (1) A short segment of a program. (2) To crop or eliminate a portion of a picture. Key clipping circuitry will cut off a limit of the white (luminance) value of a picture.

Closed caption A signal that carries subtitling information in a broadcast signal. This encoded signal is inserted into the vertical interval. Devices can be purchased that decode the information and display the text on the screen.

Close-up The camera framing of an object or person. A close-up shows a person from approximately the shoulders up, leaving headroom at the top of the frame.

CMX The company created by CBS Labs and Memorex to develop videotape editing systems. CMX was the first company to market a random-access editor and the first industry-accepted frame-accurate videotape editing system.

Coding (1) To record time code onto a videotape. (2) To print identical numbers onto film mag (magnetic tape in the shape of film used to edit, mix, and store audio) and film workprint to facilitate keeping the audio and picture in sync with each other.

Color burst A reference signal transmitted with each line of video between the end of the line's sync and the picture signal. The burst consists of a few cycles of chroma signal of known phase.

Color correction The changing of color shadings in a video picture. The process of color correction is time-consuming, so it is much wiser to get the color balance right during the production. Color correction can be as simple as changing the hue on a time base corrector or as complicated as using a machine that breaks down the video signal into its original components and then adjusts certain elements of those components. A video signal might require color correction for various reasons: (1) the camera was not white-balanced (see **White balance**); (2) one of the camera's color pickup tubes was not working correctly; (3) a playback was not properly set up to bars during an original edit, requiring that the shot be fixed to balance the color of one or several shots; (4) a color shot must be made black-and-white (see **Color burst**).

Color corrector A machine that is capable of drastically altering the color levels of a video signal.

Component video recording A technical method of recording a color picture on videotape that separates the black-and-white portion of the signal from the chroma. This method is used in half-inch professional video formats such as Betacam, Beta SP, MII, and digital recordings.

Composite   The encoding of complete video information into one signal. Originally designed for broadcasting, this process was used extensively in postproduction until the late 1980s when component switchers, video recorders, and other devices allowed for the creation of totally component signal paths. Component is a more accurate signal than composite.

Compositing   The process of combining numerous visual elements in the frame. Compositing can consist of still or action footage. With the advent of D1 and D2, along with the digital switchers and other digital devices, compositing has become a common practice in commercial and high-end postproduction projects.

Compression   (1) To proportionally lower the volume of a signal that crosses a predetermined threshold. (2) The process of reducing the size of digital information, usually by throwing out redundant information.

Computer edit   An edit performed by a computerized editing machine or the generic term for a computer on-line edit.

Computer editing system   An editing system that is capable of storing more than one edit and has the ability to manipulate the EDL for list cleaning. A computer editing system uses time code to locate specific positions on the playback and record tapes.

Computer In/Out keys   A group of keys that initiate the output of a computer EDL. Input and output can be in the form of punch tape, a printout, or a diskette.

Computer memory   Each computer editing system has a finite amount of memory for EDL storage. Some editors hold up to 100 edits, while others can hold several thousand. When the memory is full, it is time to save the EDL to punch tape, a printout, or a diskette. There is also a difference in the way that computer memory works. In some editing systems, the computer will remember the EDL even if the power is turned off. In others, the information in memory is erased when the power is turned off. Both types of computers can protect the EDL by backup to a printout or a diskette.

Continuity   The smooth flow of action and content during a program. This flow is controlled by careful attention to detail during the production.

Control track   An electronic signal recorded on videotape at each head revolution and each field that tells the next machine how to play back that particular video signal. It is similar in concept to the sprocket holes in film. Some editing machines, called control track, backspace, or pulse editors, use these pulses for editing.

Countdown   A leader at the head of a program, which counts backward until two seconds before the show. At two seconds, a brief audio beep is recorded as part of the countdown. See also **Two pop**.

Cross-pulse monitor   A television monitor capable of putting the horizontal and/or vertical blanking in the center of the screen so that these signals can be more closely examined.

CRT   The acronym for cathode-ray tube. This electronic device is the screen in televisions and computer displays. In most cases in this book, CRT refers to the computer display on an editing system.

Crystal-controlled playback   The audio playback to which a performer lip syncs during a videotaped performance. This playback must run at a perfectly constant speed. Digital audio tapes (DATs) are most often used these days for playback. Digital tapes run at a constant rate, as a crystal-controlled machine does. A variable-speed playback will cause each take of the performance to be slightly different. Because a normal reel-to-reel machine does not run at a perfectly constant speed, an editor must use a crystal-controlled machine, a DAT, or DA88.

CU   The abbreviation for close-up.

Cut   The complete and immediate change from one image or sound to another in video, film, or audio. This was the first effect used in editing.

Cutaway   A shot, edited in a scene, that cuts away from the main action.

Cuts-only editor   An editor that performs only cuts.

D   In an EDL, an indication that the edit is a dissolve (as opposed to a cut, wipe, or key).

D mode   An EDL list which is organized in such a way that a playback reel is used in its entirety, as in the B mode assembly, but with all effects listed at the bottom of the EDL.

D1   Digital videotape format using the CCIR 601 standard to record 4:2:2 component video on 19 mm tape. Currently the highest quality videotape format generally available. The first digital videotape format, hence D1.

D2   Digital videotape format using the 4 fsc method to record composite digital video. Uses 19 mm tape and a cassette similar to D1. The second digital videotape format, hence D2.

D3   Digital videotape format using 4 fsc composite signals like D2, but recorded on 12.5 mm (one-half-inch) tape. The third digital videotape format.

D4   The number 4 is considered unlucky in Japan, so there is no D4.

D5   Digital videotape format using CCIR 601, 4:2:2 video. Uses the same cassette as D3.

D9   Digital videotape format using CCIR 601, 4:2:2 video compressed about 3:1.

DAT   The acronym for digital audio tape. A cassette format featuring qualitatively superior sound, referring to either a recorder or a tape. It has two tracks as well as the ability to record time code.

DAW   The acronym for digital audio workstation. This computerized mixing device can be used to create effects, edit audio, or mix programs, replacing or augmenting analog multi-track audio mixing.

DCT   Discrete cosine transform. A widely used method of video compression. Also an Ampex CCIR 601 digital VTR using DCT to compress the video before recording it to tape.

DDR   Digital disk recorder. A digital video recording device based on high-speed computer disk drives. Commonly used as a means to get video into and out of computers and for editing.

Demo reel A videotape that shows a production company's or editor's best work, usually made to sell that individual's talent or that company's services.

Demodulate To decode a signal that has been impressed onto a carrier frequency.

Digital A signal that is encoded in ones and zeros (binary code) rather than by modulating a carrier wave's signal.

Digital Betacam Digital videotape format using the CCIR 601 standard to record 4:2:2 component video in compressed form on 12.5 mm (1/2-inch) tape.

Digital effect A generic term for the effect(s) generated by a digital effects generator.

Digital effects generator A device that produces digital effects. Each device has different capabilities and limitations and has one or more channels. Each channel can manipulate one video signal. A multibox effect would require multiple channels or multiple video generations. In a very complicated sequence, both multiple channels and multiple generations might be used.

Digital video A video picture that is recorded digitally. Some machines can store single frames and short segments of video digitally on disks. There are also tape machines that can store large amounts of video digitally. Multiple generations of digital video look exactly like the camera original because the picture is recreated by digital signals rather than by copying the signal.

Disk drive The machine that reads and writes information on computer disks.

Diskette A computer disk with a magnetic coating that can record computer information. In video production and editing, these disks are used to store EDLs, character generator information, switcher information, and digital effects.

Dissolve The fading of one image into another. A dissolve from black or to black is called a fade. The dissolve or fade is made either in a film lab, through a video switcher, or by a non-linear editor.

Dolby 5.1 The channels used for Dolby Digital, DTS. The five channels are left front, center, right front, left surround, and right surround. The ".1" channel is the low-frequency effects (LFE) channel.

Dolly A shot created by movement of a camera (toward or away from a performer or object) that is usually on a set of tracks.

Downtime The time when equipment is unavailable due to malfunction or maintenance.

Drop frame time code Time-accurate time code. Drop frame time code is time accurate because it drops two numbers every minute to make up for the small error that results from assuming that video runs at exactly 30 frames per second. Because video actually runs at 29.97 frames per second, the numbers 00:00:00:00 and 00:00:00:01 are dropped every minute except at the 10-minute marks (01:10:00:00, 04:50:00:00, etc.).

Dropout A physical lack of oxide on videotape that looks like a silver bullet shooting across the screen. Sometimes base correctors will correct for this lack of picture by repeating the previous scan line.

Dropout compensator   An electronic device that senses the lack of oxide on a video-tape and repeats the scan line above it.

DT   See **Dynamic tracking**.

Dub   (1) A copy of another videotape or the process of making a copy of a tape. (2) To mix a final version of a film.

DV   Digital video. A digital tape recording format using approximately 5:1 compression to produce Betacam quality on a very small cassette. Originated as a consumer product, but being used professionally, as exemplified by Panasonic's variation, DVCPRO, and Sony's variation DVCam. These formats use a 25 Mbps data rate and 4:1:1 sampling. A variation, DVCPRO 50, uses a 50 Mbps data rate and 4:2:2 sampling.

Dynamic tracking (DT)   A process of reading videotape that locks to video rather than the control track. This process allows variable speeds other than sound speed and can also help unstable video recordings play back correctly.

E mode   A method of organizing an EDL for minimal source shuttle time as in a C mode list, but all effects are listed at the bottom of the EDL.

ECU   The abbreviation for extreme close-up.

Edit decision list (EDL)   A computer-generated or handwritten list of the edits performed in either an on-line or an off-line editing session.

Editec®   One of the first editing systems developed by Ampex and first sold in 1963.

Editing   The process of creating a structure from the pictures and/or audio in a program.

Editing bay   An editing room.

Editing on the fly   See **Sync mode**.

Editing session   The time spent in an editing facility during which the visual and audio portions are placed in order, creating a portion of a program or a completed program.

Editing suite   An editing room.

Editor   (1) A person who creatively and/or technically assists the owners of a visual show in creating a structure from pictures and audio. (2) A videotape controller that is capable of making edits.

EDL   The abbreviation for edit decision list.

EECO   The corporate developer of time code.

Effect   Any transition or combination of images other than a cut.

EIAJ   The acronym for Electronic Industries Association of Japan.

Electron beam   A stream of electrons aimed at a particular target. In television, the electron beam is aimed at a phosphorous tube. As the beam hits the phosphors, they glow, creating a picture.

Element   A portion of a show, graphics, audio, videotape, or film; especially used in describing materials for creating effects.

ENG   The abbreviation for electronic news gathering, the shooting and editing of news on video. The production process of ENG usually occurs on location.

Equalization   The changing of sound frequencies to alter the original sound, making it more pleasing to the ear.

Extreme close-up (ECU)   A camera framing of an object or person that is very close to that person or object and usually does not allow for any headroom. An ECU can also be of any part of a person's body.

F mode   A method of organizing an EDL according to source and record times so that the reel can be edited with the minimum amount of shuttling from either machine.

Fade   A dissolve to or from black, a dissolve to or from a key, or the raising or lowering of audio levels. See also **Dissolve** and **Black**.

Field (of video)   Each frame of video in the NTSC signal (the United States' television format) consists of two fields. NTSC television creates a picture through vertical lines, and each field has 262.5 lines of video. The lines are displayed on the television tube in an interlace pattern. The odd lines of each frame are scanned, producing one field, then the even lines are scanned, producing the other field. Together, the two fields create a frame.

HDTV can be either a field or complete frame recording. The letter "i" in the format (1080i) would indicate an interlaced frame, or one that is comprised of two fields.

Field dominance   The field at which an editing system begins an edit. Field 1 dominance begins the edit at the first field of a frame of video. Field 2 dominance begins an edit in the middle of the frame, on the second field. When a random-access editor runs footage backward, an inverted field dominance (field 2 then 1) should be engaged. In a linear system, this dominance is automatically reversed because the tape is physically running backwards.

Film   A strip of silver-coated acetate or polyester base, coated with a light-sensitive material, and perforated with sprocket holes on the side. The silver reacts when exposed to light. This was the first visual recording medium that could be projected. Also see **Videotape**.

Film camera   The machine that exposes a controlled amount of light to film.

Film lab   The place where film is developed and where film effects are incorporated into a project.

Film-to-tape   The process of transferring images from film positive or negative onto a videotape.

Foley   The process of creating sounds that will eventually be edited into a sound track while viewing footage of a project.

Foreground   That portion of a key signal that appears over the picture (which is called the background). In a key using a title over a newscaster, the words are considered the foreground and the newscaster the background.

Frame (of video)   A frame of NTSC video consists of two fields (see **Field**). Each second of video consists of 29.97 frames, which is usually rounded off to 30 frames a second. See **Drop frame time code** and **Non–drop frame time code**. HDTV can be comprised of either two fields or a single frame.

Frame accurate   An adjective describing an editing machine's ability to make accurate, color-framed, quality edits. Most computer-based editing systems are field accurate, meaning that an edit is performed on a specific field and can be repeated accurately.

Frame store   An electronic device that stores multiple frames of video.

Frame synchronizer   A device that accepts nonsynchronized video, stores it for a full frame, then sends the signal back out, properly timed with the rest of the video system.

Freelance   An editor, stage manager, director, or other professional who is self-employed and works for numerous employers.

Freeze frame   A frame of video that has been frozen. A freeze frame can be accomplished through the use of several electronic devices, including a video machine with dynamic tracking, a digital effects device, a frame synchronizer, a slow-motion disk, a videodisk, a frame store device, a paint box, or a high-end character generator.

Front porch   The portion of the horizontal blanking from the end of a picture to the leading edge of the sync.

Generation   One copy of a videotape. An edited master is usually one generation away from the camera original. A submaster is two generations away from the camera original. In a pure digital signal path, there is little, if any, signal degradation from one generation to the next. An analogue generation suffers greatly from each generation.

Glitches   Any oddity in a video signal. The causes of glitches run the gamut from power surges during recording to poor tape stock, control track hits, and gremlins in an editing system.

GPI   General-purpose interface. Many devices can be triggered by an electronic pulse. This trigger device is a GPI. GPIs are used to put digital video devices and other peripheral equipment into a predetermined function (play, rewind, record, or freeze).

Handles   An additional length of audio and/or video. Handles are the extra heads and tails recorded when dubbing sections of footage. The extra material ensures that there is more than enough program material for editing purposes.

HDTV   The abbreviation for high-definition television, a widescreen format with greatly improved resolution. HDTV is a catchall for a group of proposed, standard, widescreen video formats. There are six proposed HDTV formats. HDTV formats are 16:9 aspect ratios, three with 1920 × 1080 pixels and three with 1280 × 720 pixels. The 1080 formats include 1080i (interlaced) at 30 frames per second (FPS) and 1080p (progressive) at 24 and 30 FPS. The 720 formats are all progressive, 720p at 24, 30, or 60 FPS.

Headroom   The area above a person's head in the camera framing. Every shot of a person, except an extreme close-up, should have headroom.

Helical scan   A method of recording video on tape at an angle to the tape's travel, also called slant track recording. All videotape recordings are helical scan, with the exception of quad recordings.

Heterodyne   A method of viewing the unstable video signal from a videotape without the use of a time base corrector. The picture appears stable to the eye, but cannot be used as a signal for direct switcher input.

High-definition television (HDTV)   See **HDTV**.

Hiss   Unwanted background noise in an audio recording.

Horizontal blanking   The time during which the electron beam is shut off, or blanked, to allow the beam to retrace to the beginning of the next horizontal scan line. See also **Blanking**.

House   A word used in place of facility. For example, there are editing houses, dubbing houses, production houses, and sweetening houses.

Hue   The shade of a particular color.

IEEE   The acronym for Institute of Electrical and Electronics Engineers.

Image enhancement   The digital process of sharpening the image of a video picture. Often noise reduction is performed at the same time as image enhancement.

Industry standard   A term applied to a machine or format that is commonly used within a certain area of production. For instance, digital Betacam is a broadcast industry standard.

In-house   A term meaning within the company. For instance, if a show was totally edited by a corporation's video department, you would say that the show was edited in-house. If all or part of the show was edited at another facility, you would say that the show was edited out-of-house.

IN point   The beginning of a video edit. Each edit has two IN points: the IN point of the playback tape and the IN point of the record tape. Two IN points and an OUT point define a video cut.

Insert editing   The process of putting a shot between two other shots.

Insert recording   A method of video recording that does not affect the tape's control track. To make a proper insert recording, an editor must first record unbroken video and the control track on the tape in an assemble recording to ensure a continuous signal. This is the only type of video recording that can perform an audio-only or video-only edit. See also **Assemble recording**.

Interface   The electronic component that receives computer command signals and translates those signals into a command that another machine can understand.

IRE   A measure of video devised by the Institute of Radio Engineers, now called the Institute of Electrical and Electronics Engineers (IEEE).

Joystick   A device used as a variable-speed control of a videotape machine, or a device that manipulates any electronic device. Joysticks are found on digital effects generators, switchers, and home computers.

Jump cut   A cut to a similar shot, resulting in one or more objects in the frame appearing to jump into position. The most obvious example is when an edit of a person is made using the same camera angle, but the person has moved. This gives the illusion that the person, or even just the person's head, has jumped from one spot to another. Often a cutaway is used to cover jump cuts. Occasionally, jump cuts are used as an effect to make objects or people disappear. See also **Cutaway**.

Key cut   A signal from a video device to the switcher that indicates the specific area in the background where the key is to be cut. See also **Background**.

Key frame   In an electronic device, an event in a series of events that represents one step in the sequence. Key frames are used in random-access editor effects, DVE devices to define moves, and switchers to define a series of events.

Kinescope   A video-to-film transfer, often used for archiving or as a picture reference for negative cutting.

L cut   Also referred to as a split edit, this cut has either the audio or the video preceding or extending beyond a both cut.

Lay back   A sweetening term that means to record the audio mix from a multitrack recording on the original edited master. This process erases the edited production audio and replaces it with the final audio.

Lay over   A sweetening term that means to copy an edit master's audio and time code to a multitrack tape.

Layering   The building of effects, one layer at a time, that can encompass from one to hundreds of layers.

Lightworks   The brand name of a random-access editor used primarily in the editing of feature films.

Limiter   An audio circuit that stops loud noises at a predetermined level. Some video record machines have built-in limiter options.

List management   The cleaning and tracing of an EDL before an on-line edit. See also **List cleaning** and **Trace**.

Lock   Video must be locked in several ways before a technically acceptable edit can be made. Time code lock occurs when the computer has moved the record and playback tapes into their proper positions during the preroll. The tape machines must also be locked vertically and horizontally before a proper edit can be made. Most computer editing systems check these areas before going into edit, and if anything is not locked up, the edit is aborted. Occasionally, an edit is performed even though one of these variables is not locked. If this occurs, the edit may have to be performed again.

Lower thirds   Graphics keyed over an image that describe a location or state a person's name and title in the lower third of the screen.

LTC   Linear time code. Time code recorded on a linear analog track on a videotape. Also called longitudinal time code.

Luminance   The white value of a video signal.

Luminance key   This key senses the dark or light portion of a signal and cuts an electronic hole in the background in the shape of that signal. The hole is then filled with another source of video. See also **Key cut** and **Background**.

M&E   An abbreviation for music and effects tracks. Often shows that are prepared for international distribution require M&E tracks because the dialogue and narration will be translated, but the music and effects will remain in the show.

Master log   The record of a particular show that contains the reel numbers and the footage on those reels, production notes, the show's script, the EDL, where the off-line and camera original masters are stored, the time code start and stop times of each reel, credit notes and spellings, and any other information pertaining to the program.

Matte   (1) A colorized key. (2) A high-contrast image used to cut a hole in the background in a shot. Mattes are used in video and film.

Matte camera   A video camera whose purpose is to turn art cards into a video signal, allowing the switcher to combine these graphics with other video. Matte cameras can be color cameras but are usually capable of producing only black-and-white images. The black-and-white signals can be colorized in the switcher by making a matte key.

Matte key   A key cut made from a luminance key, key cut, or chroma key and filled with a switcher color.

Medium shot   A camera framing of a person or object. A medium shot of a person is usually from the waist to the head, with headroom at the top of the frame. See also **Headroom**.

Mixer   (1) A device used to combine various audio sources. (2) A person who operates an audio mixing device.

Mixing   The process of gathering and combining audio elements for a visual production.

Modulate   To encode an audio or video signal onto a carrier frequency by altering its amplitude or frequency.

Modulated wipe   A wipe is electronically bent out of its regular shape. Modulation of a wipe can curve, bend, or oscillate straight lines. A vertical wipe could be modulated into a wavy line or a circle into an oval shape.

Montage   A series of relatively quick edits, often made to a music track.

MS   The abbreviation for medium shot.

Multitrack   An audio recorder/player that has more than one audio track. A multitrack machine usually has four or more tracks. The multitrack has been replaced, for the most part, by digital audio tape, DA88s, and digital audio workstations.

Mylar®   A strong, flexible base used for the manufacture of videotape.

Network   In television, a company that delivers programs to a group of stations. There are cable networks and loosely knit station networks (sometimes called ad hoc networks). The major networks are NBC, ABC, CBS, FOX, WB, and UPN.

Nonadditive mix   A combining of two video sources, with each source having a 100% video level. In a dissolve, the highest level that two video sources can reach is 50% of each signal.

Non–drop frame time code The original time code, calculated at 30 frames per second. Since NTSC video runs at 29.97 frames per second, an error in timing builds up. The other type of time code is drop frame time code, which is time accurate.

Nonsynchronous time code Time code that is out of sync with the video it was recorded with. Time code is recorded in the middle of the video frame. If the code is not recorded in its proper place, the computer editor will think that the video frame is in one place and the video playback deck will think that it is in another. The two will fight for control of the deck, rendering the code unusable. If this happens, the reel should be rerecorded. See also **Time code generator, Regenerated time code,** and **Lock**.

NTSC The acronym for National Television Standards Committee, which created the standards for American television. This acronym also refers to the standard formulated by the committee. See the Appendix.

Off-line edit The decision-making editing session. Not all of the edits recorded during the off-line session will end up in the final version of a program.

Offset A time code duration used to find specific locations on a reel with time code different from the original.

One-inch A videotape format that is one inch wide. The two subformats of one-inch videotape are Type B and Type C, which use different recording processes and different types of videotape.

On-line edit Any video editing session that produces a master that will be used in the final product. This session might be a prebuild session designed to create portions of the final show or the assembly of various elements to build the final show.

Open-ended edit An edit that is performed without a defined OUT point. The OUT point is determined during the edit.

Opticals The film term for effects. Opticals can be anything from titles to complex computerized animation.

Original master A first-generation audio, video, or film recording. See also **Camera original**.

Oscilloscope A device that displays electronic signals on a screen. Waveform monitors and vector scopes are two types of oscilloscopes.

OUT point The end of an edit on either the playback or the record side. The OUT point is found by adding the edit duration to the time code of the IN point.

Oxide In videotape, the easily magnetized, brown, ferrous oxide material onto which the video and audio signals are recorded. Usually the oxide is on a strong, flexible backing such as Mylar. Oxide is also used on diskettes and audio tape.

PAL The acronym for phase alternate line, a recording format used in Europe and Great Britain that derives its name from the fact that the burst phase inverts every scan line.

PAL plus A widescreen (16×9) television standard used in Europe compatible with existing 4×3 TV sets. Non-16×9 TVs show the picture in a letterboxed form.

Pan   A shot created by swiveling a camera horizontally. See also **Tilt**.

Pedestal   The lowest IRE portion of the video signal. Also called the setup. In standard broadcast signals, the pedestal should not be below 7.5 IRE units. See also **Blanking** and **Black**.

Phasing   Phasing occurs when frequencies of the audio recorded on two different tracks of a tape are not synchronized. The symptoms of the problem are heard when the two tracks are played back together. If the tracks are out of phase, or slightly out of sync, the common frequencies will cancel each other out. If phasing occurs, the phase of the audio on one of the tracks must be reversed. Many audio mixers have phase reversals which, at the press of a button, can reverse the phase of one of the sources to eliminate the phasing problem.

Phosphor   A substance that will exhibit luminescence when struck by light of certain wavelengths.

Pick-up tube   A device in a video camera that converts light into electrical impulses. The pick-up tube has generally been replaced by a newer device called a charge-coupled device (CCD), which accomplishes the same task but is a computer chip rather than a vacuum tube.

Pixel   Short for picture element. The basic unit from which a video or computer picture is made. Essentially a dot with a given color and brightness value. D1 images are 720 pixels wide by 486 high. NTSC images are 640 by 480 pixels.

Playback IN   The first frame of material that will be copied onto the record tape. See also **IN point**.

Playback OUT   The frame after the last frame of a playback reel that will be recorded onto the record tape.

Postproduction   All tasks required to finish a program after the body of the show has been shot. This includes, but is not limited to, scoring, dubbing, automatic dialogue replacement, Foley, editing, conforming, creating effects, mixing, off-line editing, on-line editing, and negative cutting.

Prebuild   A videotape built to be used in an on-line session. Prebuild sessions are on-line, but usually take place before the show's on-line session to create complicated effects.

Prelay   Locating, transferring, and editing the audio portion of a production and placing those elements onto a two-track or other mixing medium.

Preproduction   All tasks required to create a program before the body of the show is shot. This includes, but is not limited to, writing the script, booking talent, scouting locations, locating funds, analyzing the script breakdown, reviewing the storyboard, and renting equipment.

Preread   The ability to read a video and/or audio signal and record that signal onto the same tape at the time that the signal is being read. A few digital video formats are capable of prereading.

Prereader®   A computer program that organizes an EDL so that the preread function is optimized in the EDL.

Preview   To rehearse an edit without actually recording it. See also **VVV**, **BVB**, and **VBV**.

Preview keys   The keys on an editing machine that instruct the machine to perform a preview.

Producer   The person responsible for the final version of a visual production. Often the producer is also responsible for paying the bills.

Production   The recording of a show's picture and audio on film, videotape, audio tape, or all three.

Production audio   The audio that is recorded during the production of a show. Most often, pictures are being recorded simultaneously with the audio.

Production company   A company that makes audio and/or video shows.

Progressive scanning   A process for transmitting and displaying video images. Commonly used in personal computers and some HDTV and SDTV formats. Progressive scanning refers to displaying horizontal scan lines in sequence from top to bottom of a full frame.

Pulse cross monitor   See **Cross-pulse monitor**.

Quad   Short for quadruplex. Another name for two-inch videotape. It is called quad because the machines that record the quad signal have four video heads, each recording or playing back one-quarter of the tape.

RAM   Random-access memory, the amount of memory a computer has available for volatile and unsaved memory. RAM information is lost when the computer is shut off.

Random-access   An editing system that can preview multiple events and immediately change any of them. Also referred to as nonlinear.

Random-access editor   An editing system that has instant access to playbacks and has the ability to adjust any edit IN or OUT point immediately, then play back the results of these changes at once. Also referred to as a nonlinear editor.

Rank Cintel   A well-known, high-quality, film-to-tape equipment manufacturer.

Reality programming   Usually segment programs that employ historical footage, reenactments, or on-location footage that deal with human-interest stories.

Record   To make a copy of video or audio on a video or audio machine. A recording could be from a camera original, a transfer of a camera original, or any other source of picture or sound.

Record IN   The first frame on which an edit is to start on the record (copying) side.

Record master   The record tape that is used in an editing session. See also **Record stock**.

Record OUT   The OUT point of an edit on the record machine. See Chapter 14 on logging control track edits.

Record stock   The tape on which the edited master will be built. For best results, new videotape should be used for this purpose. Ideally, it should be coded with the same time code used by the majority of the playback systems.

Reel number   The number assigned to a source reel of videotape. Only one number should be assigned to each reel, and that should be the only time that number is used in the show.

Reel summary   A sheet of paper in the master log that lists all the reels in a show and briefly describes what is on them.

Regenerated time code   Time code is a digitally encoded signal that should be not just transferred but should be fed into a time code generator and regenerated, ensuring a fresh signal. A time code generator locks to the original code and sends out new time code identical to the original. Without regeneration, extraneous noise on the tape might render the code useless.

Ringing   The apparent crawling of color at the edges of colorized letters due to the inability of the NTSC signal to rapidly change from one frequency to another.

Room tone   The natural sounds that are present at any location. Thirty to sixty seconds of room tone should be recorded at each location.

Rough cut   See **Workprint**.

Safe title area   The area of the screen in which graphics can be seen by most television viewers.

Safety   See **Submaster**.

Sampling   Measuring a signal's strength at regular intervals. The samples are used to create a digital representation of that original signal.

Saturation   The amount of color.

Screen direction   The direction of action across the screen. A specific real-life direction of action does not always translate to the same direction on the screen. Screen direction depends on camera placement.

Screening   The viewing of tape or film. There are many reasons to screen a show, from viewing the original footage to considering the purchase of a finished show.

Script   The written plan, both audio and visual, of a program.

SDTV formats (standard definition television formats)   The ATSC has proposed a set of SDTV formats including 640 × 480 pixel and 704 × 480 pixel formats. The 640 × 480 pixel formats, with 4:3 aspect ratio, include 24 frames per second (FPS), 30 FPS and 60 FPS progressive, and 30 FPS interlaced scanning formats. These are unlikely to be used other than for computer applications. The 704 × 480 formats may be either 4 × 3 or 16 × 9 using the same 24, 30, 60 FPS progressive and 30 FPS interlaced scanning. DVD implements a minor variation with 720 × 480 pixels using either 4 × 3 or 16 × 9, 30 FPS interlaced scanning.

SECAM   A foreign standard for television broadcasting.

Second track   Track two of a two-track audio system.

Setup   See **Pedestal**.

Shuttle time   The actual time that it takes a particular videotape to go from where it is sitting to where it is supposed to be, at full speed. Most often, shuttle time refers to the time it takes to go from the head of the tape to the tail at full speed.

Single-camera production   The shooting of a program with one camera (as opposed to using multiple cameras).

Sitcom   Short for situation comedy.

Skew   The adjustment on a video machine that corrects the tension on the tape. Many newer tape machines automatically adjust the skew. Misadjusted skew results in a bend at the top of the video picture.

Slate   The audio or video identification of the take and location of a particular show or shot. Slates on the edited master usually include audio information (mixed or unmixed, sweetened or unsweetened) and running time.

Slaved time code   See **Regenerated time code**.

Slow-motion   The effect of slowing down the playback speed of a videotape. Slow-motion can be accomplished using a machine with dynamic tracking a nonlinear editor or a video slow-motion disk. Also called slo-mo.

SMPTE   The acronym for Society of Motion Picture and Television Engineers, a group of people dedicated to the improvement and standardization of the visual industry.

Snow   Video noise seen when playing a blank videotape.

Source select keys   Keys on the editing keyboard that select auxiliary sources or videotape machines. Once a machine is selected, other keys may be used to control that machine.

Splice   To physically cut a piece of film or video and add another section to it.

Split edit   An edit with sync sound that begins with only picture or only audio before becoming a both edit.

Spotlight   A video effect that darkens a portion of the frame, usually through the use of a switcher wipe pattern.

Sprocket holes   Holes in film that allow it to be physically pulled a certain distance.

Staff   A company's permanent employees.

Steadicam®   Trade name for a hand-held steadying device for cameras, usually bracing the camera to a person's body.

Storyboard   An illustrated plan for a film or video project.

Stripe   To record time code onto a videotape.

Subcarrier   A group of frequencies impressed onto a main carrier frequency. In composite video, chroma is transmitted by encoding a subcarrier, which is impressed onto the luminance carrier frequency.

Submaster   An exact copy of an edited master, usually made as a backup in case the master is damaged.

S-VHS   An improvement over the popular VHS video format that utilizes metal tape.

Sweetening   The audio portion of video postproduction that is done on a multitrack audio machine.

Switcher   The switcher takes all the video sources and combines them to make a composite picture that is either broadcast (live television) or recorded on tape. Most linear computer editing systems have some sort of switcher.

Sync   This term is used in several ways:

1.   Audio sync is when the picture and audio are in sync with each other. Audio could become out of sync with the picture through repeated dubbing, using a frame synchronizer, or as a result of a poorly planned audio-only edit.
2.   The video signal is composed of horizontal and vertical sync pulses. If these pulses are not properly recorded or played back, the picture can lose sync, resulting in a glitch, picture roll, or other video abnormality.
3.   The time code must be synched with the video that is being recorded. If the time code is not in sync with the video, the time code is useless for editing.
4.   All inputs to a switcher must be timed to each other. If a signal is out of time (out of sync) with the other inputs to the switcher, effects will not be possible.

Sync mode   The rolling of two or more playback machines and editing on the fly, by pressing source keys to select which source tape to go to (edit) next. It is like cutting a show live, except that you can stop to make corrections.

Syndication   When a television show is not carried by a network, it is often sold on a station-by-station basis. This process is called syndication. The people and companies who sell these shows are called syndicators.

Take   (1) A word meaning *attempt* at the beginning of a scene or shot. "Take One" would be the first attempt to get everything (camera, audio, lighting, effects, acting, and background actors) just right. (2) To select another camera or source in a program through the use of a switcher. "Take Two," the director will shout to the technical director, who will select camera number two to be on the air or be recorded.

Tape delay   The practice of taping a broadcast, then replaying it at a later date. Most of the programming seen on the west coast of America is tape delayed three hours from its east coast broadcast.

Tape operator   In most on-line facilities, the editor works with a tape operator in the editing bay. The tape operator loads and unloads tapes and is responsible for the technical setup of the video. The tape operator is vital to the on-line edit and is invaluable to the editor.

TBC   The abbreviation for time base corrector.

Telecine   A type of editing bay or the process of transferring film images to videotape.

Three-quarter-inch   A video format that is widely used for both broadcast and industrial productions. Three-quarter-inch is about to be phased out. Replacing it will be DVDs, CDRs, and DV formats.

Three-two pulldown The method of transferring four film frames to five video frames by repeating a field of visual information every other frame. Thus, three fields of information are recorded, then two, then three.

Tilt A shot created by pivoting a camera vertically. See also **Pan**.

Time base corrector (TBC) A time base corrector synchronizes video signals with other devices such as switchers. TBCs usually contain a dropout compensator (DOC), which senses a lack of oxide on the videotape and replaces that scan line with the information from the line above it.

Time code A digitally encoded signal that is recorded on videotape in the format of hours:minutes:seconds:frames. The purpose of time code is to label each frame of video. An example of a time code signal would be 05:15:18:23.

Time code generator A machine that creates time code.

Time code keys Keys used in an editing system to enter time code into the computer.

Time-of-day time code Time code that is generated by a time code generator set to the actual clock at the time of production.

Toaster A visual effects device that can perform switcher effects and create digital video effects.

Tone An audio reference signal that is recorded at the head of any audio recording and is used to calibrate the playback of that signal. On a video recording, bars are usually recorded at the same time as tone.

Tracing powder A very fine powder that was used in the early days of tape editing when tape was physically cut. The powder was sprinkled on the videotape to make the frame line visible.

Tracking The adjustment of the videotape playback position to phase the video tracks against the video read heads. This is usually an adjustable function of all helical-scan recordings (half-inch, three-quarter-inch, and one-inch videotape). The best tracking will produce the best picture.

Track slippage A method of moving a digital audio track out of its originally recorded sync relationship. This might be used to place audio in a different location (off camera) or to slip a music track a few frames to make a more pleasing sound edit.

Transport keys Keys on an editing system that, when used with the source keys, command the videotape machines to stop, fast-forward, play, or fast-rewind.

Trim (1) The process of altering time code that has been entered into an editor. (2) The remainder of a shot after the chosen portion has been edited into a film project. A trim can be many feet long and stored in a box, or consist of a few frames and kept in an envelope.

Two-inch See **Quad**.

Two pop An audible beep placed on a film or video countdown two seconds before the start of a picture or show.

Type A The original one-inch format created by Ampex. Type A is no longer used.

Type B   A segmented format of one-inch videotape recordings created by the Bosch-Fernseh company.

Type C   The Sony/Ampex compromise one-inch video format.

Ultimatte®   The brand name of a highly refined chroma keying device.

User bits   An area in time code set aside for client use. Numbers or selective alphanumeric characters (A through F) can be recorded along with time code and subsequently read back. User bits require additional equipment to encode and decode the information.

VBV   The abbreviation for video-black-video. A preview that shows a portion of the outgoing record picture, then black, then the portion of the record tape that will follow the planned edit.

VCR   The abbreviation for videocassette recorder, used to indicate any video player or recorder. Most often it is used to describe home-use machines.

Vectorscope   An oscilloscope used in video to display color values and phase relationship.

Vertical interval   The frame line between fields and frames of video, also called the vertical blanking. Information such as time code and instructions for automatic color tuning can be recorded in the vertical interval.

Vertical interval switcher   A switcher that will perform a cut only during the vertical interval. All professional switchers are vertical interval switchers.

Vertical interval time code (VITC)   Time code that is recorded in a visual, digital form in the vertical interval.

VHS   A popular home-use half-inch format being replaced by DVD disks.

Video   An electronic signal created by a camera or signal generator that can be broadcast over the air or recorded in various ways with different record machines.

Video assist   A video recording of the output of the film camera so that a take can be viewed as it is being shot or immediately after shooting.

Video-black-video preview   See **VBV**.

Video camera   The machine that changes a light source to a video image. The video camera also creates blanking. Any camera to be used on a production should be registered and tested before the actual production begins.

Videodisk   A circular disk that has video etched on it. A videodisk can be read only by a videodisk player.

Videotape   A strip of Mylar with an oxide coating that reacts to electrical impulses.

Video-video-video preview   See **VVV**.

VITC   The acronym for vertical interval time code.

VTR   The abbreviation for videotape recorder. Occasionally, VTR also refers to a videotape player.

VU meter   A meter that measures the volume units of audio.

VVV   The abbreviation for video-video-video. The most-used preview, this shows a portion of the outgoing shot on the record tape, the incoming shot, and a portion of what will appear on the record tape after the edit.

Waveform monitor   An oscilloscope that measures the white and chroma levels of a video signal.

White-balance   The process of shooting a white card with a video camera and pressing a button labeled "White Balance." This activates the camera circuit that adjusts the internal settings of the black level, white level, and the three colors (red, green, and blue) to the white card. Since the color temperature from interior lights is vastly different from sunlight, this white balancing must take place in each new location. See also **Color correction** and **Video camera**.

Wide shot   A shot that includes a wide area of a scene.

Window dub   An exact copy of original audio and video, usually on three-quarter-inch or half-inch videotape, with a visual representation of the time code burned into the picture. See also **Burned-in time code** and **Off-line edit**.

Wipe   A transition from one picture to another through the use of some sort of design (such as a straight line, diamond, or circle).

Workprint   The rough draft of a television show or film, created through an editing process.

Zoom   (1) A lens with movable elements that allows the operator to change the focal length of the lens. (2) A shot in which a zoom lens is used to change the focal length within the shot.

Index